# WILD THING

Lew Yates is a former unlicensed boxer who has also worked as a nightclub bouncer and civil engineer. He lives in Cambridgeshire.

Bernard O'Mahoney is the author of a number of true-crime books, including the bestselling *Essex Boys*, *The Dream Solution*, *Bonded by Blood* and *Wannabe in my Gang?* He lives in Birmingham.

www.bernardomahoney.com

# WILD THING

## THE TRUE STORY OF BRITAIN'S RIGHTFUL GUV'NOR

# LEW YATES
# AND BERNARD O'MAHONEY

MAINSTREAM
PUBLISHING

EDINBURGH AND LONDON

First published in Great Britain in 2007 by
MAINSTREAM PUBLISHING COMPANY
(EDINBURGH) LTD
7 Albany Street
Edinburgh EH1 3UG

ISBN 9781845962692

This book is a work of non-fiction based on the life, experiences
and recollections of Lew Yates. In some cases names of people
and locations have been changed to protect the privacy of others.
The author has stated to the publishers that, except in this minor
respect, the contents of this book are true.

A catalogue record for this book is available
from the British Library

Typeset in Badhouse and Galliard

Printed in Great Britain by
William Clowes Ltd, Beccles, Suffolk

To:
My late father, Bill, and mother, Gwen
My brother, Jim, and sisters, Jean and Barbara
My first wife, Jean, and my second wife, Margaret
Our children, Glynn, Joanne, Billy, Lewis, Vicky, Danielle and
Sarah-Jane
George Gilbody Snr and family, and all of my friends – too
numerous to mention.
You know who you all are!

# ACKNOWLEDGEMENTS

Thanks to Bill Campbell, Kevin O'Brien and everybody at Mainstream Publishing.

A special thanks to Bernie for the work he put into this book. It was a pleasure working with him.

Thank you to Peter Koster for all of the faith he has shown in me since we first met and the kindness he has bestowed upon me and the children.

Last, but by no means least, a sincere thank you and a ridiculously large reward awaits the person who returns my blue and silver dressing gown that I wore on the night I fought Roy Shaw. It was left in the back of a black taxi on a journey from St Pancras to Camden Town in 2001, and I haven't seen it since. If you have it or know of its whereabouts, please do get in touch through bernardomahoney@bernardomahoney.com.

God bless and thank you all.

*Lew 'Wild Thing' Yates*

# CONTENTS

# FOREWORD

MIDDAY, 2 MARCH 2006, ELY, CAMBRIDGESHIRE: I AM STANDING OUTSIDE THE railway station waiting to meet Lew 'Wild Thing' Yates (real name Lewis Martindale), a huge ex-boxer, bouncer and unlicensed fighter with an awesome reputation. A large green four-by-four vehicle sweeps onto the car park. The electric passenger-door window is activated and a voice calls out, 'Is that you, Bernie?'

Like the man I am greeting, I had once worked as a nightclub doorman in Essex and London. The cycle of violence perpetrated by gangs in clubs and elsewhere has never and will never change or end. A group of young villains will make a name for themselves by committing some sort of diabolical act against another human being. After a brief spell at the top of the heap they will either be imprisoned or taken out by a more powerful gang. The names change, but the story always remains the same.

It's no different with many of the doormen who are employed to try to control these gangs: they often end up forming gangs, or 'firms', themselves. A formidable new bouncer will arrive on the scene, punch his way to the top and ultimately fall in a bloody heap. I know, because I have witnessed the scenario many times, my former business partner Tony Tucker and his two associates Patrick Tate and Craig Rolfe being prime examples. One day Tucker was working as a bouncer, driving a second-hand Granada and living in a modest semi-detached three-bedroomed house; the next he and his associates were importing drugs, rampaging around nightclubs and believing they were Mafia Dons. Inevitably they were all found shot dead. Their bullet-riddled bodies were discovered in a Range Rover, which was parked down a deserted farm track. I think the police were more concerned about the vehicle not being taxed and that the deceased driver was disqualified than the fact three drug-dealing thugs had been murdered. The police knew their passing wouldn't bring about the end of mindless acts of violence being committed in and around nightclubs or the cessation of the drug trade in Essex. Within weeks other hopefuls would replace them, ensuring that the cycle remained unbroken.

Very rarely somebody does manage to rise to the top and, against unbelievable odds, walk away unscathed. Lew Yates is such a man. During my time as a bouncer with Tony Tucker and the firm that became known as the Essex Boys I heard a lot about the legendary big Lew Yates. But I have always associated legends with myths and thought the remarkable stories about him must be either made up or, at the very least, embroidered.

Big Lew, went one of the stories, would put his hands in his pockets and ask the troublemakers to go away or he would knock them out. They would usually be drugged up, pissed or feeling lucky and refuse to leave. Lew would then say, 'Pick a hand, left or right.' Seconds after the person had sneered and uttered their choice, they would be lying horizontal on the pavement, having being knocked out by the fist they had been foolish enough to choose. Others would talk about Lew fighting four or five men single-handedly, defeating them and remaining unscathed.

I used to think that no man was capable of such punching

power or, even if such a man existed, that somebody would have stopped him with a gun or a knife. These stories just had to be bullshit. I now have to admit, after meeting and researching Lew Yates, I was totally wrong. I have spoken to Lew's friends, former sparring partners, former colleagues on the door and a few of the people who have been stupid enough to call his bluff. Every one of them had a story to tell that usually included Lew's ability to end a fight with just one punch. 'Love him or hate him,' one villain told me, 'Lew is one hard bastard. He punched me so hard in the head I started to imagine that the wife was good-looking.' This man's wife was with him when he spoke to me, and all I can say is that Lew must have hit him very, very hard indeed. In addition, as I had guessed, Lew has had attempts made on his life, but even when confronted with knives and guns he has displayed remarkable courage.

When I got into Lew's car and shook his shovel-like hand, I wasn't sure what to make of him. This man mountain looked extremely dangerous; he oozed violence. He certainly wasn't the type of guy you would want to upset. But Lew was polite and good humoured, and went out of his way to make me feel welcome.

This contradictory character confused me at first. I was unsure about how I was ever going to portray him. Over the next 12 months, while we wrote this book together, I got to know big Lewie very well. I witnessed the man go through every possible human emotion: rage when he talked about the way people had dragged the sport he loves into the gutter; laughter when he talked about the good times in his life; tears when he spoke about the death of his parents, loved ones that had deceived him and his own failings as a human being. Nothing I witnessed was false. I concluded that there is no one way to describe him. Lew is without doubt an incredibly hard man who fears nobody, but he is also a very decent man who, like us all, has made mistakes. Lew Yates, in my opinion, is the real deal, an all-round genuine guy. This is his life story. I hope you enjoy reading it as much as I enjoyed hearing Lew tell me it.

*Bernard O'Mahoney*

# INTRODUCTION
## LADIES AND GENTLEMEN, LEW 'WILD THING' YATES

TUESDAY, 27 OCTOBER 1981: I AWOKE AT 8 A.M. AND OPENED THE CURTAINS OF my ground-floor flat. Forest Gate, which is in London's East End, looked as dull and depressing as it did any other day. But this was not going to be just another day. Today I had an opportunity to earn more money than I had ever earned in my life. More importantly, today could help me fulfil a lifelong dream. Roy Shaw, prizefighting legend and then reigning Guv'nor, had been interviewed on BBC Radio One and challenged any man to take him on. I had accepted that challenge. A prestige title and a small fortune were going to be the winner's prize; a bruised and battered body awaited the loser. Shaw, an ex-Broadmoor mental patient, had defeated every fighter that had been put in the ring with him, but I felt no fear. In fact, when my challenge was accepted, I felt excited. I was bursting with confidence; I thought my time had come. I opened my wardrobe and laid my kit out on the bed: one pair of blue and white shorts, one pair of boxing gloves, boots and a blue and silver dressing gown with 'Lew "Wild Thing" Yates' emblazoned across the back in

15

red letters. Having carefully laid the kit out, I left my flat and walked briskly around the local streets for approximately a mile and a half. I needed to open my lungs up; it was important that I got them functioning properly before the fight. When I returned home, I made myself breakfast. I then spent the rest of the morning shadow-boxing, lightly punching a bag I had hanging in the lounge and relaxing. That afternoon I packed my kit into a training bag but left my dressing gown on the bed as I did not want it to get creased. Everything about me had to function and look just so for this fight; no detail, however trivial, could be overlooked. The clock on the wall, which I was unable to take my eyes off, appeared to be turning so slowly I thought it had stopped.

I called my two dogs, an English bull terrier and a Staffordshire bull terrier, and took them to the park in an effort to kill time. Around 6 p.m. I picked my kitbag up, draped my dressing gown over my arm and walked to my car. I knew I wouldn't be fighting until much later that night, as my bout with Shaw was billed as the main event.

I wanted to get to the venue early so that I could soak up the atmosphere and get accustomed to my surroundings. Preparation, preparation: winning fights is all about preparation. Driving away from home, I kept thinking about the night ahead. I had been to watch Shaw fight three or four times. He was no fool but I knew if I caught him with the full force of either hand, I would knock him spark out. I had arranged to pick my good friend Ray Todd up from his home in Stratford. Two short sharp blasts of my car horn brought Ray to his front door. He raised his hand, disappeared back inside his flat and moments later came bounding towards me with his coat thrown over his shoulder. At approximately 7 p.m. we arrived at the Ilford Palais nightclub, where the fight was due to take place. I couldn't quite believe the number of people that were milling around in the High Street. There were literally thousands of them trying to get in to witness the fight. When Ray and I pulled up outside the Palais, people gathered around the car and started asking whether I felt confident, whether I was going to win, whether I feared Shaw. I asked those standing in the road to move aside, as I was going to pull away. 'Where are you going, Lew?' they asked. 'Surely you haven't changed your mind?'

'I have bottled it,' I replied. 'I'm scared; I'm going home.'

Everybody was laughing; nobody who knew me thought for a moment I had changed my mind. Ray and I drove down Ilford High Street in search of a parking space. We eventually found one in a side road. I grabbed my kitbag off the back seat and we made our way back to the venue. When we reached the front door, a huge guy named Ginger Ted was collecting tickets. 'Hello, Lew,' he said. 'Come on in.'

The scene inside the club was even more chaotic than outside. So many people had purchased tickets that they had to stand on tables, chairs and even the bar to see the ring. Ray and I were led upstairs to a dressing-room, where my corner men Neville Sheen, Mickey Kane and his cousin Roy were waiting. We sat talking tactics for a while, and then I got changed. Shortly afterwards a doctor came in to see if I was physically fit to fight. He checked my blood pressure, listened to my heart, looked into my eyes and gave me the thumbs up. As the doctor was leaving, a man entered the dressing-room and introduced himself. 'Don Atyeo,' he said, extending his hand for me to shake. 'I am a journalist from *Time Out* magazine. I would like to interview you about the fight tonight.' Atyeo asked me how I was feeling, about my fights as an amateur and about my current physical condition. I told him that I had weighed in at 18.5 st., I intended to defeat Shaw, I felt fit and was raring to go. This was not entirely true: I was 21.5 st., had only trained for six weeks for the fight and was suffering from a stomach hernia. I lied because I knew Atyeo would talk to Shaw at some point and I didn't want him to know that I was too heavy or that the mere six weeks Shaw's camp had given me to train for the fight hadn't allowed me to reach the peak of my physical fitness. This wasn't paranoia taking over; when Shaw was training for a fight with Donny 'The Bull' Adams, he had been watched by film producer Bob Brown. Afterwards Brown, who was considering making a film about unlicensed fighting, told Shaw that he was going to watch Adams train so that he could compare the two fighters. Later that night Shaw had telephoned Brown and asked how Adams appeared to be shaping up. Shaw later admitted that after hearing how impressive his opponent had been, he had begun to doubt that he could win the fight. I didn't want Shaw knowing anything about me or the condition I was in. From the dressing-room I could hear the crowd roaring as the other fighters on the bill slugged it out in the ring.

I could almost smell the stench of violence in the air. A friend of mine named Barry Dalton, known as The Mad Irishman, was fighting a man named Chris Ball from Chingford in Essex. Barry was an awesome fighter, more crash, bang, wallop than skill, but he had the heart of a lion. I would regularly meet Barry at prizefights, gyms and the various clubs around London that fighters, bouncers and criminal 'faces' frequented. Few had a good word for Barry, but he was always well mannered and polite when in my company. Regardless of what others may say, I thought Barry Dalton was a good man. His fight was first on the bill, so I did not get an opportunity to watch it. I wasn't concerned, because I had no doubt that Barry and I would bump into each other at some stage during the night.

Donny 'The Bull' Adams is one of the greatest prizefighters

of all time. During his distinguished career he had 48 fights and 48 wins. That was until he met Roy Shaw in December 1975. When the pre-match hype had reached fever pitch, both men boasted that they were going to have a bare-knuckle 'fight to the death'. News of the fighters' intentions reached the ears of the authorities and, after all sorts of legal rumblings, which threatened to have the event postponed, they agreed that they would wear gloves. Gangster Joe Pyle promoted the fight, which was held at Billy Smart's 'Big Top' Circus tent in Windsor, Berkshire. As soon as the bell went to signal round one, Shaw threw a right hook that knocked Adams over. Instead of waiting for his opponent to get to his feet, Shaw kept punching Adams, picking him up, knocking him back down and finally stamping on his head. People in the crowd were screaming, 'He is dead, Roy. He is dead. Leave him.' Adams was not dead but he was certainly unconscious. A fight that people had expected to be an epic battle had ended in seconds, and Roy Shaw was crowned the Guv'nor.

When Donny 'The Bull' Adams walked into my dressing-room unannounced, I couldn't quite believe it. 'I wanted to wish you luck, Lew,' he said. 'Use your weight against Roy. Lean on him, push him; you can beat him.' I thought it was a nice gesture, as we had not previously met, and so I thanked him.

Just after he left, a man wearing a white shirt and bow tie put his head around the door and asked, 'Are you ready, Lew?' I told him I was. 'You're on in five minutes,' the man replied. I could hear the MC announcing on the PA system that the fight was due to start. The crowd began cheering, clapping their hands and stamping their feet. I pulled the hood of my dressing gown up over my head and made my way to the ring. Getting there was no easy task. People were reaching out, trying to shake my hand or pat me on the back. There were so many well-wishers

I ended up having to push some of them out of the way in order to keep moving. The theme song for my entrance into the arena should have been 'Wild Thing' by the Troggs, but my friend had forgotten to bring the record, so I walked out to the Emerson, Lake and Palmer version of 'Fanfare for the Common Man'. As I climbed into the ring, I could see for the first time just how many people had been packed in to watch the fight. The atmosphere that night was electric, the noise deafening. It was hard not to be distracted, but I kept telling myself to focus on the task ahead. The voice of Gary Glitter, then pop star, now disgraced paedophile, boomed out of the PA system: 'Do you wanna be in my gang, my gang, my gang?' It was Shaw's entrance theme song. As he entered the ring, I glared at him in an effort to block out everything else around me. He was wearing a white towelling dressing gown with 'Mean Machine' embroidered in large red letters across the back. We couldn't hear what the referee was saying, so he motioned Shaw and me to the middle of the ring with a wave of his hand. The MC introduced us to the crowd, which was baying for blood as if we were gladiators.

'Ladies and gentlemen, the bout everybody has been waiting for, a heavyweight contest of ten three-minute rounds. In the red corner, weighing in at 15 st. 11 lb, London's very own Mean Machine, Roy "Pretty Boy" Shaw! And in the blue corner, weighing in at 21 st., Liverpool hard man Lew "Wild Thing" Yates!'

I wanted to look Shaw in the eye, make him feel uncomfortable, but he kept his head down, raising his gaze no higher than my chest. The referee checked our bandaged hands to ensure no foreign objects had been secreted to gain an advantage. It was not unknown for strips of lead or similar material to be wrapped up within the bandages in order to inflict serious injury on an opponent. The referee was happy that Shaw and I had no such items and told us to return to our corners to put our gloves on. My corner men began to advise me: 'Bull Shaw around. Use your weight, Lew. Lean on him, push him, tire him and wear him down.' As they were talking, the bell rang for the first round.

Shaw and I flew across the ring at each other, clashing like two bulls, our heads rather than our fists making first contact. I opened up with a barrage of punches and began pushing him backwards around the ring using my superior size and weight. I was surprised at how little resistance Shaw put up, to be honest. I thought that he would be much stronger. I was moving around well, jabbing him, shoving him, even dropping my hands, goading him to hit me in the hope that he would either feel intimidated or lose his temper and drop his guard. Before long Shaw began to swing wildly. Several punches missed me completely; those that did connect were ineffective. The thought of being humiliated in front of his home crowd was obviously getting to him. To antagonise him further I invited him to hit my chin, which I stuck out for him, but Shaw stood off, seemingly confused by my lack of respect for his awesome reputation. Towards the end of the round he did catch me with an explosive right hook in the ribs that temporarily winded me.

I dropped to one knee to regain my breath, then immediately stood upright to show the referee that I was able to box on. I needed to avoid Shaw for a while so that I could regain my composure. I moved around the ring, ducking and weaving as Shaw's arms flailed wildly but without effect. Before he could close in, make his punches connect and capitalise on my injury, the bell rang, signalling the end of the round. Despite succumbing to that one crippling punch, I knew I had given a good account of myself. Sitting in my corner, I decided that I was going to ignore Donny 'The Bull' Adams' and my corner men's advice about pushing and shoving Shaw. I told myself that I was going to do my own thing: stay at arm's length and box his 'pretty' head off his shoulders. As soon as the bell rang for round two, I was out in the middle of the ring and pounding Shaw. A right-hander snapped his head back, and I knew at once that I had hurt him. As Shaw tried to get in close to stop the onslaught, I pushed him away with my left and smashed him with my right. He did manage to land a few defensive jabs, but they were weak and had no effect whatsoever. One minute and twenty seconds into the round I caught him with a perfect uppercut before following through with a fast combination of punches to the head and body. Shaw staggered, and I drove him back across the ring, landing punch after punch as he went. When he hit the ropes, he dropped his hands and my fists smashed his head from side to side. He resembled a rag doll being tossed about the ring. I knew this was the moment; I knew I had defeated 'London's Mean Machine'. I caught him with a beautiful right hook that knocked his head and shoulders through the top rope. I stood back and, as Shaw ducked his head back under the rope in order to stand upright, I head-butted him full in the face. The legendary prizefighter was finished. He fell back onto the ropes, and as I moved in for the kill, the bell rang to signal the end of the round. Shaw's manager Joe Carrington was already in the ring steadying him on his feet.

I walked to my corner and was told there was still one minute and twelve seconds of the round remaining. The crowd had realised it too. 'Fix, fix, fucking fix!' they screamed. I sat on my stool, my head bowed. I could not believe they had rang the bell early just to save Shaw. The referee came over to me and was shouting about disqualifying me for using my head. 'Any more headwork and the fight is over. Do you understand?'

'Sure, sure,' I replied. I was upset that the round had been cut short, but I was confident I could finish the task in hand because Shaw was out on his feet. He'd had little to offer at the outset; now, after less than two full rounds, he had nothing. When the bell rang at the start of the third round, I walked out feeling totally confident of victory. I wasn't as strong as I had been in the second round, but I still out-boxed Shaw and I still managed to toy with him. I could see he was still dazed from the force of my head-butt, and I sensed he had lost the will to come hard at me. To be honest, I was enjoying myself. My eye was swollen from when we had clashed heads in the opening round, but, apart from that minor injury, I was unharmed. At the end of the third round I returned to my corner. Without warning, and without even examining me, the referee said, 'I am stopping this fight because of your eye. It's over.'

'What's up with my fucking eye?' I shouted. 'What's up with my eye? There is fuck all wrong with me!' My corner men were equally surprised and irate, and they too began shouting and swearing at the referee. 'It's over, it's over,' the referee kept shouting back at us as he waved his arms and walked around the ring.

The crowd realised what was happening and went wild, booing and chanting, 'Fix! Fix! Fix!' I wanted to get out of there; I felt absolutely disgusted. As I climbed out of the ring and headed for the dressing-room, a fighter named Kevin Paddock got in and challenged Shaw to fight at a later date.

He was pushed aside by a man mountain named Lenny McLean, who offered to fight Shaw and Paddock together there and then. When both men ignored him, McLean began brawling with Shaw's manager Joe Carrington, but they were quickly hauled apart. The scene descended into total chaos. People were shouting, others were threatening one another.

The crowd engulfed me, patting me on the back and shaking my hand. None of them seemed in any doubt that I had won. They were saying 'You were robbed, Lew' and 'That was a fix, a fucking set-up.' Back in the dressing-room I couldn't quite believe that victory had been snatched from me. As I sat there, Joe Carrington walked in and presented me with a huge bottle of champagne. 'This is for you, Lew,' he said. I looked at the champagne, looked at Carrington and told him to stuff his poxy bottle where the sun doesn't shine. The champagne was left on a table and Carrington walked out. As he stepped into the corridor, he was confronted by a group of men who started shouting at him. 'That fight was a fucking fix, Joe. You're taking the piss if you try and say it wasn't.'

Don Atyeo, the *Time Out* journalist, stood nearby taking notes, and Carrington saw him. 'Take no notice of them,' he said. 'Lew Yates can't see out of either eye in there, and they say it's fixed? Come on, let's go celebrate.'

Neither Roy Shaw nor I had cause to celebrate that night. It seemed obvious to me that the art of boxing, which had been my lifelong love, had been dragged into the gutter and shamed by faceless men motivated by money. I may have lost in their eyes, but I firmly believe the best man walked away from that fight with the support of everyone in the crowd who witnessed it. The fighter who had been crowned king was little more than an impostor.

# ROUND ONE

I WAS BORN ON 3 JUNE 1945 AT 105 EDGEWORTH STREET, SUTTON OAK, St Helens in Lancashire. The German Army had surrendered to the Allies in Europe four weeks earlier. The war, everyone said, was finally over. For me, though, war had just been declared: Lewis Martindale was going to take on anybody that stood in his way.

St Helens is situated 12 miles from Liverpool and 25 miles from Manchester at the heart of the north-west's busy motorway network. The borough comprises the town itself and smaller settlements such as Haydock, Newton-le-Willows and Billinge. Two-thirds of the area is rural land. Famous for its glass factory, Haydock Park horse-racing track, all-conquering Saints rugby club and little else, opportunities for its inhabitants were and are, at best, limited. My father, William Martindale, was a keen rugby player and more than capable of holding his hands up (fighting) if he had to. Bill, as he preferred to be called, was a hard-working, decent, down-to-earth man whom everybody in our neighbourhood liked. I am extremely proud and privileged to have had him as my father. Times were tough for everybody after the war: unemployment was high; jobs and money were scarce. In an effort to make ends meet, my father undertook an array of jobs, the most unusual of which was breeding mice. The garden shed always held up to 350 of these creatures. Once or twice a week my father would pack some of them into boxes and cycle to towns as far away as Widnes and Wigan, where he would sell them to pet shops for nine pence each. My mother, Gwen, was Welsh and had a very quick temper. I inherited her temperament and the name of her father, Lewis.

I have one elder brother named Jim and two younger sisters named Jean and Barbara. I was particularly close to my sister Jean. I don't know why – perhaps it's because she was the baby of the family when I was growing up. I was extremely protective of her. Would-be boyfriends were often warned off with a menacing stare or a word of advice in their ear.

Home was a two-bedroomed terraced house with a huge back garden. The 'street' we lived on was in fact a dirt track rather than a tarmacked road. When it rained, which was more often than not in the north-west, the track was reduced to a flowing river of mud. The local children loved playing in it, while house-proud mothers in the neighbourhood cursed it. Mum and Dad slept in the front bedroom of the house; Jim, Jean and I in the back bedroom. (Barbara was yet to be born.)

At the age of five I started school at St Anne's Roman Catholic Primary on Monastery Lane. The school's current mission statement bears little resemblance to the mindset of its governors in my day: 'Our challenge is to build a lively school community on the foundation of shared Christian beliefs and values. In this community each child will be encouraged to develop their talents to the full.'

The only thing I was ever any good at was fighting, both in and out of the ring. I was certainly not encouraged to develop my particular talent at school. One of my earliest memories is of me fighting with another lad in the playground. I was five and he was six. I punched him as hard as I could in the head and he ran away crying. A nun grabbed me by the hair and marched me into the main school building. I was taken to a dormitory, which had several beds in it. A coal fire heated the room, but it was rarely lit. From the mantlepiece hung a thick leather belt with a large metal buckle. Unruly or disobedient children were usually flogged with the leather strap of the belt, but for some reason I was thrashed with the buckle. The steel pin cut and blistered me so badly I had difficulty walking for days. That is the way problem children were dealt with back then.

Spare the rod and spoil the child, they would say. Sick perverted bastards. Because my elders had just endured the horrors of a bloody world war they seemed to think the use of threats and violence was the way to maintain order. Right or wrong, threats and violence were undoubtedly the preferred instruments of control. When my mother saw the injuries that the nun had inflicted upon me, she was horrified. Mum made her feelings known to the school governors and I was moved to Robins Lane non-Catholic school shortly afterwards. I knew from that first beating that school was never going to be beneficial for me, nor was I ever going to be of any use to it. Using violence was apparently acceptable when punishing children, but children following their elders' example were thrashed and demonised. It's hardly a justifiable policy. I have always loathed bullies, and I saw those nuns as nothing more than power-crazed thugs.

One day I got into an argument with a group of boys outside my home. The most vocal, Wilf Peel, pushed me in the chest and a fight started. Wilf and I stood toe to toe trading punches; neither one of us was prepared to give any ground. I sidestepped a left hook from Wilf and, as his fist whistled past my head, I caught him with a good right hand to the chin. He looked at me in disbelief before crashing to the floor, where he remained motionless until his friends helped him to his feet. The fight had taken place outside my Uncle Bob's house, who, unbeknown to me, had been watching from his living-room window. When Uncle Bob came out and called me to him, I thought I was going to be told off, but to my surprise he said the punch that floored Wilf was one of the best he had seen a young boy throw. Uncle Bob had seen plenty of young boys throw plenty of punches. He ran a boxing club named the Roundhouse, which was situated above a local pub of the same name. Uncle Bob, or Robert Jones as he was known to others, was an ex-boxer whose nose meandered aimlessly across his face, the result of taking too many punches.

Bob was a giant of a man who reminded me of the comic-book character Desperate Dan, except Bob didn't have Dan's large beer gut. 'If you can punch like that, Lewis, you ought to take up boxing,' Uncle Bob said. 'Come down the gym with me tomorrow and we will see what you can do.'

To gain access to the gym, I had to climb a ladder, which was fastened to the wall. At the top of the ladder was a trapdoor, which I had to use all of my strength to push open. It fell to the floor with a crash, sending a cloud of dust into the air. In the room I climbed into were punchbags, weights, skipping ropes, the odd medicine ball and a boxing ring. Uncle Bob showed me how to block punches, land punches, duck, weave and move around the ring to avoid an opponent. I loved every minute of the hours we spent in the gym that day and every day thereafter. Boxing became my life; every spare moment I had was spent training. Shortly afterwards my enthusiasm infected my brother Jim, and he began training with me. Once while sparring, I hit him so hard that he flew out of the ring via the bottom and middle rope. Unfortunately the trapdoor, which was only about 3 or 4 ft from the ringside, had been left open. Everybody thought that Jim was going to disappear head first down it. As I watched him slide across the floor to a certain death, all I could think was what on earth was I going to tell Mum and Dad? Fortunately Jim, dazed but uninjured, ground to a halt with his head hanging precariously over the large drop.

I trained at Uncle Bob's gym until I was eight years old. A row with my parents concerning my reluctance to attend church and Sunday school brought my boxing career to an abrupt halt. I had said I wasn't going to attend church, and they said if I didn't, I couldn't go to the gym, and that was that. Neither party was prepared to give an inch. Uncle Bob tried in vain to make me see sense, but, like my mother, I was fiery tempered and extremely stubborn.

Giving in to their demands was accepting defeat, and that's something Lew Martindale has never and will never do. Being out of the ring didn't mean I could no longer fight. There were countless contenders at school who were trying to make a name for themselves. Few, if any, were familiar with the Queensberry Rules and the noble art of boxing. During a gardening class a boy I was arguing with tried to hit me across the head with a shovel. I retaliated by pinning his foot to the ground with a gardening fork. He did a deranged one-legged dance before falling to the floor, where he screamed loudly while clutching his impaled foot. Incident after incident resulted in me spending more time outside the headmaster's office waiting to be punished than I did in class. My behaviour earned me the nickname 'Rowdy Yates', who was a character played by Clint Eastwood in the television series *Rawhide*. It was about a group of cattle drovers and their weekly adventures as they tried to guide a herd of cattle up the Chisholm trail from Texas to Kansas. 'Rowdy Yates' was always getting into fights and was described by TV critics at the time as a hot-headed punk. It was a nickname I thoroughly deserved.

At the age of ten I asked my parents if I could take up boxing again. They could see that I was going to end up in trouble for the rest of my life if I didn't have somewhere to channel the vast amounts of aggressive energy I had. For that reason, and that reason alone, they relented. Before Mum and Dad had finished lecturing me, I was out the back door, on my bike and pedalling like fury to the Britannia Boxing Club in Peasley Cross, St Helens. The club was housed in an old church building, which had a huge spiral metal staircase that led to the gym. Mr Owens, a slim but muscular man in his 30s, was the trainer. I can remember walking in and seeing all these big men hitting punchbags alongside kids my age. I was buzzing – a church where the congregation came to practise the same thing I believed in: violence!

Mr Owens asked me if I had any experience, and I told him I had done a bit with my uncle. 'We train here three times a week,' he said, 'Monday, Wednesday and Friday. Go home, get your kit sorted out and we will see you next week.' Riding home, I was bursting with excitement. I could not wait for the weekend to end so that I could pull on my gloves and climb into a ring again. From that first Monday onwards I was at the Britannia Club training three times a week without fail. I was always the first person to arrive and always the last to leave. Mr Owens, realising just how keen I was, even gave me the gym key so I could go in earlier and leave later. I would park my bike up at the front door and use this huge old medieval-looking key to let myself in. Switching on the fluorescent lights, I would have to stand in the darkness while they flickered madly before finally coming on and flooding the room in light. All the boys used to say that the back room was haunted. It was full of old books, half the windows were missing and the wind would howl through it. It really was scary for a boy of my age. I would stop pounding the punchbag or stop skipping, thinking I had heard voices or footsteps on the concrete stairs. I never could really relax until I heard the front door crash open and Mr Owens call out, 'Lewis Martindale, are you up there, lad?'

At the age of 11 I had my first competitive fight for the Britannia Boxing Club. I was matched against a boy who had 14 previous fights under his belt, and I was warned that he had given a good account of himself in all of them. To be honest, I was totally outclassed and beaten on points fair and square. For the first two rounds I was punching him all around the ring, but he kept backing away and wouldn't go over. By the time the bell went to signal the start of the third round, I was exhausted, and so my opponent was able to jab and score points almost at his leisure.

After the fight Mr Owens was furious. He ranted and raved, saying I should have paced myself and could have won if I had done so. Defeat was not something I had experienced before; it wasn't something I intended to experience again. Training just three nights a week was never going to be enough to make my dream of becoming a champion come true. Next door but one from our house lived a man named Mr Keeley. A quiet thickset balding man in his 40s, Mr Keeley was a keen boxing and rugby fan who kept himself extremely fit. After regularly seeing me leave home with my kit to go training, Mr Keeley called me over one day and asked me if I enjoyed boxing. For the next hour we stood talking about the sport we both loved. When I told him about the defeat I had suffered, he advised me not only to train but to attend boxing matches so I could watch, learn from others and, more importantly, get used to the atmosphere of a fight, because so many good boxers get into the ring and become distracted by the noise and crowd and end up losing. 'I will take you to a boxing match if you like, Lewis,' he said.

The following Saturday Mr Keeley took me to Lowe House Boxing Club in Halefield Street, St Helens. I will never forget walking in there with him. The walls were covered in photographs of men and boys boxing, and numerous glistening trophies were displayed in cabinets. Formed by Father Robert Finnemore in the early 1930s, Lowe House had produced some great fighters. In 1951 Bill Connor had become the ABA (Amateur Boxing Association) light welterweight champion (Mr Connor is the current secretary of Lowe House Boxing Club) and in 1960 Johnny Ould became the ABA light heavyweight champion. Other boxers who honed their pugilistic skills at Lowe House range from Jimmy Molloy and Jack Hughes to former British light middleweight champion, now Hollywood star, Gary Stretch. Sitting in that smoke-filled room hearing the crowd roar their approval as two men slugged it out in the ring filled me with excitement. The buzz I got from being there has never really gone away. The thrill of boxing infected me, and I have never wanted to be cured.

During the interval Mr Keeley bought me a dodgy-looking meat pie and a drink. When he handed me the pie, I told him I couldn't possibly eat it, as it was smothered in gelatine and didn't smell too healthy. Mr Keeley laughed, 'If you want to get fit and be the best, son,' he said, 'you will have to eat these pies every day.' I looked down at the lump of saturated fat, thought about what had just been said and sunk my teeth into the foul-tasting concoction. It made me feel sick, but if it was going to help me, as Mr Keeley claimed, then I was more than happy to eat the muck.

A short while after getting to know Mr Keeley, he set up a boxing ring in his back garden, and on Saturday afternoons kids would travel from all over the area to fight. Mr Keeley supplied the gloves and refereed the bouts. Crowds of local people would gather at his garden fence to watch. Mr Keeley did not make any money out of staging these fights, because no money ever changed hands. He organised everything, and we competed because we all loved boxing. I can recall one particularly mouthy kid who lived near me. He fancied himself as a good fighter and told everybody that he was going to make me look stupid if I ever got into the ring with him. The following week he was at Mr Keeley's, so I jumped into the ring and offered to fight him in front of everybody. After all of his boasting and bragging to his friends he could hardly refuse my challenge. Within moments of him entering the ring I was pounding his head and body. As he lifted his head to try to regain his composure, I hit him as hard as I could in the forehead (or straight down the middle, as I call it). He went down instantly and was so badly concussed that Mr Keeley and his friends had to carry him home. Mr Keeley continued to stage these fights for a couple of years, but complaints from the parents of damaged and defeated combatants forced him to stop.

I remained at the Britannia Boxing Club for approximately five years. During that time I had become a super-fit, powerful and courageous fighter. My Achilles heel was my temper. However hard I concentrated or trained, I could never control it. In the ring it got me disqualified; out of the ring it got me into trouble. 'If' and 'only' became the most commonly used words in my vocabulary.

For at least 200 years fairground boxing booths were the seedbed for many of this country's greatest fighters. There was a time when each county had three or four fairground booths travelling the circuit, with boxers fighting for championships at both regional and national level. Booth boxing has been set aside by some historians as being sleazy and immoral, somehow responsible for bringing the sport into disrepute. But booth

33

fighters were all good professionals, strong and healthy enough to fight in all kinds of conditions.

Freddie Mills, Randolph Turpin, Rinty Monaghan, Jimmy Wilde and Benny Lynch were all world champions. All had learned their trade in the booths and were proud of it. I loved going to watch booth fighting at Sutton Oak fairground. Licensed fighting was sterile and all about discipline. Unlicensed fighting did maintain a degree of discipline, but rules could be broken and the perpetrator would not always be penalised. I think that's why the more competitive unlicensed fighting world appealed to me. I could not only box, but I could bend and break the rules without having to face punishment. I told my parents that I wanted to leave home to travel and work on the fighting booths, but they would not allow it because a friend of Uncle Bob's had done so and ended up permanently punch-drunk. Still a teenager, I had little choice but to accept their decision – but I wouldn't always be a teenager. The fight game had become my life and, one way or another, I was determined to earn a living using my fists.

The day I left school was, without doubt, one of the happiest days of my life. I can remember standing in the main hall with all of the other children who were leaving that day. An air of excited expectancy filled the room. The headmaster clambered onto the stage, cleared his throat with a series of grunts and called for silence. For the next ten minutes we were forced to listen to him drone on about just how successful he had become. Gazing through the window at his rusting second-hand motor on the staff car park did make me wonder if he was being entirely truthful. 'You're all going out into the big wide world,' he said. 'It won't be easy; I know that. When I was your age, I didn't think I would make it, but look at me now. Who knows, in twenty years, one of you could be standing here doing my

34

job.' The thought of standing in his cheap plastic shoes filled me with dread. There was no way I was going to be wearing a tacky navy-blue bri-nylon suit like his and teaching brats like me for a living in the future. Surely there was more to success than having a menial steady job, a tired-looking wife, two snotty kids and a second-hand car? I did crave success, but I wanted to achieve my success in the boxing ring. I wanted to defeat all challengers. I wanted to become the British champion, no, the undisputed world heavyweight champion. OK, it was only a dream, but surely my dream was better than aspiring to become my fucking headmaster?

Before I had even walked out of the school gates for the last time, I had managed to secure employment. After hearing about a vacancy for an apprentice mechanic at Crows Nest garage in Clock Face, Bold Heath, I had telephoned Mr Critchley, the proprietor. Initially Mr Critchley cast doubt on my suitability for the post, as Bold Heath was a small village located two or three miles from central St Helens, with little or at best infrequent public transport servicing it. 'I wouldn't get the bus even if there was one,' I told him. 'I'm a boxer. I'm in training. I cycle everywhere.'

'I take it you don't smoke and don't drink then, lad?' he asked.

When I told Mr Critchley that I did neither, he offered me the job straight away. He obviously thought I was a good, honest, clean-living lad – a very rare specimen on Merseyside.

Billy Redfern was the head mechanic, and it was his task to assist Mr Critchley in teaching me the tricks of the trade. Billy was a decent guy who would spend time with me explaining how things worked and how to fix them when they didn't. I felt that Mr Critchley, on the other hand, treated me like his underpaid overworked personal servant. The only thing we seemed to have in common was the fact we disliked each other immensely. Any menial mind-numbing thankless job that Mr Critchley had to undertake was handed down to me with a grunt and a snigger. Not once did he attempt to teach me anything about the mechanics of a car. It would be clean this car out, Martindale, sweep that mess up, Martindale, or make me a cup of tea now, Martindale. Only God above knows how I managed to restrain myself. God also knows that Mr Critchley would never have drunk his tea if he had known what I used to top it up with. The walk to the toilet was always too much of an effort for me.

In fairness to Mr Critchley he did organise, via some local government scheme, to have me sent to night school, where I was to be taught the finer points of my trade. The downside of this was that my tuition clashed with my training nights at the Britannia Boxing Club. My training should have taken priority, but I was a teenager who wanted to wear the latest fashions, be seen in the right places and have cash to splash. Reluctantly I quit the Britannia Boxing Club and trained alone at home in the garden when I had the time – which, to be honest, wasn't all that often. The dream was temporarily put on hold.

In my defence I have to say that this was no ordinary era for a teenager to be growing up in. Had it been any other decade, I may have reached a different decision, but this was the dawning of the swinging '60s. Liverpool, a short trip down the East Lancs road from St Helens, was reverberating to the sound of the music that was to become known around the world as the Mersey Beat. Local bands such as The Fourmost, The Searchers, Gerry and the Pacemakers, The Merseybeats, The Mo-Jos, The Swinging Blue Jeans, Billy J. Kramer and the Dakotas, Billy Fury and, of course, the four lads who went on to shake the world, The Beatles, were all teetering on the brink of global success. As well as the exciting music scene Merseyside was revelling in the fact that it was dominating English football. In the 1962–63 season Everton FC were league champions. The following season Liverpool FC claimed the title. In 1964–65 Liverpool won the FA Cup for the first time, and in 1965–1966 they won the league title. Everton lifted the FA Cup in the same season. In the world of boxing local lad Alan Rudkin was crowned both British bantamweight champion and British Empire bantamweight champion in 1965.

Merseyside was alive, brimming with confidence and well-deserved pride. And I was determined to savour every possible moment of it. My friends and I would catch the train from St Helens to Liverpool Lime Street station, then walk the short distance to the famous Cavern Club in Mathew Street, where The Beatles regularly played. The first time we made the journey to watch them perform, we arrived an hour before the doors were due to open, but the queue was so long there was absolutely no chance of us getting in. The following week we arrived two hours early, but the queue was twice as long. The more popular The Beatles became, the larger the crowds became and the longer the queue grew. Eventually, after striking up a friendship of sorts with the bouncers, we got in to see them play on four occasions. Those nights I shall never forget; the atmosphere was unbelievable. I knew I was witnessing the birth of legends.

The Beatles were not the only ones giving off sparks around Liverpool at that time. My night-school teacher was constantly giving me grief – not about my work, but about petty meaningless things such as the way I was sitting, the way I leaned on my desk or the way I spoke. Snide remarks descended into open hostility. We began to argue until one day matters came to a head.

My father owned a Mark IV (SS) Jaguar, which needed a new needle for the carburettor. There happened to be one lying around in the workshop at college, so I took it home for him.

I honestly didn't think anybody would be bothered about it. However, one of my fellow pupils saw me take it and informed the teacher. Relishing an opportunity to punish me, the teacher ranted about getting me thrown out of college, before ordering me to report to his office at home time. To be honest, by the time he had finished shouting I knew my college days were over, so I couldn't have cared less about his threats. I did care about the boy who had grassed me up, though. I grabbed hold of him as soon as I saw him and gave him a good hiding. As he lay on the floor moaning, I poured a can of brake fluid and a tub of Vim scouring powder all over him. The teacher appeared just as I was tipping the last of the Vim over his informant's head. 'Martindale! Martindale! Get in my office, boy!' he screamed.

I shouted back, 'Boy? Boy? Who are you fucking calling boy?'

The teacher put his hand out to grab me, and I hit him with a right hook that dropped him to his knees. All of the other pupils were laughing and cheering. The college principal was summoned, but all he did was lecture me about respect and manners. I'd had enough of advice, so I chased him down the corridor. Running with his eyes flickering madly as he looked over his shoulder in fear, the principal managed to lock himself in his office before calling the police. The teacher I had assaulted refused to press charges. He told the officers that he was afraid to do so in case I sought revenge. However, he made it plain that he no longer wanted me in his class or anywhere else on the premises. Mr Critchley was far from happy when he heard the news. He droned on for hours about the unique opportunity I may have thrown away. Eventually, after much hand-wringing, he agreed to keep me on until he had looked into the matter.

I knew I was on borrowed time, so my interest in the job waned dramatically. One of my daily tasks was to go to Mr

Critchley's taxi office in Shaw Street, St Helens, and clean any vehicles he had hired out for weddings or other special occasions. At lunchtimes I would be left alone on the premises, so I began driving the cars around the yard at speed, showering the buildings and other vehicles with small stones as I swerved, skidded and attempted handbrake turns. As well as the fleet of taxis Mr Critchley kept his pride and joy at this yard. It was an American Chrysler 300F in pristine condition. I truly did not mean to do it, but one afternoon, while reversing a taxi into the garage at speed, I misjudged the stopping distance and slammed into the back of Mr Critchley's car. When he saw the crumpled rear end of his beloved vehicle, he jumped up, jumped down, clutched his chest and then sat on an old bench mumbling and cursing. To put it mildly, Mr Critchley was distraught. When he finally stopped gasping for air and got to his feet, he escorted me to the yard gate, pointed the way to St Helens and told me never to set foot on his property again.

It wasn't long before I found another job. A man named Tommy Hankins took me on as an apprentice mechanic at his garage on King Street in St Helens. Tommy had lost his right hand in an accident and had made a crude steel hook which he wore in its place. Tommy drove an old MG sports car, and in order to manoeuvre it he had bolted a circular socket to the steering wheel. Tommy would unclip his hook when he wished to drive and replace it with another attachment, which had a steel ball bearing welded onto the end. The ball bearing was designed to clip into the round socket on the steering wheel, so in effect the wheel became an extension of Tommy's arm. To this day I will never know how he managed to drive around St Helens at speed like he did. The lads in the garage used to call him Captain Hook. In a bygone age he probably would have been a pirate. He certainly was unorthodox, if not slightly mad.

He would dangle the kettle from his hook and shout through an unnecessarily loud PA system that he wanted tea. In fact the whole PA system, loud or not, was unnecessary, as his voice didn't actually need amplifying at all. The office was so small and positioned so close to the mechanics' pits that we would have been able to hear Tommy if he was whispering. The PA system was also used to 'encourage' the labour force to work harder. Like some deranged tin-pot dictator Tommy would stand in his office, microphone in hand, bellowing abuse, or encouragement, as he preferred to call it, at anybody within sight.

To be honest, I liked Tommy. He was a real character, and I enjoyed working for him. While employed at the garage, I got to know many of Tommy's regulars, one of whom was George Gilbody, a trainer at Lowe House Boxing Club. George used to come into the garage in an old Standard Vanguard car that I used to service for him. Inevitably we talked about boxing, and I told him how much I was missing it. 'Come down to Lowe House,' George said. 'Show me what you can do.' I no longer had to attend night school, so I told George I'd love to go to his club.

George is undoubtedly one of the toughest guys I have ever met, and I have met more tough guys than most. His training techniques were merciless, but they made me hard, both physically and mentally. I am not exaggerating when I say this, but if somebody had hit me with an iron bar after a training session with George, I doubt very much if they would have put me down.

Confirmation, if any were needed, of George's training credentials and ability can be found in his sons' boxing records. George Jnr was ABA champion five times and British Olympic boxing team captain at the 1980 Moscow games. He fought boxing legend Tommy 'Hit Man' Hearns in a hotly disputed bout that kept him out of the British team for the Montreal Olympics in 1976. George's other son, Ray, won three ABA titles in his career and was crowned British bantamweight champion in 1985. In 1979 and 1980 George Jnr and Ray were the only brothers ever to win senior ABA titles on the same night.

I started boxing on a regular basis for Lowe House. Before too long I began to have difficulty in getting sparring partners. The other boys at the club complained bitterly to George that I was really hurting them. In an effort to make me more powerful, rather than request I take it easy on the other lads, George invited professional boxers into the gym to spar with me. One of these was a local man named Johnny Chisnall, who had enjoyed a run of first-round knockouts. Chisnall was about eight years older than me, well built and a very experienced fighter. He had become a bit of a local hero, so much so that his photograph adorned the walls of most of the pubs in St Helens. As well as being successful in the ring he was a well-respected street fighter. Chisnall and a friend named McManus more or less ruled the roost in the town's nightspots. Like me, Chisnall's problem was his explosive temper. During his fight with Jack London (brother of the famous Brian London, who fought the likes of Muhammad Ali, Joe Bugner, Jerry Quarry, Henry Cooper, Billy Walker and Jack Bodell) Chisnall had knocked Jack down, jumped on top of him and continually pounded him until the referee had dragged him off. Unsurprisingly Chisnall was disqualified for his outburst. When he came to Lowe House to spar with me, I couldn't wait to get into the ring. At first Chisnall seemed to be taking things easy with me, but after I caught him a few times his punching power increased. He backed me into the corner of the ring but he wasn't hurting me. To prove the fact, I dropped my hands and taunted him by laughing and saying, 'Hit me harder.' I'll never forget his face or his response: 'You cunt! You drop your hands and I'll knock you out.'

Undaunted, I kept my hands down and replied, 'Come

on then, do it.' Chisnall came at me and we traded punches until eventually I drove him back out of the corner. I couldn't believe it. Chisnall had knocked a lot of professionals out, he had this awesome reputation and here was young Lew doing him. George could see that our sparring session was developing into something far more sinister, so he jumped into the ring and separated us. After that Chisnall refused to spar with me again. He did come in the gym about a week later to collect some kit he had left there, and George called out to him, 'Are you going to get in the ring with Lew? He needs somebody to spar with.'

Chisnall picked up his kit and replied, 'Yeah, some other time,' before heading towards the door.

George was shouting, 'What, don't you want to spar with my boy? Don't you want to know my boy?'

But Chisnall just kept walking.

I saw Chisnall some time later around St Helens and said, 'I thought you were going to come and do some sparring with me?'

He replied, 'Yeah! I will, I will,' but he never did turn up.

In time Johnny Chisnall and I became friends, and he would always offer advice before I fought. He went on to train young kids around St Helens who loved the sport, starting at the Britannia Club, followed by St Helens Amateur Boxing Club (ABC) and finally Lowe House Boxing Club. Johnny sadly passed away in 2005 after suffering from cancer.

George Gilbody's enthusiasm and the faith he showed in my ability undoubtedly boosted my confidence. In the dressing-room George would get so excited and hyped up about a bout that he would often come close to fighting with my opponents' trainers. Before I got into the ring, I would hear George shouting at the opposition, 'Nobody can hurt my boy – nobody can hurt my boy.' I could tell that he was really proud of me, and I would give my all not to let him down. If I did make mistakes, he wouldn't hesitate to bollock me left, right and centre. He certainly had no qualms about shouting and screaming abuse at me, but nobody else was allowed to do so. I remember sparring with George one day. He hit me below the belt as hard as he could, and I immediately went down. My head smashed into the ring floor, which was made of hard wooden blocks. I felt no pain in my head because the pain between my legs was so intense. George was bending over me and asking, 'Are you all right, you all right?'

Almost vomiting, I rolled onto my back and looked up at him through swirling unfocused eyes. 'Fuck off, George. Please just fuck off,' I mumbled. I tried to get back on my feet but I was unable to do so. The pain felt like a severe cramp that stifled any movement from my groin to my neck. Eventually I got to my feet and went home. The next morning the pain was so acute and the groin area so inflamed that all I could do was hobble to the toilet, piss blood and stagger back to my bed. My condition did not improve for at least a week.

George really was a dirty fighter, and he showed me all of the tricks: how to head-butt, bite and bang an opponent's ears. Whenever I employed these tactics in the ring and was penalised, George would shout and scream, 'You didn't do it right! Do it on the referee's blind side. Don't let him see you.' I was disqualified several times for head-butting and biting, but George never did advise me to stop; he just told me not to get caught.

Whether I was in the ring or out of it, I was never good at avoiding being caught. Then again I was never ashamed of my actions, so I didn't put a great deal of effort into covering them up. Like all young lads I would play pranks on my workmates and have moments of forgetfulness while daydreaming. I was changing the wheel of a car in Tommy's garage when all of a sudden the axle started to spin. I thought that it was one of the other mechanics playing a practical joke on me, so I shouted out, 'Leave the axle alone, wanker. I'm trying to change a wheel.'

'Who the fuck are you talking to?' came the reply.

Within seconds I was being pulled away from a man I later learnt was Tommy's son. Tommy hauled me into the office and told me that acts and threats of violence would not be tolerated in the workplace. A week later I drove a high-sided vehicle onto the ramp in the garage and, after activating the button that raised it up, I began to talk to my friend. Moments later we were showered with debris from the garage roof as the vehicle smashed into it. Tommy ran from the office, saw his customer's vehicle wedged firmly in the garage roof and began ranting and raving at me. 'One more chance,' Tommy said. 'One more chance and then you're out of a job.'

I think I did well, considering the sort of person I was. Tommy thought otherwise as he chased me out of the tea room two days later. We had all been sitting in silence sipping our tea. Tommy had been reading a broadsheet newspaper that hid his upper body from our view. The temptation was too great for me. I picked up a cigarette lighter and set fire to the paper that he was reading. The flames engulfed the newspaper and threatened to engulf Tommy, who jumped up screaming. I ran from the tea room laughing and Tommy followed. He didn't catch me and ended up having to shout the news at my back that I was sacked.

# ROUND TWO

A GIRL ONCE SAID TO ME THAT IF ROMANCE EVER DIED, I WOULD BE TAKEN in for questioning. Those were not her only words of wisdom that night. She actually said a lot of things, but they are far too explicit to repeat here. To say she said anything is actually wrong, because she spat the words at me rather than uttered them as she stormed off down the street. I have never been much of a ladies' man. Romance is for fantasists; I am more of a grounded, practical, realistic creature – qualities females tend to label as ignorance, selfishness or stubbornness. I am not saying no woman has ever melted my heart. There has been the odd woman from time to time who captured my attention. Calling them odd is not being disrespectful; I say it in recognition of the outstanding patience and tolerance they showed in the face of extreme adversity. I was simply not the easiest guy to live with.

During the periods I found myself banned from the ring, I had to find something else to occupy my mind and time. I had various casual girlfriends over the years, but I never really hit it off with any of them. That was until I met Jean Baldwin, who turned out to be the first true love of my life. One evening I was driving through St Helens when I noticed a really pretty

45

girl sitting on a bus that was picking up passengers outside the Co-op supermarket. I don't know what came over me. I pulled up level with the window she was sitting at and started waving my arms frantically and mouthing, 'Get off the bus.' The girl began to laugh and looked away, so I jumped out of my car and banged on the window. The driver put his head out of his window, shouted, 'Piss off, son,' and drove away. The girl turned around, smiled at me and waved. I have never avoided a challenge and I was determined not to avoid this one. I jumped in my car, slammed it into gear and sped after the bus. I hadn't thought about where this vision of beauty might reside, but I did begin to wonder when I had been driving for twenty minutes.

Throughout the journey we continued to wave and smile at each other like demented Cheshire cats. I was still gesturing for her to get off the bus, but she just kept laughing and breaking into the smile that had stolen my heart. After several miles I saw the girl stand up and start walking towards the front of the bus. At long last I was going to get my chance to talk to her. I pulled over, clambered out of the car and ran towards the bus. 'My name's Lew,' I said. 'What's yours? Do you live around here? Do you want to come for a drive in my car?'

The girl just looked at me and laughed before turning and walking away. I went after her and asked if she would like to come out on a date. 'Which question do you want me to answer first?' she asked, still laughing. I told her I didn't care which question she answered so long as she agreed to see me one night. 'I don't know,' she replied sheepishly. 'I don't even know you.'

'Exactly,' I said, 'and you never will unless you come out with me.'

'My name is Jean. Pick me up from here at 7 p.m. on Wednesday. Bye, Lew.'

Before I had time to reply, Jean had turned and walked

away up a nearby garden path. 'See you at 7 p.m. then, Jean,' I shouted after her. Driving home I felt elated. There was something about Jean that I couldn't explain, but it made me feel extremely happy.

For our first date I took her to a pub called The Bear Paw at Frodsham, a small picturesque village located midway between Chester and Warrington. Jean told me that she was a stylist at a hairdressing salon called Leahy's in St Helens. The salon had been in the news at that time because the proprietor, Edward Leahy, had put a loaded shotgun to his own head and pulled the trigger. His wife, according to the girls in the salon, had been having an affair and had said she was leaving him. If Mr Leahy hadn't blown his own brains out, he may well have taken his wife's life, her lover's life or both. Love, Jean and I concluded, was a very powerful emotion that third parties should not become entwined in.

When I drove her home that night, we shared our first kiss and agreed to meet the following evening. From that day on we spent every available moment in one another's company. We would go to the cinema, Chester Zoo or for long drives out to country pubs in my car. To say we were happy is an understatement; we were on cloud nine!

If Jean could not meet me for any reason, I would go for a drink with my mates. One of the places we used to socialise in was the Plaza in St Helens. When I say socialise, I actually mean fight. The place was full of heroes and bullies, all eager to knock out anybody who dared to question their fighting ability. After several particularly bloody battles the door staff told me that the management no longer wanted me on the premises. It was the first place I had ever been barred out of. I was pretty sure that it wasn't going to be the last. Just before Christmas my friends said they were all going to the Plaza. There were a lot of works parties being held around town and they said all of the office girls would go there when the parties ended. 'Come down, Lew, it will be a laugh,' they said.

'Maybe for you lot, but it won't be much fun for me standing outside. I'm barred,' I replied.

After much encouragement from my friends, who were adamant the door staff would never remember me, I agreed to go. As we stood in the queue, I could see the bouncers scanning the faces of everybody waiting to get in. 'They have recognised me,' I said to my friends. 'They are pretending they haven't, but when I get to the front they are going to tell me I can't come in.'

My friends were laughing at my insecurity, but I just knew the bouncers had clocked me. As I put my foot on the step to enter the club foyer, a hand gripped my shoulder. 'Lew, can I have a word with you?' a bouncer said.

'There's no need,' I replied. 'I know I am barred. I will just go.'

To my surprise the man laughed and said, 'Don't worry about that. I want to talk to you about something else.' Cautious, but not sensing any danger, I followed him out to a fire exit. 'Do you fancy working here, Lew?' he asked.

'Working here doing what?' I replied.

'As a bouncer,' he said. 'I have seen you fight more than once, unfortunately, and we could do with a handy guy like you here.'

A bit of extra cash was always welcome, so I said, 'OK, I will give it a go.'

The bouncer stuck his hand out. 'Welcome aboard, Lew. I will see you here tomorrow night at 8 p.m.'

I shook his hand and thanked him. 'By the way,' I said. 'I take it I'm no longer barred, and as I am already in the club I won't have to go back out to reception to pay?'

The bouncer looked at me and laughed. 'Go on, Lew, fuck off inside and join your mates before I change my mind.'

The following night, dressed in my best black suit, I walked into the Plaza. It seemed odd that I was going to be paid for fighting in a club that had recently banned me for fighting. Taffy, a fellow bouncer who I correctly guessed was Welsh, took me to one side and asked me how I was feeling. 'Bit nervous, I bet,' he said. 'I know it's your first night. If it will make you feel better, you can borrow this.'

Taffy offered me a leather-bound cosh, but I told him I wouldn't need it. 'Thanks all the same,' I said, 'but I prefer to use my fists.'

Taffy laughed, patted me on the back, said, 'You'll learn, mate,' and walked away. I was introduced to the other three doormen who were working that night and informed that the manager was expecting a full house. 'That means there will be eight hundred and fifty of them, Lew, and only five of us,' the head doorman said. 'I know you have been in here as a customer, but working here is a different ball game. As a punter you don't see half of what goes on. As a doorman you should only miss a quarter of the shit.' He advised me that the reputation for trouble that the club had earned at that time was well deserved. 'People only come in here for two reasons, Lew: they either want to fuck someone or fight someone.' While still absorbing these prophetic words of wisdom, I was pointed in the direction of the main bar and dance floor.

'Your mission,' the head doorman said, 'is to go mingle and ensure drunks don't lay, sit, fornicate or fight in that area.' I felt uncomfortable walking around sober in my best suit seeing drunken friends and enemies of my own age enjoying themselves. While pausing momentarily to take in the chaotic scene, I felt two arms wrap around my chest and hold me in a vice-like grip. Without hesitating I threw my head forward then smashed it back as hard as I could into the face of my attacker. I felt his hold on me loosen, so I turned, ready to unload a barrage of punches. Taffy was doubled over, holding his nose, trying to stem the flow of blood that was quickly turning his white shirt red. 'You bastard, you bastard,' he said as he sank to his knees. 'I was only messing about, Lew. It was a fucking joke.'

'Just as well I didn't have that cosh, then,' I replied laughing. Taffy never did see the funny side of his own joke, nor did he ever offer me advice on how to look after myself again.

Despite having an income from working on the door at the Plaza, I realised that I would have to find full-time work in order to make ends meet. Running a car, looking good and taking Jean out was certainly not cheap. Instead of pursuing a trade, as I had done in the past, I went to work as a labourer on a building site. It was hard graft, but to be honest I enjoyed the work and it kept me extremely fit. For the first time since leaving school I felt content with the way my life was going. I had a beautiful girlfriend, a car that was almost reliable, a day job and a part-time job at weekends. Money appeared to me as if it was in abundance, and I was happier than I had ever been. Nine months after meeting Jean she told me that she had something important to tell me but I had to promise not to get annoyed. My heart sank: she had found somebody else, was moving away or didn't like me any more. Every possible dark scenario swarmed around my tortured mind. 'I promise I won't get annoyed,' I lied. 'Just tell me, Jean, tell me.'

'I think I am pregnant, Lew,' she said. 'I think we are going to have a baby.'

I was overjoyed but also concerned about how our parents would react. 'Are you sure?' I asked her. 'We can't tell anyone until you know for definite.'

A week later Jean's doctor confirmed what she already knew: she was having my baby. I offered to go and break the news to her parents, but Jean was adamant that it was best coming from her. Eventually we agreed that I would tell my parents and she would tell hers. My father took the view that what is done is done and we would just have to get on with it. My mother was unhappy. She told me that I had thrown my life away. I was, according to her, incapable of looking after myself, let alone a woman and child. Jean's father hit the roof when she told him. He vowed never to let me in his home again. Her mother, on the other hand, accepted what had happened and said that she would do all that she could to help Jean, our baby and myself. When everybody had come to terms with the news, tempers mellowed and within a month Jean and I were living together at her parents' home. Acceptance did not mean forgiveness: Jean's father would make sarcastic comments about me and sit in silence if we found ourselves alone together in the same room. It didn't bother me because I had never thought much of him or his opinions.

In those days unmarried mothers were a rarity, and unplanned pregnancies generally resulted in shotgun weddings. Before Jean and I had even been consulted, our mothers were making the arrangements. One evening after work Jean and I had to attend a meeting with a vicar at St Matthew's church, where our wedding was to take place. Sitting in the vestry counting the seconds until it was time to leave, I listened to the vicar drone on and on about God, the sanctity of marriage and the importance of the vows Jean and I were going to make. 'Of course, Lewis and Jean,' he said, 'before this marriage does take place, I expect to see you both here every Sunday.'

'You won't see me here every Sunday,' I replied. 'I am a busy man.'

'I am afraid you don't understand, Lewis,' the vicar said. 'You have to attend if you wish to get married in church.'

I told the vicar it was him that didn't understand. 'I am not coming here every Sunday, and if that means I can't get married in your church, fine.' With that I stormed out, with Jean following closely behind in tears.

When Jean's mother heard what had happened, she went to speak to the vicar, and another appointment was made for the following week. 'It's a different vicar, Lew. Please just go and keep quiet,' she pleaded. Reluctantly, for Jean, I complied.

Jean's mother had obviously briefed the second vicar. The meeting was very brief and businesslike. 'You will stand here, Lewis. Jean will enter through that door. You'll say a few words, kiss your bride and be on your way,' he said. Before I knew it, Jean and I were back in the car and heading for home; our big day had been arranged.

When the wedding did take place, I was pleased I had allowed myself to be talked into cooperating. Jean looked absolutely beautiful. After the ceremony we climbed into my old Ford Anglia and headed for our honeymoon destination. Somebody had used red lipstick to scrawl 'Just Married' all over the windows. Old boots and a dozen tin cans had been tied to the bumper. The noise as we trundled along the M6 was horrendous. One hour or fifty-five miles later we reached our destination: Blackpool Pleasure Beach. I know it is hardly Barbados or Hawaii but it was all we could afford at the time. We had not bothered to book a room in advance because we thought at least one of the countless guest houses would have a vacancy, but we were wrong. I drove around looking for a room until the rattle of the cans tied to the bumper tested my sanity. 'Fuck this, Jean,' I said. 'We will have to sleep in the car.' Moments later I found a parking space just off the Golden Mile and pulled in. It may not have been the ocean view Jean may have once dreamed of looking at from her honeymoon suite window, but it was certainly a view she was unlikely to forget.

The following morning a milk cart rattling past awoke us. I started the engine and resumed my search for somewhere to stay. Jean sat next to me in silence; her first night as Mrs Martindale had hardly been magical. The tin cans, which were still attached to the bumper, rattled along the street disturbing the early morning silence and destroying my concentration. After what I had endured, fortune just had to smile on me. The first guest house I found had a vacant double room, which we booked for a week. I was overjoyed. We had a roof over our heads, and a bed, but the icing on the cake was the fact the landlord was an ex-fighter who had adorned the walls of every room with photographs of boxing legends. Happy? I was in heaven.

When we returned from Blackpool, Jean's mum greeted us with good news. A lady she knew had advertised a flat to rent in Thatto Heath, St Helens. Jean's mother had been to see her, explained we were looking for our first home and she had agreed to rent it to us. Jean cried, she was so happy. I too was happy, mainly because I hated being under the same roof as her father. Over the next few weeks our mothers helped us to furnish and decorate the flat, which was above a chip shop in Grange Park Road. Shortly after moving in, Jean went into labour and was rushed to hospital. When I heard the news, I drove to the nearest public telephone box. 'It's a boy, Mr Martindale,' the nurse said. 'You have a son.' I went home, got changed and rushed to the hospital. It's hard to explain how I felt when I first set eyes on my son. It's a unique experience that only people with children can appreciate. We named him Glynn, in recognition of my mother's Welsh heritage. My future appeared to be mapped out. I had my menial steady job, a wife (who didn't yet look tired), one snotty kid and a second-hand car. Jesus Christ, I thought, I'm turning into my old school headmaster.

I don't know what possessed me to do it – visions of leapfrogging my headmaster's success, perhaps – but I exchanged my reliable Ford Anglia for a Ford Zodiac Executive with a Scouser who had 'don't trust me' written all over him. The vehicle looked the part, but halfway home the oil light came on. I pulled into a garage and topped the engine up, but a few miles further down the road the light came on again. After topping the engine up a second time, I managed to get the vehicle home despite a glowing engine that threatened to melt the bonnet. Parked outside the chip shop, the car looked the business. Mr and Mrs Martindale, the neighbours must have thought, were doing very well for themselves. We were in fact doing far from well. The truth was the car was a heap of scrap and the wedding, honeymoon, flat and birth of our son had left us in debt – so much so that I couldn't afford to tax the car, so I 'acquired' somebody else's tax disc and altered the details on it. A few days later a policeman pulled me over for a routine check and spotted the tax disc had been tampered with. I was arrested, taken to the local police station and interviewed. I told the police that I had no idea who had stolen the tax disc and altered it. 'I only purchased the vehicle three days ago, and the tax disc was on it,' I lied. I was released on bail, while the police made further enquiries. When I returned to the station a week later, I was told that there would be no further action against me.

'That Scouser had plenty of previous convictions for this,' the policeman told me. 'We searched his garage and found lots of false paperwork. I'm sorry for troubling you.' I had to laugh to myself. I had taken the tax disc from a car in a scrapyard, but I didn't feel guilty about the Scouser getting nicked for it because he had told me the Zodiac was in good condition when he must have known it was a mechanical wreck.

I read in the local paper that a man named Johnny Sullivan was appealing for top amateur fighters to join him at a gym in Preston and turn professional. I knew all about Johnny. He had started his remarkable boxing career in his father's 'Battling Sullivan's Boxing Booth', with which he travelled nationwide fighting all comers. After brawling in the booths, Johnny had turned professional at 16 and soon earned a reputation for being a very stylish, exciting, heavy-handed puncher with the ability to analyse his opponents' style very quickly. Every one of his ninety-seven professional fights was a crowd-pleaser. After knocking out an opponent named Ronnie Grogan in the second round of a bout, Johnny was awarded the prestigious *Boxing News* 'Fighter of Merit' award. He then went to America and topped the bill at Madison Square Garden against top opponents Gordon Wallace, Mike Gillo, Rory Calhoun and Joey Giambra. On his return to Britain Johnny knocked out Gordon Hazel in the first round to win the British middleweight and Commonwealth (British Empire) middleweight titles aged just 22. But a controversial decision later saw him lose these titles to Pat McAteer. He returned to have six more bouts in America, then became a light heavyweight in Britain, where he finished his career against Tonga's Johnny Halifihi and Trinidad's Yolande Pompey.

The opportunity to have such a seasoned fighter as Johnny as my manager was too good to miss. I telephoned the gym, and Johnny invited me over to assess my ability. I don't know what came over me, but even before meeting Johnny I told Jean that we were moving to Preston. 'Are you mad, Lew?' she asked. 'We have a home here. You have a job. In Preston we have nothing.'

'And we will end up with nothing if we stay here,' I replied.

'I want to do something for us. I want you and Glynn to be proud of me. I want to be a champion fighter.'

Jean looked at me as if I had finally gone mad. 'Unfortunately you're the boss, Lew,' she said, shaking her head, 'so if that's what you really, really want, we will go.'

I didn't know it at the time, but leaving St Helens, where Jean and I had been so happy, was going to prove to be one of the biggest mistakes of my life.

When I arrived at the gym for my assessment, I was told that I would have to spar with three separate opponents. 'Each of these fighters has a different technique,' Johnny said. 'I want to see how you defend against different attacks and how you attack different defences.'

When I turned to go and get changed, Johnny's father, 'Battling Sam' Sullivan, stood in front of me. 'Show me some moves,' he said. As I took up various poses, ducked and weaved, Sam began jabbing me. I thought he was testing my jaw, because half-hearted taps into my face soon became explosive hard thuds. Determined to impress both Johnny and his father I took the punishment and stood my ground. 'You will do, lad,' Sam said. 'Get changed. Show me what you can do in that ring.'

In the very first round of the first bout I knocked the guy I was fighting down, and there he remained. In the second round of my second bout the referee stepped in, saying I was too strong for my opponent. In the third round of my third bout I knocked a tall lad with a long reach clean out. Sam came into the dressing-room as I was getting changed and said that the fighters were complaining because they had never been hit so hard. 'We want you to turn professional,' he said. 'Believe me, lad, you have what it takes. Johnny has applied for his licence to manage fighters. We will be able to get you big-money bouts in America. You can go all the way, Lew, I know it.'

When I got home, I could not wait to tell Jean what Sam had said. Visions of me winning titles and earning vast amounts of money swirled through my head. My dream could now become reality, but I would have to move nearer to Johnny's gym in Preston so that I could train regularly. A house became vacant opposite Jean's brother Bob's in Blackburn. The gym was only a 20-minute journey away, so we made enquiries about it.

We were told the property was for sale rather than to rent. Jean and I had enough money saved for a small deposit, but I knew I would need a regular full-time job in the area if we were going to take on a mortgage. Jean's brother came to our rescue. Bob said that he would be able to offer me full-time employment in the joinery and shuttering company that he owned. Three months later Jean, Glynn and I moved to Blackburn.

While I waited for Johnny to obtain his management licence, I trained exceptionally hard. The other lads who used the gym were reluctant to get in the ring with me so, in an effort to give them confidence, Johnny put on a pair of gloves himself and climbed in. 'Come on then, Lew. Show me what you can do,' he said. Johnny was a big man, so I kept my distance in the first round. I thought if I made him work, I could wear him down and then attack. In the second round, as he advanced towards me, I hit him so hard that he flew into the ropes. As he got to his feet, I could see that he had been shocked by the power of my punches. 'You bastard,' he shouted. 'You bastard.' Johnny took off his gloves, threw them on the floor and then climbed out of the ring.

'Don't call me a bastard,' I shouted after him before getting out of the ring myself and heading towards the dressing-room. When Johnny calmed down, he began telling everybody that I was good enough to become the next Rocky Marciano. The only comparison I can draw today between myself and Marciano is the fact that his life and my boxing career ended in much the same way: unexpectedly and abruptly. Marciano died in an aeroplane crash and my hopes and dreams fell to earth when Johnny's application for a manager's licence was turned down. Johnny owed tax in America from his own fighting days, so the boxing board deemed him unsuitable for management.

Distraught but not deterred, I telephoned one of my old trainers, Herbie Goulding, at the Raven ABC in Warrington and asked if he could pull a few strings and get me in the ABA's North-West Counties Championships. Herbie said that it was extremely unlikely, as applications for the current year's finals should have already been submitted. 'I will give it a go, though, Lew,' he said, 'but don't get your hopes up.' Three days later Herbie telephoned me and said he had managed to get me a place in the competition. I could not quite believe my luck. If I boxed well and won the competition, I still had a chance of turning professional.

I was chosen to fight Billy Aird, who was the northern counties amateur champion for three years running. The fight took place at Liverpool Stadium. I really liked fighting at that venue because it was like a proper professional fighters' arena. The only thing I didn't like about the place was the fact the dressing-rooms were always freezing cold. I fought there several times and also watched a lot of fights there. On the night I fought Billy Aird, I was feeling confident but anxious. I knew he was no mug, so I wanted to get stuck into him early and finish the job as soon as possible. The moment the bell rang to signal the start of the first round, I laid into him, pounding his ribs and torso. I knew I was hurting him because he was trying to hold my arms, grabbing me like a crab. In the second round Billy continued holding on to me, preventing me from landing any decent punches. I began to get frustrated and decided I would have to employ one of the dirty tricks George Gilbody Snr had taught me. Billy was 6 ft 2 in. tall, a nice height for my head, so I let him feel it a couple of times. As his legs began to buckle, the referee grabbed my arm and dragged me away. I couldn't hear what he was saying because the crowd were cheering and clapping, but when he pointed his finger and then pointed at each of the three judges, I knew I had been given a public warning. I shouted, 'Fuck off!' at the referee before grabbing him and throwing him across the ring. The referee staggered and stumbled before falling into the ropes. Billy stood in his corner with a look of astonishment on his face. I don't think he knew what to say or do.

When the referee regained his composure, he stood pointing at me and began shouting, 'Out! Out! Out!' Despite his apparent sense of outrage he wouldn't come anywhere near me. The crowd were on their feet, waving and cheering. They were loving it. When I got back to my corner, I noticed Joe Erskine was in the front row watching me. Joe was British heavyweight champion in 1956–7. He fought Henry Cooper on five occasions, of which he won two and lost three. Joe was an absolutely fantastic fighter. Alongside Joe was Harry Scott, a Scouse boxing legend who had fought Alan Minter, Kevin Finnegan, Chris Finnegan and Rubin Hurricane Carter twice. As I climbed out of the ring, Harry Scott looked at me, winked and then started laughing. It's a moment I shall never forget. You can't get much better than a nod of approval from one of boxing's greats.

Billy Aird later turned professional. He fought four heavyweight title bouts, three of which he lost, but in September 1970 he did defeat Richard Dunn (who went on to fight Muhammad Ali) to claim the Central Area heavyweight title. As for me, my euphoria was short-lived. A rather formal letter informed me that, for assaulting the referee, I was banned from the ring for 12 months. The dream was back on hold.

They say that bad things happen in threes. I had failed to turn professional; I had then been banned from boxing; and then one afternoon at work I had an argument with my brother-in-law Bob and he sacked me. Fearing I would be unable to pay our mortgage and end up homeless, I tried hard to secure a new job. I had kept in touch with Johnny Sullivan in the hope he would one day get his management licence. When I told him that I'd been banned from boxing and had then lost my job, he suggested we meet, as he had a proposition for me. 'Do you think you could look after this place?' he asked, as we sat together in the Hibernian Club in Preston.

Looking around at the mainly Irish working-class clientele, I could see no reason why I wouldn't be able to maintain order. 'Sure, Johnny, I could do it,' I said. 'Is there a vacancy, then?'

Johnny explained that a group of pro-Republican Irishmen had started frequenting the club and were causing trouble. In one incident they had beaten up a customer simply because he was English. 'There is a doorman employed here,' he said, 'but to be honest he is not up to much. The management want somebody to restore order, and I suggested you. The job's there if you want it.' Without hesitating I agreed to take the job and thanked Johnny.

The doorman I inherited at the Hibernian turned out to be an all-singing, all-dancing action hero. What he did not know or had not done was not worth knowing or not worth doing, or so he thought. In reality he was an incompetent fool, incapable of throwing himself downstairs, let alone some of the Neanderthal men we were expected to sort out. Every time a fight broke out, the hero would disappear into the toilets or go for a walk around the car park. I was not aware that we were responsible for patrolling the local neighbourhood, but the hero certainly dedicated a lot of time to doing so.

One evening I asked the three pro-Republican Irish guys if they would leave because they were becoming increasingly intoxicated and loud. 'Fuck you, you English bastard!' one of them shouted. Without replying, I grabbed him in a headlock and charged towards the exit door. His head smashed into the push bar and the door burst open. As he began to stumble, I released him and he fell to the floor. I walked back inside the club and asked his friends once more to leave. Somebody had either told them that I had parents or they had decided they no longer wanted trouble, because I wasn't referred to as a bastard again. They simply drank their drinks and left.

Later that night, as the hero patrolled the neighbourhood, he saw the Irishmen kicking my car, which I had parked some distance from the club. Instead of confronting the men, the hero ran back towards me shouting, 'Lew, Lew, they are smashing up your car!'

I ran outside, and when I reached my vehicle, the men were still kicking it. When they saw me, they began shouting, 'Come on, you English bastard! We will kill you!'

Two hit the pavement after I unleashed a left and right hook in quick succession. The third and loudest mouth I held against the car so I could really punish him. Blow after blow landed in his kidneys and head. He was semi-conscious and still trying to vomit when I eventually let him fall to the floor. I looked at my car and then looked at the three men lying alongside it. The red mist came down. 'Bastard, bastard, bastard!' I shouted as I kicked and stamped on each of them. The hero and several customers came out of the Hibernian and tried to calm me down.

A woman began screaming, 'Stop him! For God's sake, stop him! He will kill them.' I think it was the sheer panic in her voice that brought me to my senses. Another, calmer, female voice was demanding that an ambulance be called. I knew that when an ambulance did attend, the police would not be far behind. I looked at the men, who were spattered with blood and lying motionless. It was time for me to go and never return. I told the hero, who was visibly shaking, to get everybody inside so they could not see which car I was going to get into.

'An ambulance is on its way,' the hero shouted. 'Please can you all go inside?'

As soon as the last person entered the club, I jumped in my car, started the engine, put my thumb up to the hero and sped away.

Johnny Sullivan later told me that the three men had all suffered injuries that required hospital treatment. 'Luckily for you, Lew, they hate the police more than they hate the English, so they refused to talk to them. Had they done so, you would be going to prison for a very long time.'

I knew Johnny was right. Losing my temper had caused me to lose my boxing licence and my job, and now I had come close to losing my liberty. I knew I had to try to control my rage. I also knew that it was not going to be easy.

# ROUND THREE

WHETHER I WAS GOING TO BE BOXING IN THE RING OR BOXING ON THE DANCE floor of a nightclub, I knew that I had to maintain my fitness. In an effort to do so, I drove 200 miles per week to get to and from St Helens ABC, where I had started training. Tony Smart, the trainer at the club, noticed how keen I was and urged me to re-apply for my boxing licence. 'Fuck that. I am not grovelling to them,' I said, but Tony was adamant.

'What's the point of putting this much effort into training if you're never going to box again?'

Reluctantly I agreed to sit down and write a letter of apology for hurling the referee across the ring during the Billy Aird bout. I didn't mean a word of what I wrote, but I wanted my licence back. It took a few months and three ridiculously long letters of major sucking up before my licence was finally reinstated. Lew Martindale was once more getting ready for the boxing ring. I had the required physique, I had the willpower and I had an abundance of new sparring partners: the customers at my latest place of work.

The Cavendish Club on Lords Square, Blackburn, regularly attracted 2,000 revellers when it was at its height of popularity.

Trends change and inevitably numbers dwindled before the club underwent various refurbishments, name and ownership changes. The last I heard, it had regained its popularity and is again one of the north-west's most exclusive clubs but is now called Heaven and Hell. If I had been asked to think of a name for the club when I worked there, I too would have called it Heaven and Hell, as it contained elements of both under the same roof. The Cavendish could be a joy to work in. It had a casino, a silver-service restaurant, a discotheque and a stage on which artists such as Dusty Springfield, Slade, Alan Price, Kiki Dee and The Troggs would play. The clientele were, in the main, the more affluent members of the local community. Being paid to be entertained by successful pop stars, control well-mannered non-violent people and hang around a casino looking at beautiful girls was heaven to me. It was the groups of wannabe gangsters who tried to get in every night that made it hell.

There were eight doormen employed at the Cavendish. The head doorman Ray Copeland and Big Jack Holt (who is now involved with the running of Bolton Amateur Wrestling Club) were top men, but the rest were, at best, useless. In order to get into the club, which was situated above the main shopping precinct in Blackburn, customers had to use a lift. As the doors opened and the occupants spilled out, we would soon gauge whether they were going to be trouble or not. It's not something I can explain; it's an instinct or skill that you develop while working on the doors, but unfortunately it's not infallible.

One evening three coaches full of rugby players from Wigan arrived. We didn't normally allow large groups of men into the club, but these appeared sober and courteous enough as they entered reception and so were welcomed. Just before closing time the door staff were called to a disturbance at the main bar.

When I arrived, I saw that several of the rugby players were pushing one another and their friends were trying to intervene. I positioned myself between the two factions and told them to get out of the club. Four men dressed in smart blazers informed me that they were rugby-club officials and they were going to sort it out. 'There's no need for anybody to leave,' they announced. 'We will resolve this.'

'I am not sure what language you speak in fucking Wigan, mate,' I said, 'but here in Blackburn and most other parts of the UK, get out means fucking leave.'

The officials looked at me, looked at the door and started walking towards it. The players followed meekly behind. The last three to leave were huge thickset men, and I sensed that they would want to have the last word. As they stepped outside the door, one of them said to me, 'I will have it with you.'

By the time I reached him, he was standing on the steps that led to the multi-storey car park. 'You'll have it with me, will you?' I said. I still can't believe what happened next. The man raised his hand to his face, popped his false eye out and put it in his top pocket. Crack! I punched him in his gaping eye socket and knocked him straight out.

When his friends saw what had happened, they ran down the stairs and onto the car park screaming, 'Kicker, Kicker, get up here quick!'

I have no idea who Kicker was because he ignored his friend's appeals for help and remained elusive. I picked up my semi-conscious one-eyed opponent and threw him down the short flight of stairs onto the car park. I then looked to see if his friends were leaving or coming back for more, but they were doing neither. For some unknown reason they were involved in a pitched battle against one another. The police eventually arrived, herded them onto their coaches and escorted them out of town.

I have no idea how the one-eyed guy got home. He was still staggering about long after his teammates had left. As I say, the instinct and skill you develop on the door concerning the likely behaviour of people unfortunately isn't always an exact science.

I ejected an Asian guy one evening who had been involved in a minor scuffle. As he waited for the lift to take him to the street, he became abusive and threatened to assault me. I told him in no uncertain terms that he was welcome to try, but he remained where he was and continued to shout abuse. Eventually the lift arrived, he got in, the doors closed and I thought I had seen the last of him. Ten minutes later the lift doors opened and the Asian guy re-emerged. 'You wanker! Die, you wanker!' he screamed as he ran towards me. I stood in the door and waited for him to get within striking distance of me. With arms flailing wildly, he crashed into me. I managed to knock him back out of the door, but not before he had lunged at me with a knife and stabbed me through the right forearm. Blood poured out of the wound. I looked down at the hole in my jacket, looked down at my assailant and moved towards him. The expression on my face told him all he needed to know. Before I could grab him, he was on his feet and moving rapidly in the opposite direction to me. Instead of waiting for the lift, he jumped down the short flight of steps that led onto the multi-storey car park and ran down the exit road until he reached the ground floor. I chased him out into the street, and when he realised I was not going to give up, he sought sanctuary in a pub. I didn't care where I caught him or who witnessed what I was going to do to him, so the fact he was in a public place meant nothing to me. The bastard was going to pay wherever he was. As I entered the pub, he stood next to the bar and picked up two glasses, one in each hand. 'Stay back, you mad bastard!' he shouted. 'Stay back, or I will glass you.'

I was so relieved I had caught him and so pleased he was clearly terrified that I began to laugh. 'You're fucked, son,' I said. 'Glass me. Go on, glass me, because I am going to cut you a new arsehole.' I picked up a glass and walked slowly towards him. Before I could reach him, two police officers burst into the bar and told me to put the glass down. My assailant was crouched down trembling in the corner of the room, so they assumed I was the aggressor and arrested me. Once outside I explained that I was a doorman and the Asian guy had stabbed me for no reason. The officers looked at my wound, told me to remain where I was, then went back into the pub to arrest the man. When they brought him outside, he was struggling and shouting that he was going to 'do the bouncer'. Being public spirited, I decided to help the officers. I grabbed the Asian by the hair with one hand and by the seat of his trousers with the other. I lifted him until he was waist high, asked the police to open the back door of their car and then launched him head first into it.

I returned to work, but it was made clear to me that my way of dealing with unruly customers was not acceptable. Nothing was said to my face, but there were constant snide remarks made by the management about unnecessary violence and the number of customers who were complaining. It seemed as if they were looking for an excuse to get rid of me. Inevitably they found one. Like most door staff of that era, we had a fiddle going. Customers would come in, purchase a ticket from the cashier and then hand it in to the doorman at the point of entry. These tickets would then be counted by the manager at the end of the night to ensure the cashier's till tallied up with the number of customers who had paid to get in. For instance 1,000 tickets sold at £5 each meant there should have been £5,000 in the till. I would collect the tickets, wrap an elastic band around ten or twenty of them and then drop the tickets to a friend, who would be waiting 50 ft below in the shopping precinct. This person would then sell them to people waiting to get the lift up to the club at a discounted rate. Those who had purchased a ticket would then come into the club, show the cashier the ticket and say they had been in earlier but had popped back out for something. The cashier would wave them through, and the ticket would be handed back to me. It wasn't exactly lucrative, but it doubled my meagre wage every night.

One evening a man who regularly purchased my discounted tickets came into the reception area drunk and stuffed two or three pound notes into my top pocket in front of the assistant manager. Before I had a chance to ask the man what he was up to, the assistant manager pointed at me and said, 'Come here, Lew.'

I had always disliked this guy. In my opinion he spoke down to the door staff. 'Who the fuck are you talking to?' I replied.

Without answering, he walked away in the direction of the manager Sid Stuart's office. I did not wait to be summoned; I followed him and burst through the door just as he was grassing me to Sid. 'Calm down, Lew,' Sid pleaded. 'We don't want any trouble, but you have been caught fiddling. I am going to call the police.'

'Really, Sid,' I replied, 'and how the fuck are you going to do that?' I grabbed the two telephones that were on his desk, threw them on the floor, stamped repeatedly on them and then ripped the wires out of the wall.

The assistant manager ran shouting from the office, 'Help, help, Paul! Lew has gone mad!'

Paul, a muscular young barman, entered the office. I told him to fuck off or he'd get it as well. He ran off without saying a word. I informed Sid that he could stick his job and walked out of the office. The assistant manager was in the corridor outside. I grabbed him by the lapels of the ridiculous-looking green velvet suit he was wearing and pulled his face close to mine. 'If you ever dream of grassing me, I will pull your useless fucking head off. Do you understand?' He wasn't listening; he was trembling with fear and pleading with me to let him go. 'Do you fucking understand?' I shouted.

'Yes, yes,' he replied. 'I understand.' With a lapel in each hand I stretched my arms out. As the velvet cloth tore, he was lowered to the floor. When I walked away, he was on his knees clutching his shredded suit and sobbing uncontrollably.

Jean was happy when I told her that I was no longer going to be employed on the door. I had been working six nights a week, which meant we rarely had an opportunity to go out together. The violence I encountered at the club and the endless stream of threats I received down the phone while at home worried Jean. 'Get a normal job, Lew,' she begged. 'We have a young son to think about now. We don't need all of the aggravation.'

The trouble with women is they are usually bloody right, so, with a heavy heart, I agreed. I started work at the Lion Brewery in Coniston Road, Blackburn. I was employed in the keg room, stacking and cleaning out aluminium beer barrels. It was mundane work, but I enjoyed it – not only because the pay and working conditions were good, but also because I was able to train throughout the day using the full beer barrels as weights.

My boxing career had undoubtedly been hampered by my marriage to Jean and the nomadic life we had led. Including junior and schoolboy bouts I had, to date, fought more than 40 opponents in the ring. I had been disqualified five or six times for head-butting, biting or some similar violation of the rules, been beaten on points approximately eight times and had won the remainder. Had I boxed at one gym with the same trainer, which would have helped me to focus exclusively on developing my craft, I am confident I could have fought and defeated any British heavyweight. Ifs, buts and maybes: I accept that everybody's life is tainted by those phrases, but I know I had the ability, and a lot of respected people in boxing think I had it too.

A month after I started work at the brewery, Jean announced that she was pregnant with our second child. Both of us were excited and extremely happy about the prospect of another addition to our family. Nine months later our daughter Joanne was born. After all of the numerous ups and downs we had endured since we first met, stability and normality appeared to have finally arrived in the Martindale home. Jean saw an advertisement in the local newspaper regarding a hairdressing salon that was for sale. Owning her own business had been a long-term ambition of Jean's, so I told her to ring the number. I had been chasing my dream with little success since we had first met, so I felt it was only right that Jean should be given the opportunity to pursue hers. The salon was situated in Colne Road, Burnley. Above it was a spacious flat, which was to be included in the sale. Jean fell in love with the salon and the flat as soon as she saw them. 'We have to take it, Lew,' she said. 'It's too good an opportunity to miss.'

Within a few weeks we had sold our home, purchased the salon and flat and moved in, to begin our business venture. J.L. (Jean and Lew's) Hairdressing Salon soon attracted enough custom for us to employ two other stylists – not that I was involved in any way in the shop; my job was looking after our two children and doing chores around the flat. When the children were old enough to attend nursery, Jean took care of them and the shop, and I went back to work as a builder. These were years that I remember with great affection; life was simple but rewarding.

In late 1972 Jean fell pregnant with our third child. I'm not sure if it was her hormones playing up or her intuition, but Jean was convinced that if she allowed anybody to manage the salon for us he or she would be dishonest. Jean was equally adamant that nobody could be trusted to babysit our as yet unborn child when it arrived, so the salon was put on the market and we went in search of a new larger home. In July 1973 Jean gave birth to our son Billy. Life for the Martindale family just seemed to be getting better and better. Having disposed of the shop and flat, we purchased a house amongst the hills in the beautiful Rossendale Valley, which is just outside Burnley. The views from our windows were breathtaking. It was certainly the ideal location to bring up three small children. I was working on a construction site at a place called Mellor in Blackburn around this time doing paving and tiling. The money wasn't great, but work in the building industry was becoming increasingly difficult to come by.

One of the guys on site was a painter who fancied himself as a bit of a kung-fu expert. He would talk to people like shit, strut around whooping like Bruce Lee and kick piles of bricks. I hated the bastard and knew it wouldn't be long before we fell out. Everybody else on the site feared him, as they considered him to be a bit of a nutter, but I could see through his charade. One day I was sitting having lunch in a bathroom I had been tiling when he entered. I was having a laugh and a joke with a couple of other builders when Blackburn's answer to Bruce Lee shouted out, 'Oi, Bluto, keep the fucking noise down.' I didn't reply. I just got to my feet and smashed my fist into his sneering mouth. He flew across the room before ending up on the floor in a crumpled heap. 'My head, my head,' he moaned. When he looked up at me, I saw that he had plenty to moan about. His face had ballooned so much that his features had become distorted, and it was continuing to swell. To be honest, I became quite concerned, as a huge lump appeared to be growing out of his cheek under the eye. It looked as if his head was going to explode. Bruce Lee sensed he was in trouble too. He got to his feet while clutching his oversized head and ran from the room screaming, 'Help me, help me!'

When the site manager saw the state the man was in, he immediately called an ambulance. 'Fuck this, lads,' I said to my workmates. 'I'm going, and if anybody asks, you haven't seen me.' I jumped into my van and sped away from the site, never to return. I later learnt that Bruce Lee had suffered a burst blood vessel when I had punched him. He was kept in hospital overnight for observation but released the following day when the swelling had subsided.

Finding employment was becoming almost impossible in the north-west of England at this time. Even if you did manage to find a job, your days were spent on strike rather than working. It is difficult to comprehend today how much power union barons wielded in those days. There were endless strikes afflicting the Post Office, the steel industry, the construction industry, the ferries and much more. In 1977 a staggering 49 per cent of self-employed people in the construction industry went bankrupt. Throughout the 1970s industrial disputes alone cost the country between six million and ten million lost working days a year. The introduction of the three-day week and the arrival of 'stagflation' (the combination of inflation and recession – an economy that begins to shrink while prices still continue to rise) brought the country to its knees.

To keep myself occupied and in shape, I started training at Eric Wilson's gym, which was in the old town-hall buildings in Burnley. Prior to Eric's arrival at the gym, a wrestling club had used it, but he had 'evicted them' and encouraged boxers, cyclists, weightlifters and anybody else interested in developing their physique or skills to train there. Eric was 69 years of age and had been involved in boxing all of his life. For his age Eric was very fit. He would work out in the gym and cycle everywhere he went, regardless of the distance. Eric's home, like his gym, was cleaned with military precision. Everything had its place and everything was spotless. The walls of his home were adorned with his excellent drawings, mainly of Disney characters. Autographed photographs of boxers, famous singers and actors, all in praise of Eric, surrounded the fireplace. He would not listen to any music other than country-and-western, and woe betide anybody who tried to handle his prized record collection.

In his younger years Eric had worked as a bouncer. During one incident he had been blinded in one eye after being stabbed with a drumstick. This made reading and some other tasks difficult, so I would do his weekly shopping, sort out his mail and do anything else that he had problems doing himself. Eric did not seem to be generally liked around Burnley. I think it was because he spoke his mind and didn't care whom he upset by doing so. That is what I liked about him: his almost brutal no-nonsense approach to life. When Glynn and Joanne were at school, I would take my youngest son, Billy, to Eric's home. One lens in Eric's spectacles was made of slightly misted glass to hide his damaged eye. Billy used to drop a coin behind the lens and howl with laughter while shrieking 'Penny Head'. When it was time to leave, Eric would give Billy a pile of drawings to take home for his brother and sister. Eric really appreciated all I did for him, and I appreciated all he did for the children and me.

In an effort to save money, I would go out in search of work on my bike rather than using the car (and this also helped to keep me fit). One lunchtime after yet another fruitless search I returned home, put my bike in the back garden and walked into the kitchen. It had been my intention to have a cup of tea and a sandwich before resuming my search. As I entered the kitchen, my old khaki-coloured transistor radio was playing some awful '70s music. David Cassidy, Donny Osmond and the Bay City Rollers all sounded pretty much the same to me: crap. I picked it up to turn it off just as the presenter introduced a guest. 'Welcome to Radio One, Roy,' he said. 'It's great to have you on the show.'

The man didn't reply; he grunted. Deciding against turning the radio off, I sat down and listened. Roy turned out to be Roy Shaw, a respected fighter who had made his name on the unlicensed boxing circuit in London. I had heard of Shaw through my good friend Ray Todd, who shared a flat with Brian Jacobs, Shaw's weight-training partner. Ray had told me that Shaw was an awesome fighter; few that had fought him had lasted more than a round. 'Despite his record,' Ray had said, 'I reckon you could beat him.'

As I sat listening to Shaw on the radio, I started to laugh. Shaw told the presenter that he wanted to fight Muhammad Ali. 'I could beat him,' he said. 'In fact I can beat anybody.'

The presenter, astonished as I was by Shaw's boasting, asked, 'Anybody, Roy? Are you claiming that you can beat anybody?'

'Yes,' replied Shaw, brimming with confidence. 'In fact if anybody is prepared to fight me, I will wager £10,000 I'll beat them.'

I nearly choked on my lunch when I heard this. Here I was, struggling to find work to support my wife and children, and a guy my friend had told me I could beat was promising £10,000 to anybody who could defeat him. At that time the average cost of a house in London was £13,500; today it is approaching £300,000, so the wager Shaw offered was quite substantial by anybody's standards. I ran out the back door, jumped on my bike and pedalled like fury to the nearest telephone box. 'Ray, Ray, listen to me,' I said when my friend picked up the phone. 'Get in touch with Roy Shaw and tell him your friend Lew has just heard his challenge on Radio One. Tell him that Lew said he wants a part of Roy Shaw. He wants to meet him, beat him and take his ten grand.' Ray said that he would contact Shaw as soon as possible and get back to me.

When Jean came home, I sat her down and said I had some good news. 'You've found a job, haven't you, Lew?' she beamed.

'Kind of,' I replied.

Jean's face displayed her disappointment. 'Kind of' could only mean there was some sort of catch. Jean knew the good news would be followed by a devastating big 'but'. 'What's the story then, Lew?' she asked.

'I am going to London to fight a guy named Roy Shaw,' I replied. 'They say he is the best, but if I beat him, and I know I can, I get £10,000 in prize money.'

Jean was neither excited nor despondent. She just looked up at me and said, 'If you have to go, Lew, then go.'

The following morning I headed for London. When I arrived at Ray's flat, I was introduced to Roy Shaw's friend Brian Jacobs. He told me that he was going to be acting as a go-between for both parties, and I said I had no problem with that. 'Has Roy ever met you, Lew?' Brian asked.

'No, he hasn't,' I replied. 'Why do you ask?'

'No reason,' Brian said. 'I am just looking at the size of you and imagining he hasn't.'

Moments later Brian left to begin the process of arranging

the most lucrative fight of my life. There was not a shadow of doubt in my mind that I would win. I had been training hard at Eric's gym and every ounce of my 17.5 st. muscular frame was bursting with energy. I was physically and mentally sharp. Eric's experience, expertise and training skills had perfected my ring craft. With all due respect to Roy Shaw, I didn't think he stood a chance against me.

When Brian returned from his meeting with Shaw and his manager, I could tell by the expression on his face that my challenge had not been accepted. 'There's a problem,' Brian said. 'Roy will fight you, but he now wants you to pay £10,000 up front. He will match it, and at the end of the fight it will be winner takes all.'

Shaw couldn't have hit me as hard as this news hit me. 'Where the fuck am I going to get £10,000 from? He didn't say all this when he was on the radio.'

Brian, unable to answer for his friend Shaw, said, 'That's what I have been told to tell you, Lew, and more than that I cannot say.'

The journey home to Jean and the children was torture. I was dreading facing them. I had departed with promises of wealth and was returning home empty-handed. My face said it all when Jean opened the door. She didn't speak; she just hugged me and said, 'Never mind, Lew, you tried.' But I had not tried; the fight with Shaw had not taken place. I had been robbed of my chance to succeed.

After just a few days of hanging around the house in a dejected mood, I decided to do something about our intolerable situation. The prospect of finding local work was nil and our debts were mounting. I told Jean that, while in London, Ray had told me there was plenty of work available in the building industry. I had decided to go down there, stay at his flat, work and send money home until the employment situation locally had improved. Neither of us wanted to be apart, but it was a case of needs must, so, with a heavy heart, Jean agreed. That weekend I kissed my wife and the children goodbye and headed back down the motorway to London.

# ROUND FOUR

WHEN I ARRIVED IN LONDON, I WENT STRAIGHT TO MY FRIEND RAY'S FLAT IN
Windsor Road, Forest Gate. His flatmate Brian Jacobs had
moved out, so Ray had agreed to let me rent his room. After
dropping off my meagre possessions, Ray introduced me to a
friend of his named Fat Joe, who lived two doors away. I made
small talk with Joe and mentioned that I was a keen boxer. Joe
said that he was a friend of Terry Lawless's, one of the most
successful managers in British boxing history. At first I thought
Joe was winding me up, but he insisted he knew Lawless and
told me to go down to his Old Royal Oak Gym in Barking
Road, Canning Town, the following day. After being reassured
by Ray and Joe that I was not the subject of a practical joke, I
said I would go and introduce myself.

When I entered the gym early the next morning, Terry Lawless
was standing to my right near a line of shadow-boxing mirrors.
I recognised him immediately. The boxer Jim Watt was training
nearby. Watt was to become world lightweight champion after
Roberto Duran left the title vacant in 1979. He knocked out
Alfredo Pitalua in 12 rounds to claim the title. On the walls of
the gym there were photographs of other fighters that Lawless

had managed, such as John L. Gardner from Hackney, who had thirty-nine fights, winning thirty-five and losing just four. Gardner's speed and aggression were to take him to the edge of world-class boxing at the turn of the 1980s. He won the British and Commonwealth titles by stopping one of my old opponents, Billy Aird. Gardner also stopped Rudi Gauwe and Lorenzo Zanon, a world-title challenger from Italy, in European title fights. There were also photographs of world welterweight champion John H. Stracey, world light middleweight champion Maurice Hope and Charlie Magri, the world flyweight champion. As I stood there in awe of these great fighters, Lawless approached me. 'Can I help you?' he asked.

'My name is Lew Martindale,' I replied, 'and I would like to train at this gym if that's possible.'

Terry shook my hand, introduced himself and said, 'I can see you have had cut eyes in the past. It certainly looks as if you have been around a ring before.'

After talking about my boxing record and the various trainers I had worked with, I was told by Terry that I was welcome to train at the gym.

The following evening, while working out and training, Lawless approached me. 'I have been watching you for a while tonight, Lew,' he said. 'It's obvious that you're a powerful, skilful fighter. Have you ever thought about turning professional?'

I explained to Terry that I had been through the motions before with Johnny Sullivan but nothing had come of it because Johnny had been denied a management licence. 'Keep at it, Lew,' he said. 'I will certainly be keeping my eye on you. I think you have the makings of a great heavyweight.'

I thanked Terry and asked him if he knew where I could find a bit of door work. I explained that I was struggling to find a job in the construction industry despite assurances from friends that there would be plenty when I arrived in London. Terry suggested that I speak to a Nigerian guy named Jamie, who regularly used the gym. When I contacted Jamie, he said they needed a couple of guys at a club called the Room at the Top in nearby Ilford, Essex. There had been an incident at the club recently that had resulted in a man losing his life. The police were treating the man's death as murder, and two members of the door staff had been arrested and bailed while enquiries continued. A condition of their bail was that they could not enter the club, so replacement door staff were required. Jamie advised me to go to the club and ask for a guy named Peter Koster.

That evening I drove to Ilford and found Peter sitting at a table in the club. I asked him if he was looking for door staff. Peter replied that he was, shook my hand and asked me my name.

'Lew Martindale,' I replied.

Peter looked me up and down and said, 'Not your real name, Lew. What name do you want to use if you end up working here?' Doormen back then, for a variety of reasons, including tax avoidance and evading police enquiries following incidents where customers had been hurt, used to give false names to the head doorman. I thought for a moment but couldn't think of a pseudonym to give to Peter. 'Any name will do,' Peter urged.

I suddenly remembered the nickname that other children had given me at school: Rowdy Yates. 'Yates,' I said to Peter. 'You can call me Lew Yates.'

We sat and talked about the various nightclubs that I had worked in and the men I had worked with and boxed in the ring. I liked Peter from the moment I met him. Despite being 6 ft 2 in., weighing 17 st. and being a broad-shouldered, very strong man, he was unusually calm and very diplomatic. I've never been able to explain it, but when Peter Koster has something to say,

81

regardless of the situation, people stop what they are doing and listen. Peter said that I sounded as if I knew what I was talking about regarding working on the doors, so I could start work that weekend. 'I will give you a night this week and see how you get on, Lew. If you're OK, I will give you more shifts next week.'

On my first night at the Room at the Top club a guy named John Chinnery showed me around. The club was situated approximately 120 ft above the street on top of Ilford shopping centre. Two or three doormen worked at ground level, where a lift, which held nine or ten people, would take customers up to the club. When they got out of the lift, they would enter the main reception area. Beyond that to the right was a restaurant and through a set of glass doors was the main room and dance floor.

It was a trendy club, which attracted in excess of 1,000 people a night at weekends. If there was any trouble in the club or at the front door a 'panic' button would be struck by a member of staff, which would illuminate a light on the DJ's console. The DJ would know which panic button had been pressed by looking at the particular light that was illuminated. He would then announce, 'Door staff to the front door,' 'Door staff to the dance floor,' or door staff to wherever. It was certainly a well-run club, but it needed to be because of the area it was in. The good people of Ilford were no mugs, and the local hard men were premier division. Times change, fortunately, and these days the Room at the Top is relatively trouble-free, but that wasn't my experience of it.

Early in the evening during my first shift there was an altercation outside the lift near reception. Three men were refusing to leave and one in particular was getting very aggressive. 'Leave now or I will knock you out,' I said.

The man looked at me and laughed. 'I will go in my own time.'

Before he hit the floor, I had sent his friend crashing into the wall with a right hook. 'Do you want some?' I asked the third man who was with them. He looked at his two friends, who were lying motionless in a heap, turned and ran into the lift. I assumed he didn't want trouble, so I stepped over one of the men and walked back into the main room of the club.

Peter Koster and the other door staff who had witnessed the incident laughed and said, 'Fucking hell, Lew, we are glad you're on our side. We could do with you being here every night.'

Two weeks after starting work at the club, I saw Roy Shaw bowl into reception with a few friends. This was the first time I had set eyes on the Guv'nor, the king of the unlicensed ring, whose crown I had come to London to take. It was definitely him; I recognised him from the numerous posters that had been plastered all over walls, billboards and bus shelters around the East End and Essex. I walked over to a man I knew named Peter Lee, who was with Shaw, and said hello.

'Hello, Lew,' he replied. 'Let me introduce you to Roy Shaw.'

'All right, mate,' Shaw grunted.

'Lew's a fighter,' Peter said.

Shaw looked at me and replied, 'Yeh, he looks like one.'

We shook hands and exchanged pleasantries, but throughout the brief conversation Shaw hardly looked at me. I was staring at him thinking, little do you know, I have come to this town for you and your title. I had not mentioned my challenge to Shaw to any of the door staff, because people were so in awe of him they would simply have told me that I was mad to even consider fighting him. They certainly wouldn't have taken me seriously. Knowing that and realising Shaw hadn't even remembered my name angered me. When I later calmed down, I had to laugh at my own stupidity. Shaw couldn't possibly have remembered my name, because when I first challenged him I was known as Martindale. Peter Lee had introduced me as Lew Yates. It didn't matter; Shaw was going to get to know me soon enough and regret doing so. I now not only wanted to take Shaw's crown; I wanted to shatter the illusion held by so many people that he was unbeatable. My chance, I hoped, would come eventually.

One evening I was walking around the club with a doorman named Ricky asking people to drink up. To be honest, it was the only part of the job I really disliked. There would always be some drunken arsehole staring down a glass at the last inch of his pint mumbling 'OK, OK, I'm leaving' but who in reality had no intention of moving. A group of about 15 heavy-looking guys were standing near the bar, and when Ricky asked them to drink up they totally ignored him. I walked over to them and said, 'Come on, lads, drink up. We want to get home tonight.' One of the group, whom I later found out was named Arnie, threw his drink over his shoulder. I immediately grabbed Arnie and said, 'You're out.' One of his friends lunged at me, so I hit Arnie, knocking him clean over a table, and started fighting with his friend. To this day I don't know who hit me, but I saw a heavy 'dimple'-type glass coming towards my face. I ducked, and it exploded on my forehead. The glass cut me to the bone just above my right eye. Blood gushed out and soaked my clothing. I went absolutely fucking berserk.

As I advanced towards the man I had been fighting with, I threw punches at everybody who tried to get in my way. The man I wanted started walking backwards, trying to distance himself from me. A large black guy stood in my way and put his hand inside his jacket, indicating that he was carrying a weapon. I ran towards him; he turned and sprinted towards the safety of the lift. A doorman named Neville Sheen was shouting, 'Watch him, Lew, watch him! He's got a blade!' When I got to the reception area, the black guy was with four or five of his friends in the lift. The door staff were holding me back. The lift doors closed and the men were gone. I went back into the club and knocked down two men who had been with the group. They didn't offer any resistance, so I left them lying where they fell. I searched the club for the man I had been fighting with when I was glassed, but he had vanished.

I was losing a lot of blood, so Peter Koster and another doorman said they would take me to King George's Hospital on Eastern Avenue. While we were in the accident and emergency department waiting room, a man came in and called Peter over. I couldn't hear what was being said, but when he left, Peter told me that it was Billy Blundell's driver. 'Who's Billy Blundell?' I asked.

Peter said that Billy was the guy I'd been fighting with when I'd been glassed. Peter explained that Billy's driver had been told to find out if I was going to look for them with a shooter. 'I told them you don't need a shooter, Lew. You can sort out problems with your hands.' Peter told me that Billy and his brother Eddie Blundell were 'top-drawer faces' who had been involved in a bloody turf war during which some of their rivals had been shot. 'They're nice enough geezers, Lew,' Peter said, 'but they don't mind going to war.'

'Neither do I, Peter,' I replied, 'especially when I am in the right.'

When the doctors had finished stitching me up, Peter dropped me off at home, and I thought no more about it.

A few weeks later I was in a car being driven by a doorman named Steve Ryan. We were passing a garage in Forest Gate called Ted's, which repaired not only cars but also commercial vehicles. I noticed there were two ice-cream vans on the forecourt. A thickset man sitting in a car parked next to them was talking to a mechanic. As we pulled up in the traffic, this man jumped out of his car and approached ours. It was Billy Blundell. 'Hello, Lew,' he said, extending his hand. 'I don't want any more trouble with you. I need to speak to Stevie.' I eyed Billy with caution as Stevie reversed into a parking space and got out of the car. When they had finished talking, I too got out. Billy apologised about the trouble at the club, laughed and said, 'Do you know something, Lew? I have never been hit so hard in my life. I have still got the fucking lumps on my head.' I could hardly be rude or aggressive to such an upfront guy, so we shook hands and agreed to put the matter behind us. In time Billy and I became friends, and we still laugh about our bloody introduction every time we meet.

A month or two after the row with Billy, a tall Scottish lad came to the door of the club. 'Are you a bouncer, mate?' he asked, while smirking at me.

'What makes you think that, Jock?' I replied.

'Because you have got a bow tie on,' he said.

'No, I'm not a bouncer. I just collect the fucking tickets and stand here entertaining the local idiots. The show's over for now. If you're going in the club, go in. If you're not, fuck off.' I was surprised to learn that this man, whom I'll call Iain, managed one of Billy Blundell's businesses. After he left the club that night, I told the door staff that I would appreciate it if they didn't let him in again. I had resolved my differences with Billy and assumed this mug had heard about the trouble and had come to the club to try to cause more.

The following week Iain turned up at the club and was told that I had said he couldn't come in. Iain turned, walked away and returned five minutes later with a car jack. 'Tell that cunt Lew I am going to do him,' Iain shouted at the door staff.

'No problem,' the door staff replied. 'Somebody will let him know.'

By the time I had been informed of his threats, Iain had left the building and was walking away down the street. I got into the lift and, once at ground level, ran out after him. Iain heard me coming up behind him, ran to his car, opened the passenger door, dived in and locked himself in. I ran around to the driver's door, managed to get my fingers in the top and began pulling the door off its hinges. Screaming in terror, Iain leapt from the car and ran. Halfway down the street he stopped running, turned and began shaping up as if preparing to box. He was throwing punches, ducking, weaving, and, I have to admit, he looked good. When I got near him, he changed his mind about fighting me and ran away again. In frustration I returned to his car, smashed every window, kicked in every panel and even bent his steering wheel. I heard no more from him until a few months later when one of the door staff said to me, 'That Scotsman's in here.'

'Where?' I asked. 'Where? I'll fucking kill him.'

The doorman pointed to Peter Koster, who was talking to a tall individual, and sure enough it was Iain the Scotsman. When I reached Peter, he was asking Iain what he was doing in the club. Iain, mouthy as always, replied, 'I will go when I finish my fucking pint.'

Without saying a word, I knocked his drink out of his hand, grabbed him by the throat and said, 'You're all mine, you wanker.' I dragged him through a fire exit and through the restaurant to an area behind the lift where nobody could see us. Peter had followed me out, but I told him to leave me alone with this guy. I let go of Iain and said, 'Come on then, you and me. I thought you wanted to have it with me?'

Iain struck the beautiful boxing pose he had displayed months earlier in the street. Acting is fine on stage, but it's pretty useless in a street fight. I hit Iain so hard that one of his teeth left his mouth like a .303 bullet. As I prepared to deliver another blow, I saw that his eyes were rolling in his head, so I stepped back. Bigmouth Iain was out cold before he had even met the floor.

Some doormen would have jumped all over him, but I had proved my point; there was no need for further violence. I dragged Iain to the lift, threw him in and sent him and it to the ground floor. The door staff below dragged him outside and left him lying in the doorway of Harrison Gibson's department store. They later told me that Iain had urinated and soiled himself, which isn't unusual when somebody gets knocked out like that. Forty-five minutes later, he was seen pulling himself up off the floor and staggering away into the night.

The next time I saw him, I was entering a shop in Manor Park as he was leaving. Iain glared at me, so I turned around and walked back out of the shop. He had either vanished into thin air or ran like an Olympic athlete. Either way, mouthy Iain was nowhere to be seen, and I haven't seen him since. I did, however, get a visit from some of his friends.

Funso Banjo is not a musical instrument, as I first thought when I heard the name. Funso Banjo was destined to become, according to a national newspaper, the next Muhammad Ali. Banjo, a Nigerian prince who had been sent to university in England, was a huge man, aged around 25 and fearsome looking because of the deep tribal scars that had been carved into his face. Banjo worked on a casual basis for Billy Blundell. I was told that he wasn't happy about the way I'd dealt with Iain and that I'd be wise to watch my back. Two Jaguar cars pulled up outside the club one night containing eight extremely large black guys and two Alsatian dogs. The manager had booked a few diverse cabaret acts in his time but I was sure this wasn't another.

'Mickey the Claw', a novelty act in his own right, had a Beatles haircut, stood at 5 ft 3 in., was painfully thin, talked through his nose because of a badly deformed jaw and only had three fingers on one hand. Despite his numerous unfortunate disabilities, the Claw, as we used to call him, was a helpful and well-meaning guy who worked with us at the club. It was the Claw's job to operate the lift that took the punters to and from the street. When I arrived downstairs after being told about the men, I saw the Claw shuffling around waving and pointing his three fingers at the men in the cars. I called out to him to stay away, then walked towards the vehicles. As I got close to the men, a police car pulled up and they drove away. The arrival of the police was unconnected to the presence of the men; the officers were just carrying out one of their regular courtesy calls to check all was OK in the club. I asked the Claw if he had recognised any of the cars' occupants.

'One was a guy called Rod [not his real name],' he snorted, 'and he was driving a car owned by Banjo.' The Claw didn't know who owned the other vehicle or the identities of the men in it. I knew Rod; he was 6 ft 6 in. tall and obscenely ugly. His jaw was twice as wide as the top of his head, which made it resemble a bucket.

The following Friday I noticed Rod leaning against the bar in the club having a drink. 'You all right, Rod?' I asked.

'Yes, man, yes. I'm cool,' he beamed.

'Tell your fucking mate Banjo I want to see him,' I said. Rod sensed that I was annoyed and stared straight ahead, not daring to reply or make eye contact. At the end of the night he came over to me and tried to make a joke about the situation. He was laughing, telling me to chill out and throwing playful punches at me. I said, 'Don't fuck about, Rod. If you want to throw punches, come out the back. Let's do it for real.' Rod was wearing a woollen hat, and as he turned to walk away I snatched it from his head. I walked towards the restaurant and urged Rod to come and retrieve it, but he remained where he was. I walked back to him, stuck his hat on the head of one of the other doormen and then punched Rod in the throat. He tried to fight me, but I slammed him into the wall, shouting, 'You aren't fucking strong enough, son.'

Rod, despite his size, didn't have the heart of a fighter; he was little more than a wimp. He begged me, 'Please, sir, please, sir, don't hit me.' I threw him into the lift, but even then he continued to grovel. I may sound like a bully, but this man and seven of his friends had been waiting to attack me for no reason. I hadn't hurt him for his part in the despicable plot; I had merely reminded him that I was no fool. The next time I saw Rod, he pulled alongside me at a set of traffic lights in Forest Gate. I looked over at him. He looked back at me, then slammed his car into gear and shot through a red light, narrowly missing a tipper lorry as he sped across the junction. Our paths never did cross again.

I was working six nights a week at the Room at the Top club and earning reasonable money. Every night when I got paid, I would put most of my wages in an envelope and post them home to Jean. The remainder I used to feed and support myself. I didn't have the time to go out and socialise as I was working nearly every night, so my existence was very cheap to maintain. Although I rang home regularly, I missed Jean and the children terribly. Some nights, after I had finished talking to them on the telephone, I would replace the receiver and be close to tears. The children would always ask when Daddy was coming home, but Jean was growing increasingly distant. I realised bringing up the children alone could not be much fun, so I suggested that she return to work. It would provide her with a bit of additional money, get her out of the house and give her a break from the kids. Jean agreed and started working part-time at a hairdressing salon in town. Billy was looked after by a close friend of Jean's, who also met the other children out of school. Initially Jean seemed much happier, but after a while she became distant again. I don't know what it was, but a voice in my head was telling me over and over that something was not right back home. However hard I tried to dismiss it, my sixth sense, intuition, call it what you will, would not let my troubled mind rest. I had been working for seven months in London when I asked for my first weekend off. 'I want to surprise the wife and children,' I confided in Peter. 'Would you mind?'

'Not at all,' he replied. 'A break will do you good, Lew. We all need to get away from this place now and again.'

I almost skipped home that night, I was so happy. The following day I bought presents for Jean and the kids, stuffed them into a big hold-all and headed for Euston station. Approximately three hours later I arrived in Preston, where I had to change trains for Burnley. I had a 15-minute wait, so I sat in the station buffet. Should I? Shouldn't I? I sat staring at the public telephone in the corner wondering whether I should call Jean to tell her I was coming home or not. The voice of uncertainty that had haunted me for months returned. I told myself that whatever I thought or felt, I should not make the call; I should arrive unannounced. An hour later I was getting off the train at Burnley and striding towards the hairdressing salon where Jean worked. The voice in my head had not gone away, and it was still telling me something was wrong.

Reluctantly, and with a sense of impending doom, I stopped at the first public phone box I found and picked up the receiver. 'Could I speak to my wife, Jean?' I asked the receptionist at the salon. 'Tell her it's Lew, her husband.'

As soon as I heard Jean's voice, my heart sank; she sounded worried rather than pleased to hear from me. 'Hello, Lew. Where are you?' she asked.

'London,' I lied. 'Why is that? Is everything OK?' Jean said that I sounded closer. I pretended to laugh and told her I was: 'I'm in Burnley, Jean. I will be with you in ten minutes.' There was a sense of panic in Jean's voice as she mumbled OK and quickly replaced the receiver. I stepped out of the phone box and walked as quickly as I could to the salon. I was terrified of learning the truth about whatever had been or was happening, so instead of going into her workplace I stood across the road from it. After ten minutes Jean hadn't emerged, so I bit my lip, crossed the road and walked in. 'Is Jean here, girls?' I asked.

'No, I'm sorry,' the receptionist replied. 'She has had to leave early.' I ignored the receptionist and made my way out to the staffroom at the back of the premises. 'You can't go out there!' the receptionist shouted.

Continuing to ignore her, I looked for Jean, and when I was satisfied that she wasn't in the salon, I left. My heart was either pounding, breaking or both by now. I'm not sure what it was doing, to be honest. Up until this point in my life I had never loved any woman other than my mother and my wife, and so had never suffered any sort of emotional trauma. I knew that whenever I did find Jean, whatever she had to tell me wouldn't be good news. Regardless of what that news might be, I just had to hear it so I could try to put things right. I ran to the bus stop as the rain began to fall. When I turned the corner, I was just in time to see the bus disappearing up the street. Unlike the first time I had set eyes on Jean, I was on foot and therefore unable to pursue it. I ran into the road and stood in the path of an oncoming car, which was forced to brake violently.

'What on earth are you doing?' the female driver shouted out of her window. 'I nearly ran you over.'

I hadn't got a clue what to say, so I blurted out the first thing that came into my head: 'I have to get to Crawshaw Booth. It's an emergency,' I said.

The woman could see I was in a distressed state, so she told me to get into her car. 'Put your foot down,' I said when I climbed in next to her. 'I don't have much time.' Eyeing me with a degree of suspicion, the woman put the car into gear and sped away, ignoring speed limits and traffic lights. We arrived at my home in record time. I got out of the car and asked the woman to wait a moment. At the front door, soaking wet in the pouring rain, stood my children Glynn and Joanne. When they saw me, they ran towards me, and I hugged them both. 'What are you doing out here in the rain?' I asked. 'Where's your mother, and where is your brother Billy?' The children explained that they didn't know where their mother was, they were locked out and Billy was with a childminder. I carried the children to the woman's car and asked her if she would give us all a lift to another house, as we had no key for our own home.

The woman must have thought that the emergency I'd spoken of involved the children being locked out and left alone, so she kindly agreed to take us to the house where Billy was being looked after. I had no idea that my son Billy was being cared for by somebody other than one of our close friends; Jean had certainly never mentioned the fact to me. Glynn and Joanne told me that the arrangement had been in place for some time. I found it hard to believe, but it turned out to be true, as they had no difficulty in pointing out the house where 'our Billy's carer' lived. When I knocked on the door, the woman who answered was initially reluctant to let me take Billy, because she had no idea who I was. When Billy emerged from a room, he shouted 'Daddy, Daddy' and ran towards me. It was only then that the woman agreed to let me take him.

Fortunately she also had a spare set of keys for my house, which she handed to me. I returned to the car with the three children in tow and asked the woman if she would take us back to our home. Displaying the patience of a saint and not some woman who had been hijacked by a madman, she smiled and said certainly. When we arrived, I thanked my rescuer and took the children to the house of some nearby friends.

I explained the situation to the friends and asked if the children could stay with them until I had located Jean. Fortunately they agreed to assist me. I kissed the children goodbye, assured them I wouldn't be long and walked back to our home struggling to hold back my tears. I let myself in and walked around the house calling Jean's name, but there was no reply. I went into the main bedroom and began to look through the drawers in Jean's bedside cabinet. What I found struck me like a knife through the heart. A man named Paul Smith had been prosecuted for driving the wrong way along a one-way street, and his summons was in my wife's bedside cabinet. I had never heard of the man, so I assumed the presence of his property in my home could mean only one thing: the woman I loved, the mother of my three children, was having an affair.

I ran out of the house and down the road to a friend of Jean's named Connie. 'Where's my wife?' I asked, 'and who is Paul Smith?'

Connie looked shocked and very worried. 'I don't know where Jean is, Lew,' she replied, 'and I have never heard of Paul Smith.'

I could tell by Connie's face that she was not telling the truth, but I could also see that she was too scared to say anything that might upset me further. I turned and ran back to where my children were being looked after. I felt as if my world was falling apart, and I needed to cling on to what I had left. I thanked my friends for looking after the children and walked with the kids to a public phone box.

Huddled inside, safe from the driving rain, the children clung to me as I telephoned my parents, Jean's parents, our brothers, sisters, friends and anybody else who could possibly have enlightened me as to what was going on. Each and every one of them denied being aware of anything untoward. The children began to cry because of my demeanour, so I picked them up in my arms and carried them home. That night we all slept together. The children kept asking for Jean. I lied, telling them that Mum had gone out with a friend for the night and would return in the morning, but they sensed that all was not well. My emotional state, like my wife, had betrayed me.

# ROUND FIVE

THE NEXT MORNING I WASHED AND DRESSED THE CHILDREN, AND THEN MADE them breakfast before taking them to a friend of Jean's who had offered to babysit. Once I knew that the children were together, safe and being looked after, I went in search of my wife and the man who had assisted her in destroying my family.

Unfortunately for Smith the police officer who had stopped him for committing a relatively minor traffic violation had written his parents' address on the summons. With every step I took towards their house, I grew increasingly angry. I was no longer wondering whether or not Smith had taken my wife; she had confirmed that when she ran away when I turned up in Burnley. I was now considering how I was going to kill him, having tried, convicted and sentenced him to death in his absence. The door of his parents' home shook as I hammered my fist against it, but nobody answered. 'Come out, you useless bastard!' I shouted through the letterbox, but again there was no reply. I knocked on the neighbours' doors, but they said they had no idea if he was home or not.

As I was walking back towards Smith's parents' house, an elderly couple asked me what I wanted. I told them I was looking for Paul Smith. 'Paul's our son,' the lady said. 'Is there a problem?' Despite my anger I tried to be as polite as possible – his parents, after all, couldn't be blamed for anything he had done. I told them that I was looking for my wife. I described her, described our children and gave Jean's full name. The expression on Mrs Smith's face told me that she knew my wife. 'He told us it was his girlfriend,' she said. 'Jean didn't wear a wedding ring, and she certainly never mentioned having any children.'

The full extent of Jean's deception hit me like I had never been hit before. 'When I get your fucking son, I am going to pull the bastard apart with my bare hands!' I shouted. 'His bollocks will be posted through your letter box. Let the bastard know I am looking for him.'

As I walked away from the house, a police car pulled up and an officer got out. 'Oi, you,' the policeman shouted, 'stay where you are! I want to talk to you.'

I turned around and glared at him. 'Do yourself a favour, mate,' I replied. 'Leave me alone. Get back in your car and fuck off.' The policeman looked at me, looked up and down the street, took his hat off, got back into his car and drove away without saying another word.

In desperation I returned to Connie's house. I could not believe that, as Jean's best friend, she would not know anything. When I arrived, I didn't bother knocking on her door, which happened to be open; I just walked straight in. A man whom I had never seen before was sitting in the lounge with Connie. 'Do you know Paul Smith?' I asked.

'Who wants to fucking know?' the man answered with a smirk. A moment later his cocky demeanour had gone. The man's eyes threatened to pop out of their sockets as I squeezed his throat tighter and tighter. 'Nod your fucking head if you want to live to answer my questions, arsehole!' I screamed.

The man, who was struggling to breathe, nodded his bloated purple head, so I eased my grip. I asked him again if he knew Paul Smith, and he nodded furiously. 'I can hardly breathe, mate,' he gasped. 'Please help me.'

I told him to save what breath he had for my questions and advised him not to refer to me as his mate. 'I am Jean Martindale's husband. We have three children together. Tell me everything. If you lie once or hold anything back, I will squeeze the fucking life out of you.'

Every word the man uttered tore through me. He said that his best mate Paul Smith had been sleeping with my beloved Jean in my bed. 'I told him he was out of order,' the man said. 'I even told him he was wrong because Jean was married with kids, but all he said was "too bad".'

I think those words hurt me more than anything else I was told that day. Jean was forfeiting her family for a person who could not care less about whom he hurt. I squeezed the man's throat a little tighter. 'Where does Smith work?'

He could see in my face the pain his words had inflicted. He could also see that my pain was quickly dissolving into uncontrollable anger. 'He isn't my mate any more,' he replied. 'He is a lorry driver at the metal factory in town.' I let go of the man and, without saying another word, he ran from the house clutching his throat.

'Is Paul Smith here?' I asked a man sitting behind a desk in the transport office of the metal factory. The man, who didn't even look up from the newspaper he was reading, said Smith had not been in for a few days. Then, almost as an afterthought, he asked why I wanted to know. I didn't answer. I grabbed the man's shirt, pulled him out of his chair and across the desk, and pinned him against the wall. I advised him to look at people who were talking to him in future and demanded to know everything he knew about Paul Smith. The man was so scared he could not speak coherently. He just kept murmuring that he was the foreman and he had not seen Smith for days. I know my behaviour was totally unreasonable, but I was not thinking straight. I was distraught and extremely angry. My world had fallen apart.

I left the factory and spent the rest of the day roaming aimlessly around the town and anywhere else I thought I might find Jean and Smith, but they had simply vanished. Anger turned to sadness, and sadness turned into self-pity. As I sat with my head in my hands, I suddenly felt ashamed of myself. The children had not seen either of their parents all day, and here I was chasing a woman who had deserted us all. I collected the children, took them home, embraced each one of them and assured them that everything was going to be all right. 'Dad's home now,' I said, 'and wherever Dad goes, you will all be with me. I promise you will all be OK.'

The next morning I telephoned Peter Koster, apologised for not being able to go into work and explained the situation to him. Peter, as always, totally understood and offered to do all he could to help. 'Do what you have to do, Lew,' he said. 'Take as much time off as you need. Your job here is safe.'

I was not sure what I was going to do. I was more than capable of looking after the children or working, but I couldn't do both. I couldn't bring myself to leave the kids with a childminder while I went to work – not after they'd been abandoned by their mother – so I decided to stay at home and sign on the dole. It was an awful time; the children were extremely upset. They were convinced that I would leave them too – so much so that they would cling to me wherever I went. If I had to use the toilet, they would stand outside and insist I leave the door ajar just in case I 'escaped' out of the window.

Witnessing their anguish forced me to hide my own – a task that I don't mind admitting was at times unbearable. I could not bring myself to go into the bedroom I had shared with Jean. Once the children were asleep in bed, I would go downstairs, lie on the settee and endure a disturbed night's sleep. Images of Jean betraying me in our home would flood my mind, torturing me. If it wasn't for the children, I don't know how I would have found the strength to get through the ordeal. I was heartbroken. To make matters worse, the DHSS refused to give me any money because they said I had not paid enough national insurance contributions. After two or three weeks there was no food in the house. My shoes had holes in, which I covered over with cardboard cut from boxes I found at the back of a local shop. My parents could see the trouble I was in, so they brought around hot meals for the children and me.

Approximately ten months after Jean had left, a letter arrived from a solicitor, stating that Jean was seeking access to the children, as she wanted to take them on holiday. I couldn't quite believe the audacity of her. This was not the Jean I had known and loved. How could she walk away from her own children, not bother to tell anyone where she was and then, ten months later, send a letter inviting the children on holiday as if nothing had happened? I telephoned the solicitor who had sent the letter and demanded to know where Jean was, as I needed to speak to her. The solicitor refused to tell me anything other than the fact I would be taken to court and ordered to give Jean the access she had requested if I didn't agree to it now. I may have sworn at him – it's hard to remember because I was so angry. Either way the line went dead.

I consulted a local solicitor about the matter, and he advised me that opposing Jean's application for access to the children would be futile. 'The courts are always sympathetic towards mothers when it comes to children,' he said. 'My advice is you take this on the chin and comply with her request.'

With a heavy heart I contacted Jean's solicitor and told him that I would agree to let her take the children on holiday for two weeks. I still had no idea where Jean was living, so I asked my solicitor if he could find out where my children would be going on holiday. I needed to know if Jean was going to pick them up and, if not, where I was going to have to drop them off. A few days later I attended my solicitor's office. Reading a letter from Jean's solicitor, he said that her parents were going to collect the children from my home and take them to Surrey. 'More than that I am not at liberty to divulge, Mr Martindale,' he said. The letter he had been reading lay on his desk. I could see from the letterhead that Jean's solicitor was based in Leatherhead, Surrey. There would be no reason for her to travel to a distant town to employ a solicitor, so I guessed that was where she must have been living. At last, after ten long months, I knew where my wife and her lover had run away to.

My initial thought was to travel to Surrey and vent my anger on Smith, but if I were imprisoned, which I surely would have been if I had got my hands on him, my children would lose their father. I decided that, while the children were on holiday, I would sort out some form of employment and start a new life for us all. The house we had once called home held too many painful memories for me, so I decided it would be better for us all to move to another area. I telephoned my old friend Ray Todd in London and explained that I needed somewhere to stay for a couple of weeks while I looked for a flat and sorted out some work. 'You're in luck, Lew,' he said. 'The spare room is still empty. You and the children can have it if you want to.' I thanked Ray and told him I would be in London soon.

The day the children left to go on holiday with Jean was very traumatic. The three of them stood in the hallway sobbing their hearts out, pleading with me not to let them go. I did my best to reassure them that everything was going to be OK, but I wasn't even convincing myself, and the children could sense it. A loud knock on the front door signalled the arrival of Jean's mother. When I opened it, she stood there, ashen-faced, and not a word was spoken. I looked over her shoulder to see her husband sitting bolt upright in the driver's seat of their car. I glared at him, but he stared straight ahead, too embarrassed or too scared to even acknowledge me. 'Make sure my children return home in two weeks' time,' I said. 'Make sure they are safe and make sure Smith doesn't go anywhere near them.'

Jean's mother didn't reply; she just led the children out to the car and they all got in. Billy, Glynn and Joanne were still sobbing uncontrollably as Jean's father pulled away. Some things we witness in life remain etched in our memories for all time. The expressions on my children's faces as they drove away in that car all those years ago still haunt me today. I have no doubt they always will. I did not know if I was ever going to see them again, and there wasn't a thing I could do about it. For the first time in my life I felt powerless.

As soon as the children had gone from my sight, I stepped into the street and slammed the door shut on a home that represented a life that was no more. I had understandably fooled myself by temporarily believing there was a way our family could be reconciled, but harsh reality had destroyed any illusions about that dream. I knew in my heart that I had to consider a future for myself and the children that would not include Jean. Today I had to start laying the foundation-stones of the future.

Not all of my problems were difficult to resolve. The family pet was a 28.5-in-long ferret, which weighed 6.5 lb. Sniffer, as we called him, was so big that a lot of people thought he was a rare breed of dog. I don't think the good people of London town knew much about these creatures, but in Lancashire most families had a ferret, a whippet, or both. I couldn't leave Sniffer, as there was nobody at the house to feed and water him. There was only one thing for it: I would have to take him with me. I put Sniffer in a plastic bread bin and caught the train to London. Ray had agreed to meet me at Euston station. When I alighted from the train, I walked towards him, but Ray didn't seem to recognise me. 'Hello, Ray,' I said when I reached him.

'Fucking hell, Lew! What's happened to you?' Ray asked.

My hair had grown past my shoulders since Jean had left, and I hadn't taken much care of myself. I knew I was just using the fact that I couldn't afford haircuts and new clothes as an excuse. Jean's betrayal had hit me harder than I realised. I hadn't really come into contact with many friends since she had left, so nobody had commented on my appearance. Ray's reaction made me even more determined to get my life back on track. 'I have had a rough time, Ray,' I replied, 'but I will be OK.'

Ray gave me a bundle of bank notes and said, 'This is from the lads at the Room at the Top. It's not a lot, but they wanted to help out.'

I was really touched by this gesture. I asked Ray to wait a moment while I went to a phone box to ring Peter Koster and the lads, as I wanted to thank them for helping me. When I got through to Peter, he wouldn't listen to my words of gratitude. 'Don't worry about all of that,' Peter said. 'Everyone is looking forward to seeing you back at the club. If you feel up to it, you can start work tomorrow night.'

I hadn't yet left the station and I had already addressed the problem of money and employment. 'Thank you, Peter,' I replied, 'and thanks to all of the lads. I look forward to seeing you all tomorrow.'

I had never had such generosity from relative strangers bestowed upon me before. Unbeknown to me, there was more to come. When I arrived at the club for work the following night, all of the staff came out to welcome me. Mr Clive Bednash, the owner, pulled me to one side and said, 'You look like the wild man of Borneo. Take this money and go and get yourself a haircut tomorrow.' A bundle of cash was pushed into my pocket and Mr Bednash walked away.

Mr Goddard, the general manager, then approached me. 'Great to have you back, Lew,' he said. 'Go to Hyman's tailor shop in East Ham tomorrow, tell them you need a suit making and the bill is to be sent to me.'

The warmth and humanity these people showed me genuinely choked me up. I shall never forget their friendship at a time when I was in such real need. Peter Koster explained to me that during my absence he had employed other door staff to cover my shifts. 'I can't just sack them, Lew,' Peter explained, 'so I can't give you more than a couple of nights per week at the moment.'

I told Peter that I understood his dilemma. A former Room at the Top doorman named Neville Sheen had, I was told, recently taken over the security at a club called Cinderella's near Brighton. I telephoned Neville and asked him if he could give me any additional shifts. 'For you, Lew, no problem,' Neville replied. 'I have got two nights a week for you if you want it.' I now had eight shifts to work during the two weeks the children were away on holiday. At least when they returned I'd have a bit of money, regular employment and somewhere new for us to live sorted out.

Cinderella's turned out to be a real battleground. A large travellers' site was nearby, and the younger members of its community used the club dance floor as a boxing ring to sort out their differences. Neville was an instructor at a gym owned by British karate team coach Ticky Donovan OBE. He was about 5 ft 10 in., weighed about 13.5 st., had tons and tons of bottle and a heart like a lion. Neville was, to say the least, a very competent and confident fighter.

The week before I had arrived at Cinderella's, Neville had beaten the shit out of one of the travellers, and repercussions were expected. Some of the doormen were talking about burning the travellers' caravans, but Neville would have none of it. 'There's women and children in those caravans,' he said. 'It's not going to happen.'

On my first night at Cinderella's one of the travellers ordered a beefburger at the bar and then refused to pay for it. I was alerted to the problem when the traveller began shouting and about 30 of his friends gathered around the bar. 'You either pay or you go,' I said when I reached the man.

There was an uneasy silence as the traveller eyed me up and down. 'There's too many of us,' he said.

A ginger-haired giant traveller named George, whom I later learnt had an awesome reputation as an unlicensed fighter, walked over and stood between us. 'You'll pay now,' he said to the man, 'and then you and your friends will leave.' The money for the burger was handed over and the man left with his friends in silence.

Unfortunately the young travellers didn't stay away. Every night they would return, breaking into cars outside the club or causing trouble with customers as they arrived or left. To be honest, if it wasn't for Neville I wouldn't have remained there; it was a real dive.

I preferred working at the Room at the Top, but even that attracted its fair share of retards and nutcases. On my second night back there a customer alerted me to a man who was threatening people with a combat knife at the bar. When I went over to investigate, I saw a tall lad in his 20s, who was covered in tattoos, prodding people with his finger. I assumed he was either drunk or on drugs, but when I got closer I realised he was neither. 'I'm going to fucking cut you,' he was saying to a man as I came within earshot of his threats. Dave Maxwell, a member of a very well-respected Essex family, was standing nearby and shouted, 'Watch him, Lew! He has got a blade!'

I grabbed at the man's back pocket as he went to pull a knife from it. Fearing he would get his hands on the weapon first, I butted him so hard in the face that I split my own head open. He lay on the floor, the knife by his side. I picked it up, then dragged him by the leg out of the main club and into the kitchen. I threw him on a steel table that the chefs used to prepare food. 'Wake up, you cunt,' I said, slapping his face. 'I don't want you to miss this.' As soon as the man began to regain consciousness, I held his throat and threatened to cut his face off with the knife. It's funny how wankers who carry knives no longer like them when they are in other people's hands.

'Please don't cut me, sir. Please don't cut me,' he whimpered.

'Cut you?' I replied, laughing. 'You overestimate yourself, son. You're not even worth beating. Have this instead.' I head-butted him full in the face again and he passed out. The chef had been shouting at me throughout the incident about blood, bodies and the hygiene implications of a murder taking place in his kitchen. He was of course right; visions of customers complaining about pieces of a tattooed face in their soup brought me to my senses and I calmed down. I picked the man up, took him to the lift and dumped him in it. Mickey the Claw pushed the button and we descended to the ground floor.

I dragged the man into the street and dumped him outside the department store Harrison Gibson. I think that shop has had more bodies dumped on its doorstep than charity shops have had bin-liners full of second-hand clothes dropped outside. I got in my car, put the knife, which I still have to this day, in my glove box and went back to the club to get cleaned up.

Following this incident I became friends with David Maxwell. He is a genuine no-nonsense but polite man, and certainly not the kind of guy that people can take liberties with. Two or three years later David was charged with the murders of two men: David Elmore, a nightclub bouncer, and his friend James 'Jimmy the Wad' Waddington (so named because he always carried a thick wad of money around with him). The two men had disappeared on Valentine's Day 1984. According to staff at a Turkish restaurant called the Kaleli in Station Road, Barking, there had been a scuffle in the restaurant, after which the two men had been bound hand and foot, attacked with a ceremonial sword that had been stolen from a sports club, throttled to death with a tablecloth and dragged out. Brian Wilson, who gave evidence at David's Old Bailey trial, claimed Elmore began to recite the Lord's Prayer, and when he reached 'Thy will be done' he was interrupted by one of his attackers, who said, 'You're dead right, son.' The murders were alleged to have been carried out following a long-standing feud between Elmore and his family and the Maxwells. In one incident Mickey Maxwell had been struck in the head with an axe. In January 1985 the jury found David not guilty of both murders after just one hour of deliberation. 'I am off to celebrate with my family,' he told reporters. 'I have been held in prison since March for crimes I had nothing to do with. The jury accepted what I told them about prosecution witnesses lying through their teeth. We had only got the word of the police that these two men were murdered in the first place. The only reason that I can put forward as to why the staff at the restaurant implicated us is that they have something to hide and they wanted a fall guy.'

David Reader, who was acquitted of assisting in the disposal of the bodies, added, 'It's all been an ordeal. The allegations against myself, my brother Ronnie and David Maxwell are totally without foundation. Ronnie Reader was in Spain at the time of the other two men's arrest.'

Ronnie told *The Sun* newspaper in an exclusive interview, 'I shall return home after Maxwell and my brother have faced their trial. I'm taking a terrible chance. If I am found guilty, it means life imprisonment.'

After his acquittal a senior detective in the case told reporters, 'We are not looking for anyone else.'

Elmore and Waddington's severed heads turned up ten months after David Maxwell and the Reader brothers were acquitted. They were thrown at the door of Harold Hill police station in Essex.

After the heads were found, Jimmy Waddington's mother, Winifred, told the *Daily Express*, 'I felt desolation at not knowing where his last resting place might be or what exactly had happened to him. I wanted to have him found in one piece.'

I know how Mrs Waddington felt, albeit for different reasons. I'd like to have found Paul Smith in one piece, although it's unlikely that he would have been in the same condition when I left him.

A week before the children were due to return home, an official-looking letter addressed to me dropped through Ray's letter box. I knew it could only be bad news because hardly anybody knew where I was staying in London. I tore the envelope open and began to read the contents of the letter in total disbelief. 'Dear Mr Martindale,' it said. 'Due to the continued absence of yourself from the family home, your children have been placed in the care of the local authority.' I couldn't read any more. I sat on the stairs and screamed like a wounded animal. Jean had custody of the children for 14 days, and they had only been gone a week. There had to have been some sort of administrative error and the letter had been sent by mistake. My children, who were only just coming to terms with the break-up of our family, couldn't be in care. I ran down the road to the telephone box and dialled the number on the letterhead.

'I've received a letter that says my children are in care,' I said to the social worker who answered. 'That can't be right. My children are on holiday with their mother in Surrey.'

I was asked to hold the line, and a few minutes later a stern-sounding lady informed me that the contents of the letter were true. 'Your mother-in-law went to your house with the children, Mr Martindale. After knocking on your door repeatedly, there was no reply, so she and her husband took them to the council offices in Rawtestall and left them there. Somebody from this office attended your home address. You were not in, so the children were taken into care.'

I couldn't believe what I was hearing. 'My wife had custody of the children for 14 days. They are not due back yet.'

The lady wasn't even listening to me. 'It's a matter for the courts now, Mr Martindale. I am sorry. I cannot help you further.'

'They are my children!' I shouted. 'I am coming to get them, and if you or anybody else tries to stop me, I'll kill you or them.'

Probably not the most eloquent phrase I have ever used, but that's how I felt at that moment. Unsurprisingly the line went dead. I rang the office again and again until finally I found somebody who was prepared to listen to me. I was informed that my children were 'in safe custody' at a place called Rawtestall. I was also told that they had been separated and the youngest was very distressed. I begged the lady on the phone to give me a number so I could talk to the children, and eventually she agreed. Glynn and Joanne understood the situation and were in no doubt that I was going to get them out of there so that they could be with me. Billy, on the other hand, was too young to understand the situation and cried his heart out. I promised him repeatedly that I wouldn't leave him in there and we would all be back together soon. Eventually he stopped crying, and I was able to put the phone down. There was nothing I could do to help the children that night, but I could make preparations for when they were returned to me.

I turned to Neville Sheen once more for assistance. 'I desperately need a motor,' I said. 'The problem is I can't pay for it up front.'

Neville, who dabbled in second-hand motors, pointed to a Wolseley 6/110 on his drive and said, 'Take that, Lew, and pay me for it out of your wages.' The car was valued at £250. I earned £15 a night at Cinderella's plus a bit of fiddle money, so it wouldn't take long to pay it off. I thanked Neville, jumped in the car and was back in Lancashire within hours. My solicitor had spoken to social services by the time I had arrived, and a degree of common sense had come into being. The letter requesting access to the children for 14 days so that they could go on holiday and my reply agreeing to it had been produced.

Social services accepted that they might not be acting in the children's best interests by keeping them from me and it was agreed that I could take them home. It was an extremely emotional reunion for us all. Billy clung to me like a limpet; I could feel his nails embedded in my neck. He made it crystal clear that I wasn't going away from home without him again. That night we all slept together in the same bed. The following morning I put the TV on the back seat of the car, filled the boot with the children's clothing and tied their bunk beds to the roof with rope. Glynn sat in the back, Joanne in the front passenger seat and Billy on the driver's seat armrest. I tried to get him to sit with Glynn, but he wouldn't have it; he just clung to my arm and cried relentlessly. I drove away from the house we had once called home and didn't even bother looking back. I wanted to forget it, Jean and all of the happy memories that had since become too painful to recall.

Before heading back down to London, I needed to say goodbye to my old trainer and good friend Eric Wilson. 'I'm leaving, Eric,' I said when I arrived at his gym in Burnley. 'I'm going to take the children to live in London.'

Eric got very emotional and to my surprise he began to cry. 'Don't do it, Lew,' he said. 'I will sign over half of this gym to you if it will make you stay.'

I told Eric that I had to go. 'There are too many memories here for me,' I said. 'I am going to miss you, mate.'

Eric embraced me, wished me well and, with a firm handshake, said, 'Good luck to you and the children, Lew. I am going to miss you all.'

Men like Eric are hard to find. He was like a father to me and my children. He died of heart failure three months after we said goodbye. Boxing and Burnley lost a great man. I felt very emotional as I pulled onto the motorway, but Billy, who still hadn't stopped wailing, wasn't going to give me time for sentimental thoughts. I tried to console him by saying that his pet ferret Sniffer was waiting for him in London, but he wasn't having any of it.

Billy howled in my ear and clung to my arm for the entire journey. Despite the noise, a paralysed arm and the left-hand side of my face being covered in dribble, I didn't care. We were together again and going home as a family.

# ROUND SIX

AS SOON AS WE ARRIVED IN LONDON, BILLY DEMANDED TO SEE SNIFFER.
I think Billy associated the ferret with home, because when he sat
next to Sniffer's cage, he immediately calmed down and stopped
crying. I changed my dribble-soaked shirt, unloaded the car,
made the beds and then took the children over to Peter Koster's
home. His wife Jan knew the kids had been through a difficult
time and so did her best to cheer them up. It didn't take them
long to get back to their old selves. Billy was running around
the garden taunting Peter's dogs and ended up falling into the
fish-pond. When we all ran to his rescue, he stood up with a blue
woollen mitten on each hand, told us they were boxing gloves
and warned us to stay back. I'm not sure if we were all laughing
at Billy or laughing because we were all so happy.

An 18-year-old girl named Theresa O'Brien lived in the same
road as Ray, and she offered to babysit for me while I worked. 
I must admit, I was very apprehensive about leaving the children
with a stranger after the trauma they had suffered, but the grim
reality of my situation was that I had to earn money to clothe
and feed them and keep a roof over our heads. Ray knew Theresa
and her family well and assured me that they were good, decent,

trustworthy people, so I accepted Theresa's offer. The first night that I was due to go back into work, I attempted to leave home as late as possible so that the children would be asleep when I walked out of the door and still sleeping when I returned in the early hours of the morning. Billy sensed something was going on and refused to go to bed. Eventually it got so late that I had to say my goodbyes regardless and head for the door. Every shriek and scream from little Billy tore through me. 'Don't leave me, Daddy! Please don't go!' he yelled after me. The further I walked from home, the more distressed and louder he became.

When I reached the end of the road, I turned and walked back to console him. I phoned Peter later to explain my absence. 'I can't come to work,' I told him. 'The kids are in the phone box with me now. They refuse to let me out of their sight.'

Peter said that he understood and told me not to be concerned. 'Don't worry about work, Lew. Take care of them kids and call me tomorrow.'

The following night Peter agreed to let me come into work late. Even Billy had succumbed to his need for sleep by the time I was due to leave. When I returned the following morning, the children and Theresa were still in bed. When they eventually did wake up, I explained to the children that I had been to work while they had been asleep. 'But you're back now,' they said, 'so we don't mind.' I was pleased that the children were showing the first signs of settling down.

It's a pity I couldn't say the same thing about some of the childish delinquents that we had to endure at the Room at the Top club. Terry the Whale was 6 ft 1 in., weighed 28 st. and had more bellies than a herd of pigs. All I ever heard him say when he waddled in the club was, 'Hit me, hit me. You won't be able to hurt me.' Some equally stupid punter would then shape up and jab what resembled a waterbed on legs, but which was in fact Terry the Whale. When the club had closed one evening, a few people had stayed behind for a drink and Terry the Whale was performing his one and only party trick. 'Harder, harder!' he shouted as some fool pounded his bloated torso. The Whale noticed me watching and called over, 'Do you want a go, mate? I've heard you're quite tasty.'

I walked over feeling like a kid at Christmas. 'If you really think you can take it, I'll do my best to oblige,' I replied.

Terry the Whale stood with his legs apart, stuck his gut out and dared me to give it my best shot. A devastating right hook sent him sprawling across the floor, but it didn't stop him boasting. 'Not bad, not bad,' he mumbled through clenched teeth. 'Not bad at all.'

'Do you reckon you could take one on the button [head] then, Terry?' I asked.

'No, no, it's OK, mate. I have to go,' he replied as he headed for the door. Terry the Whale collapsed outside the club and spent the next five days in hospital pissing blood. He never did ask anybody to try to hurt him again.

When I initially returned to work at the Room at the Top, I was doing two or three shifts per week, but before too long I had paid Neville for the car, left Cinderella's and was working six. Theresa, who had done a fantastic job babysitting the children, said that she didn't mind doing a few nights per week but six was too much. Theresa was a teenager and wanted to go out with her friends now and again, so I fully understood her predicament. 'No problem,' I said. 'If you tell me what nights you are able to babysit, I can book the other nights off.'

'I could always ask my sister Margaret to help out,' Theresa replied. 'She would do the nights when I am not available.'

The following day Theresa introduced me to Margaret. I thought she was very mature for her age and very sensible.

I was more than happy to let Margaret babysit. The children took an instant shine to her, as they had done with Theresa. I was pleased that the degree of stability Theresa had allowed to come into our lives was going to continue. The children still asked after their mother, and naturally there were occasional tears from us all, but I knew that time would heal those wounds.

I hadn't been out socially since Jean had left, so when Neville invited me to a party at his house I jumped at the chance. Ray had recently moved out of the flat we lived in and handed the tenancy over to me. I now had my first real home with the children, so I thought it was a good excuse to go out and celebrate. When I arrived at Neville's party, the place was packed. I said hello to a few people and went upstairs to use the toilet. Two girls were sitting on the stairs talking, and as I went to pass them, one grabbed my arm. 'It's Lew, isn't it?' the girl said. 'I'm a friend of Neville's girlfriend, Mary, and I know all about you.'

'I hope she hasn't told you anything bad,' I replied. The girl laughed and said Mary had only told her that I worked with Neville and that I was single but had three children. 'Nice meeting you,' I said and continued up the stairs. The girl was extremely attractive, about 25 years old and Irish. I didn't think for one moment that she would be interested in me.

When I started back down the stairs, the girl stood up and said, 'I know your name. Don't you want to know mine?'

This has got to be the lads winding me up, I thought. This pretty girl can't want to know me. 'Tell me your name, then,' I replied, 'and the name of the guy who put you up to this.'

'I'm Pat Docherty [not her real name],' she said, staring straight at me, 'and nobody put me up for anything.'

Pat walked down the stairs, turned at the bottom and beckoned me to follow her into the lounge. We sat on the settee all night laughing and joking about nothing in particular, and when it was time to leave she gave me her telephone number. I met her several times over the next few weeks until eventually we began seeing each other as a couple. In time I introduced her to the children, and they warmed to one another – so much so that Pat said she would like to babysit for me while I was working. This arrangement resulted in Pat moving in and me having to let Theresa and Margaret go.

Things were fine at first, but Pat began to get jealous about my marriage to Jean. I tried to explain to her that I no longer had feelings for my wife, but Pat was having none of it. 'You still love her! I know it!' she would scream. I arrived home one night to find Pat, photos of Jean and an empty bottle of Drambuie lying on the floor. Pat was drunk, and Jean's head had been cut off in all of the photographs. I shook Pat until she awoke and asked her what on earth she had been up to. 'You still love her, Lew,' she mumbled. 'I know you do.'

'What are you on about?' I replied. 'We have been through all of this. I haven't seen Jean for over a year. I am with you now.'

She got off the floor and began to shout at the top of her voice about me being a liar, so I walked out of the flat and sat in my car. I saw no point in defending such a pointless allegation made by somebody who was drunk, so I remained there for about an hour. Hoping Pat had calmed down, I then returned to the flat. When I opened the door, I could smell burning, so I rushed into the lounge. She had put the waste-paper bin in the middle of the room, filled it with the mutilated photographs of me and Jean, then set it on fire. The blaze had got out of control and set fire to the carpet, so Pat had flooded the room with water in an effort to douse the flames. I screamed at her, 'You could have killed the children, you lunatic!' Pat didn't reply. She just sat on the settee sobbing her heart out. I packed her belongings in a suitcase, led her out to my car, put her and

117

the luggage on the back seat and dropped them off at a cab office in Forest Gate.

A few days later Pat arrived back on my doorstep, suitcase in hand, tears rolling down her face. 'I'm sorry, Lew,' she said. 'I really miss you.' What could I do? I didn't have the heart to turn her away. I had to let her in, make her promise it wouldn't happen again and carry on as before. Things did go OK for a while, but the green-eyed monster that dwelled within her wouldn't rest. I had a lot of feelings for her, but I also had to think about my children. After three or four more drunken scenes involving plates and similar missiles being aimed at my head, I knew that I had to call a halt to our relationship. I sat her down and insisted that she must leave. Pat didn't argue; she simply packed her bags, walked out of the flat that day and left London the following weekend. I missed her terribly, but I think going our separate ways was the best thing for both of us.

Theresa and Margaret heard that Pat had departed and immediately contacted me to ask if they could babysit the children again. I was more than happy to oblige. Theresa had by this time found a day job and soon found that staying up late and getting up early was too much. So Margaret, who at the time was unemployed, ended up babysitting nearly every night. Because of the amount of time she spent at my home, it was inevitable that we would form some sort of relationship. After my experiences with Jean and Pat I was happy to be just friends with Margaret. The problem was Margaret was single, tall, slim, very attractive and sleeping under the same roof as me. Why on earth did God burden mankind with desire?

Roy Shaw's manager Joe Carrington turned up at the Room at the Top one night. Joe Pyle, Shaw's former manager, was still on the scene but was more involved in promoting the fights.

Carrington was about 5 ft 10 in., well built, smartly dressed and spoke with a gruff voice. He came across as very confident, cocky almost, and looked as if he was no stranger to violence. Carrington introduced himself to me, and we shook hands. 'I hear you want to fight Roy,' he said.

'I do,' I replied, 'but he wouldn't take up my challenge.'

Carrington said that the game was all about money. 'If you put £10,000 on the table, a fight with Roy could probably be arranged.'

'But I don't have £10,000,' I replied. 'It sounds to me like he's making excuses.'

Carrington sighed, ignored my comment and said, 'I can get you a fight if you like. The guy's name is Donny "The Bull" Adams. He is a teetotal, non-smoking, hard-faced Gypsy. Amongst the travelling community he is king.'

'And how much would that cost me?' I replied.

'Sweet fuck all, Lew, sweet fuck all. You can mix it with The Bull for nothing.'

If Carrington could promote a fight between me and Donny 'The Bull' Adams without £10,000 being paid up front and make money, I failed to see why he couldn't promote a fight between Shaw and me without a fee being paid. The £10,000 down payment just seemed like a good excuse to avoid fighting me.

'I came to London to fight the Guv'nor,' I said. 'I don't want to be king of the Gypsies, nor do I want to fight men Roy has already beaten. It's Roy I want to meet in the ring, nobody else.'

'It's not going to happen,' Carrington replied. 'Not unless there's £10,000 on the table.' I shook hands with him. He finished his drink and left.

There was one other man I wanted to fight – not in the ring, but to the death in the street, or wherever else I could lay my hands on him. The spectre of Paul Smith and the damage he had caused my family refused to leave us. Billy, especially, had terrible bouts of sadness and would sob uncontrollably while asking 'Where has Mum gone?' or 'When is Mum going to come home?' I felt his pain and wanted to be able to ease it for him, but until I could locate Jean, I knew I was powerless.

I became friendly with a customer at the Room at the Top who said that he worked for the DVLA (Driver and Vehicle Licensing Agency). I was talking to him one night about how my wife had deserted me and how I came to be in London. He asked me if I still had the police summons that I had found in my wife's bedside cabinet. 'I have, but why do you want to know?' I replied. The man explained that Paul Smith's summons would have his car registration written on it. If I wanted, he could put the registration into his computer at work and the current address of where the car was registered would come up.

Fear was the first emotion I felt when the man handed me a slip of paper with Smith's address on it the following week. Fear because I was not sure I could control my urge to walk out of the club and kill Smith. I sat down trembling with rage. I knew I had to think rationally; I knew I had to think of the children. I unfolded the small piece of paper and saw that the car had recently been taxed and an address in Guildford had been given. The registered owner was a Mr Paul Smith.

'Fucking hell, Lew, you look like you have seen a ghost. Is everything OK?'

I looked up from the table where I was sitting and saw that big Steve Ryan, a doorman I worked with, was standing there. 'I haven't seen a ghost, Stevie,' I replied, 'but I am thinking about turning somebody into one.'

When I told Steve I had been given Smith's address, he urged me not to do anything I would regret. 'Think of the children, Lew,' he said. 'You have got to think of the children.' I knew he was right, but I couldn't just throw the address away and forget about the matter. The children had a right and a need to see their mother, so I decided to travel to Guildford and talk to her.

The following day Steve Ryan and I went in search of Jean. Steve had insisted on accompanying me, because he feared I might do something I would later regret. 'Jean was a hairdresser,' Steve said. 'Guildford isn't a huge town, so we will check out all of the salons to see if she is working before we go anywhere near Smith's address.'

By this time I had calmed down, so I agreed to look for Jean rather than wreak revenge on Smith. Once the children had made contact with their mother, I could deal with Smith. I spent the day sitting in the car as we drove from salon to salon in search of my absent wife. Steve had said that, as Jean did not know him, he would go into each salon and look for her. It made sense, because if Jean saw me approaching her workplace she might hide or flee. I gave Steve a photograph of her and he got out of the car to begin the search. I lost count of the salons I watched Steve walk into and then walk out of shaking his head. It was getting late, we had not had any luck, so we agreed to try three more before heading home. When Steve walked out of the second salon, he was nodding his head and smiling. 'I have found her,' he said when he reached the car, 'but for fuck's sake, Lew, please stay calm.' I was angry with Jean for what she had done, but I had no intention of harming her. I just wanted her to have contact with the children, because they were missing her so much. I had tried to believe that they would eventually forget her and move on, but children can't pretend their mother doesn't exist. I asked Steve to wait in the car and I walked towards the shop.

I hadn't quite reached the salon when I saw Jean and another lady walk out the front door. Jean's eyes met mine and the colour immediately drained from her face. 'It's OK, Jean,' I said, 'I just want to talk to you about the children.' Jean didn't answer; she turned and began walking briskly away.

'Is everything OK, Jean?' the other lady asked.

Jean didn't answer; she continued to walk away at speed. I assured the lady that there was no problem and went after Jean. I caught up with her, promised her that there wasn't going to be any bother and explained that the children really needed to see her. 'You've made your bed,' I said, 'you have to lie in it, Jean. This is about our children, not us.' Eventually Jean stopped walking and, after hearing what I had to say, agreed to meet me two days later. I didn't tell the children I had met their mother, because I thought she might disappear again without seeing them. On the day of the meeting Billy and I travelled to Guildford. He thought that we were going shopping. When he saw his mother, Billy cried with joy and put both of his arms out so that Jean would pick him up. Tears of joy turned to tears of pain, because, to my horror and Billy's, Jean refused to hold him. I couldn't quite believe how Jean had changed; the girl I had fallen in love with and married was no more.

I don't know what was going through my troubled mind, but I didn't blame Jean; I blamed Smith. He was responsible for turning my children's mother against them, and he had to pay. I didn't say anything to Jean about her lack of affection for Billy; I knew that if I started having a go at her, the meeting would deteriorate into an argument and nothing would get resolved. I picked Billy up in my arms. He was still reaching out towards Jean, crying and kicking in the hope that she would embrace him. Jean continued to ignore him. We sat on a bench talking, and after an hour Jean agreed that she would have contact with the children. 'I have to go now,' she said. 'I will meet you next week, and we can finalise the details.'

Billy was very distressed, so I said I would walk with Jean to the bus stop in the hope that her ice-cold heart might thaw. When the bus arrived, Billy became so upset that I genuinely feared for his well-being. He was trying to cry but was unable to catch his breath he was so distraught. Jean got on the bus and didn't even look back. I couldn't let her go with Billy in such a state, so I jumped on the bus and ordered the driver not to move until I told him it was OK to do so. I walked to where Jean was sitting and in front of all the passengers said, 'This boy, your son, needs you. Now get off this bus, give him some attention or I will drag you off.' Jean looked around at the passengers, who were staring at her, got up and walked off the bus. When Jean finally held Billy, he clung to her, digging his small hands into her clothing, ensuring they couldn't be parted. After making numerous promises, Jean calmed Billy down enough to allow her to catch her bus and go home.

The following week I arrived in Guildford to meet Jean and discuss her having contact with all of the children. As I stood at the bus stop where we had arranged to meet, I noticed a woman watching me from the end of the street. I could only see her head, which appeared momentarily but at regular intervals from behind the wall of a building. I had no doubt that the woman had something to do with Jean. I was tempted to wave at her, but I thought it best to let her play out whatever game she was playing. When Jean arrived, we agreed to go to a café for a coffee so that we could discuss the children. We walked past the woman who had been watching me, and when I looked back shortly afterwards I saw that she had followed us. We had not been in the café long when the woman entered. I'm not sure if she was deliberately making such a poor job of trying not to be noticed, but if the woman thought I wasn't aware that I was being followed, she clearly believed I was either blind, stupid or both. I stood up and walked over to the woman's table. 'I know you're following me on Jean's behalf. Do yourself a favour: get up, get out and don't trouble me again.'

The woman didn't reply. She looked at Jean, shrugged her shoulders and disappeared out the door. When I asked Jean who the woman was and why she had followed me, she denied knowing her. When I tried to arrange a time and day for the children to meet Jean, she refused to commit herself. All she kept saying was, 'We will see, we will see.' As I sat there, I kept recalling Smith's friend telling me that he had said it was 'too bad' about Jean's children. To me it seemed as if she had adopted his attitude. It was at that table that I decided I was going to kill him. Jean and I failed to agree on anything at the meeting, and to be honest I gave up caring. I felt I shouldn't have to beg, plead or try to talk a mother into maintaining contact with her own children. After what had happened, Jean should have been grateful that I was giving her the opportunity to see them. The meeting ended in an uncomfortable silence, after Jean announced she had nothing further to say on the matter.

We didn't arrange to see each other again; there seemed no point. I turned up at Jean and Smith's house instead. I didn't knock on the door or even get out of my car. I just wanted to see what Smith looked like so that I could begin to plan his death. Jean must have described my car to Smith or seen it outside the house herself. Somebody noticed it, because shortly after I arrived a police car pulled into the road and parked in front of me. Before the officer had a chance to speak to me, I started my car and drove off. The police car followed, so I turned around, drove up and down Jean's road three or four times and then headed for London. A few days later I received a letter from Jean's solicitor informing me that a court had granted her an injunction against me. I was, the letter said, forbidden from going within a ten-mile radius of her home. She had now made it official that she had no intention of having any sort of relationship with the children. My anger consumed the few rational thoughts that I had left. I asked one of my friends, Ray Todd, to travel down to Guildford in order to watch the house. I wanted to know if Smith left the house or he arrived home at a certain time. I needed to have a window of opportunity to strike. After Ray had arrived in Guildford, he telephoned me. 'The house is empty, Lew,' he said. 'They have gone.'

Dejected, but far from defeated, I went back to the friend who worked at the DVLA. I asked him to find out whether the car had been registered to a new address. Two days later he walked into the club and gave me another piece of paper. When I read it, I saw that Smith and my wife had moved to Aldershot. I know I wasn't thinking straight – I was probably teetering on the edge of insanity – but the rage that burned within me was driving me on and on to certain disaster. I thanked my friend for giving me the address and then telephoned Ray to ask him if he would meet me in the morning. 'Where are we off to, Lew?' Ray enquired.

'Aldershot,' I replied. 'I have found Smith, and I am going to rub the bastard out.'

There was silence for a few moments, and then Ray said, 'Fine, Lew, fine. I will come around first thing.'

I telephoned another man and asked him to bring 'a powerful silent tool' to the club as I needed it for a bit of business. The man, who supplied firearms to a lot of villains in London, didn't ask questions; he just replied, 'I'll be there in an hour. Meet me on the car park.' The cold night air cleared my head a little as I leant against the boot of my car waiting for the guy to arrive. The rage had died, but my mind was still swirling with mixed emotions – one moment I knew my plan was insane; the next it made sense. Images of Billy breaking his heart and Smith's words 'too bad, too bad' would not leave me. A pair of headlights picked me out on the car park, bringing me back to reality. Seconds later the armourer was telling me to open the boot of his car.

'It's a fucking crossbow,' I said when I saw the weapon the man had brought to me.

'The best there is,' the man replied. 'You said you needed something silent and powerful. The target will be brown bread [dead] before they hit the deck, Lew.' The man gave me four steel-tipped bolts and explained that if one hit a man, it would pass straight through him and take half his vital organs with it. 'If people see him go down, Lew, they'll think he's had a heart attack, because there won't be any noise.' He then advised me, 'Make sure you clean them with methylated spirits first. It will remove all fingerprints.'

This guy could sell sand to the Arabs; he certainly convinced me that the crossbow was preferable to a gun. 'How much do I owe you?' I asked.

'It's on the house,' he replied, 'a favour, Lew. Maybe one day you can do me one in return.'

I thanked the man, put the crossbow and bolts in the boot of my car and returned to the club. The following morning Ray and I drove down to Aldershot. I told Ray I didn't expect him to get involved in anything that I intended to do, but he said he was with me through choice. 'Somebody needs to look out for you,' he said. 'You're not thinking straight, Lew.'

When we arrived at the address, which was close to Aldershot military barracks, Ray looked through a dustbin that had fortunately been left at the side of the house. We wanted to find a letter or household bill that would confirm that Smith and Jean actually lived there. Moments later Ray stood up smiling and waved a piece of paper above his head. I had found Smith again. The house was situated on a main road, so I parked my car in an adjacent side road, where I had a clear view of his front door. It was starting to get dark when I saw the porch light come on. A man stepped out of the house with a small dog on a lead and closed the door. 'It's him, Ray; it's fucking him,' I said. I could hardly contain my excitement. The bastard who had caused me and my children so much heartache was going to be dead in the next few minutes. I loaded the crossbow and sat in the car. 'I will get him when he has finished walking the dog,' I said. 'I don't want to fuck the dog's night up too.' Ray sat in silence, eyeing the loaded crossbow nervously.

Twenty minutes later I saw a figure emerging from the darkness with a dog. 'That's him, Ray; that's him,' I said as I got out of the car. Ray opened the passenger door and ran around the car to me. Smith's head was in line with the steel-tipped bolt that I was about to unleash. Fearing I may miss such a small target, I lowered my aim. A bolt through the upper torso would be equally lethal. I didn't care where it hit him, so long as the bastard died. As I squeezed the trigger, Ray pushed me hard, and we fell into the side of the car.

'You mad bastard!' Ray shouted. 'You have fucking killed him! You have fucking killed him!'

I fought Ray off and got to my feet. Smith was standing at his front door, presumably getting his keys out. There was no indication that he was aware of my attempt to murder him seconds earlier.

I had missed. Ray's charging into me had caused the bolt to veer off its intended path. I went to the boot of the car to reload, but Ray jumped on me again. 'Please, Lew, please, don't fucking do it. Think about your kids.'

By the time that Ray and I had finished struggling, Smith was probably in bed. I sat in the car with my head on the steering wheel. Ray put his hand on my shoulder and pleaded with me to go home. I knew he was right: my children needed me and I needed them. The madness that had controlled me since I'd met Jean in Guildford subsided. I started up the car and headed for home. I owe Ray Todd a lot. He is a good decent man who has never turned his back on me in numerous times of need. He later told me that he was worried about my state of mind that day and had only accompanied me to prevent me doing something I'd later regret.

About a month later my friend from the DVLA approached me with another piece of paper in his hand. 'They have moved again, Lew,' he said. I thanked him and took the piece of paper. I didn't read what was written on it. I just walked to the nearest bin and dropped it in.

The responsibility of having to look after my children meant my boxing training regime had to be reduced dramatically. I had been forced to stop attending Terry Lawless's gym and had restricted myself to running in a local park and working out on a punchbag at home. When the children started school, it gave me some free time during the day, so I started training at the gym run by Neville Sheen. The harder I trained, the more pumped up and full of stamina I became. I had endured some pretty difficult times since Jean had deserted us. I was now bursting with explosive energy and wanted nothing more than to unload it and all of my pent-up anger on somebody in the ring.

Standing in the club one night, I couldn't help overhearing a man who was telling a group of people what an awesome fantastic this and that Roy Shaw was. The way the man was going on about Shaw, you'd have thought he was describing God. I shouldn't have interrupted him, but I couldn't help myself. 'Shaw's not all that,' I said. 'He wouldn't fight me when I challenged him.'

The man looked at me and laughed. 'He would fucking do you, son, with one arm tied behind his back.'

I answered his petulant remark with my forehead. The man clutched his nose and began to fall backwards. Blood gushed from between his fingers and poured down his shirt. Before he hit the floor, I lifted him into the air with a right hook. Peter and the other members of the door team ran over to find out what was going on. The man's friends began shouting about Shaw, and Peter asked me what Shaw had to do with all of this. It was then that I told Peter why I had come to London. 'I came here to fight Shaw,' I said, 'not to work the door. That prick over there reckons Shaw could do me with one hand behind his back. I have contacted Shaw's people but they said they wanted £10,000 up front before I could fight him. As you know, Peter, I'm not holding that sort of cash. The truth of the matter is Shaw is too scared to fight me.'

Peter looked at me, shook his head and laughed. 'As soon as that guy finds his head and he's been cleaned up and escorted from the club, we need to talk.' Ten minutes later I found Peter sitting in the restaurant and I pulled up a chair. 'I'm confident you could beat Roy,' Peter said. 'In fact I have so much faith in you I am going to get a consortium together and raise the £10,000.'

I didn't know what to say. I was speechless. After a moment or two I thanked Peter and shook his hand. 'I won't let you or anybody else down,' I said. 'I have wanted Shaw and his title for a long time.' Within a few days Peter, Brian Gerard, Ray Smithers and a guy named Peter 'Flat Nose' Lee had raised the £10,000, contacted Shaw's manager and agreed I would publicly challenge Shaw in the ring at his next fight. Terry Hollingsworth, the ABA champion who had been defeated by Shaw in one round not long beforehand, was entrusted with the stake money from both parties. It was agreed that the winner would take the entire purse for the fight. The dream was back on.

# ROUND SEVEN

THE LAST BARE-KNUCKLE FIGHT ON ENGLISH SOIL TO ATTRACT MAJOR and widespread public interest took place at Farnborough, Hampshire, in 1860, when the undisputed champion of England Tom Sayers and the American champion John Camel Heenan battered each other into oblivion in two hours and twenty minutes. It was a somewhat bizarre and brutal fight. Heenan appeared to be winning, but the crowd rallied to Sayers's assistance by invading the ring. When order was restored, a devastating blow from Heenan fractured Sayers's right arm, but still he boxed on. Police officers tried to stop the fight in the thirty-sixth round, but once more spectators spilled into the ring. The boxers fought five more rounds before it was finally declared a draw. Both fighters were awarded commemorative belts, and a public collection raised over £3,000 for Sayers, given on condition that he would never enter the ring again. Seven years later a Cambridgeshire undergraduate drew up a boxing code under the patronage of the eighth Marquis of Queensberry that included the obligatory use of boxing gloves.

Over a hundred years later, and less than two years after his release from prison, Roy Shaw picked up where Sayers and Heenan had left off, putting unlicensed fighting back in the limelight. After defeating numerous contenders from the travelling community at Barnet Fair, Shaw was given the opportunity to fight the king of the Gypsies, a formidable bare-knuckle fighter called Donny 'The Bull' Adams.

Shaw's close friend Joe Pyle (a south-London gangster with more connections than the National Grid) saw the fight as a unique money-making opportunity. Pyle became Roy Shaw's confidant, manager and promoter. The Krays, the Richardsons and men like Buster Edwards or Freddie Foreman may be better known to the public, but by the end of the '60s all of these men and their hangers-on were either in prison or living abroad in exile. Amongst the criminal fraternity Joe Pyle was equally notorious, equally feared and equally respected. If something major was being planned by a criminal gang, Pyle would know about it. From the events leading up to the murder of Jack the Hat by the Kray gang and the Great Train Robbery to the American Mafia's attempts to overtake London's casino scene, Pyle witnessed it all. Yet despite a few close calls – including a spell in prison on a murder charge that would have seen him hanged if found guilty – Pyle remained at liberty throughout. He was, and without doubt remains, a very, very shrewd operator. Together Pyle and Shaw made a very formidable partnership.

Traditionally, unlicensed fights had taken place at fairs, travellers' sites, pub car parks or scrap-metal yards. The Shaw versus Adams contest generated so much interest that Pyle decided to stage a larger, more lucrative, professional event. He hired a large field from a farmer and erected beer tents and a boxing ring. Pony racing was organised, along with various other forms of entertainment. For a mere ten pounds the customers were guaranteed an entire day of fun. However, the Chief Constable of Essex, where the fight was due to take place, had other plans.

Two days before the event, with hundreds of tickets already sold, he contacted Pyle and said there was no way the fight was going to be allowed to take place. Despite his best efforts to inform ticket-holders, Pyle was unable to tell everybody. On the day of the event the field was filled with disgruntled travellers baying for Joe Pyle's blood. 'We have been conned,' they told the television reporters who flocked to the scene. 'Roy Shaw and his cronies haven't heard the end of this.'

Initially Pyle was concerned, but then he realised that the publicity would create more interest in the fight. More interest meant more money, and that appealed to Pyle. Over the next few days and weeks Pyle tried in vain to put the fight on, but he was told that it couldn't go ahead unless it was governed by the British Boxing Board of Control (BBBC). Pyle conceded that the event appeared to have hit a brick wall. There was no way that Shaw and Adams were going to be granted licences to box. Both were considered to be too old, and both had criminal convictions. The hype surrounding the fight continued to grow in the media, so the police decided to take some pre-emptive action in the hope it would end all of the speculation about it ever taking place. They arrested Roy Shaw and Donny Adams and charged them with breach of the peace. Unwittingly, the police had set in motion a chain of events that would decriminalise unlicensed fighting. When the men appeared in court, Adams told the magistrate, 'You cannot stop me and Shaw having this fight. It might take place in a park, where innocent people might get hurt, but it will take place. We had hoped that by staging it in a ring, we might be able to make it safer, but now that has been denied to us.'

When Shaw was asked if he had anything to say, he told the magistrate that in Borstal he had been advised to sort his differences out with people in the ring rather than in the street.

'It was,' Shaw said, 'the way I preferred to resolve disputes.' The prosecution said that, despite the men's apparent willingness to fight, they had been forced to intervene because it was a criminal offence for any fighter not to wear gloves or to fight without a time limit.

The magistrate thought long and hard, referred to a large pile of law books on his bench and then looked up to address the court. 'As long as the defendants wear boxing gloves, employ the services of a proper referee and moderate the fight using timed rounds, the fight, should they still choose to partake in one, whether licensed or unlicensed, would not be illegal.'

Joe Pyle was ecstatic. He immediately contacted Billy Smart and secured the use of his Big Top circus tent, which was conveniently not in use and being stored in Windsor for the winter. The fight, if a ten-second brawl can be described as such, was a disappointing spectacle to watch, but it was a huge success for Pyle and Shaw. The moment Donny Adams kissed the canvas, offers to fight Shaw came flooding in from across the country. Shaw fought and defeated Mad Dog Mullins, Mickey Gluckstead and Terry Hollingsworth in quick succession. Every contest was a sell-out, and every contest indicated that the next bout would need a larger venue to fulfil the demand for tickets.

Then one day a young Frank Warren and his brother Bobby strolled into Joe Pyle's office and made him an offer he couldn't refuse. Frank Warren said that he was managing a fighter named Lenny McLean. 'He's my cousin,' Warren said. 'I know all about him. Lenny has such a big following we could fill any venue that you care to offer him.' If Pyle and Shaw agreed, they could organise a contest that would be even bigger than Donny Adams versus Shaw. After Shaw gave the nod, Pyle stuck his hand out and a fight between the two East Enders was arranged to take place at Cinatras nightclub in Croydon. Peter Koster, Barry Dalton, Phil Watford (the southern area light-heavyweight champion), two doormen I worked with, Ian Jones and Gerry O'Leary, and I all travelled down to the venue to watch the bout together. There is an awful fascination about an unlicensed fight – the same fascination that makes people slow down to look at a motorway smash. The atmosphere is full of danger, menace and impending doom. The crowd shout abuse at each other and, occasionally, scuffles break out.

When we arrived at Cinatras, somebody started shouting insults at Phil Watford, so he threw a glass, which exploded on the offending man's head. A large space in the crowd appeared and we found ourselves facing an angry mob. 'Fuck you, let's have it,' we shouted as we advanced towards them. Stewards and bouncers got quickly between both parties, and the trouble ended as quickly as it had began. Everyone's attention soon returned to the main event. None of us could say with any confidence which fighter would win. Shaw's recent victory over the ABA champion Terry Hollingsworth had done nothing but good for his unblemished fight reputation. McLean, a giant of a man, had been boasting in the newspapers that he was going to 'rip Shaw's head off'. Before the men had even entered the ring, there was controversy. McLean claimed that Joe Pyle had given him doctored boxing gloves. Every time McLean tried his gloves on, he said, they sprang open. After a heated argument between the two camps McLean sent one of his team to fetch a pair of his own. Both fighters looked awesome when they finally entered the ring; we knew we were about to witness a gladiatorial encounter.

When the bell rang, Shaw steamed into McLean, subjecting him to a barrage of body blows. The crowd were cheering and stamping their feet as 'the Guv'nor' pounded McLean, forcing him back into the ropes. Nobody could quite believe it when McLean raised his enormous head and roared back at the crowd, 'Look, he can't hurt me.' In round two Shaw flew at McLean again, hammering his body with powerful punches. I could see what McLean's tactics were: he was hoping to tire Shaw out and then finish him off when he dropped his guard. When the bell went to signal the end of the round, Shaw looked exhausted. His corner men were shouting at him, demanding that he let McLean do some of the work. When round three started, Shaw, obviously ignoring their advice, threw a flurry of punches into McLean's midriff. Suddenly McLean's huge frame began to sag. Shaw was hurting him. When McLean finally dropped his head, blow after blow from Shaw found its target. Sensing victory, Shaw stepped back and hit McLean with a volley of vicious punches. Eventually the referee stepped in and declared Shaw the winner by raising his hand aloft. No disrespect to Shaw or McLean – both men had been entertaining – but there was nothing I saw that made me think I couldn't beat either of them.

I didn't know it at the time, but the outcome of the fight I had just witnessed had been at best questionable. Shaw confessed to author Jon Hotten in his book *Unlicensed: Random Notes from Boxing's Underbelly* that when he had been hammering McLean around the ring, McLean had said, 'Tell him to stop it, Roy. Tell him to stop it.' Shaw said that he had then raised his hand in the air. I had witnessed him doing this, but I had also seen he was on the verge of collapse himself. The referee saw Shaw's signal that McLean was no contest and immediately stepped in to declare Shaw the winner. The fight, then, had not run its full and proper course. Both camps now had the opportunity to hype a rematch and double their takings.

I was aware, but didn't give it much thought at the time, that it was gangsters promoting these events and not the Christian Brotherhood. Money is their Guv'nor, their reason for getting out of bed each morning. They earn their ill-gotten gains by hook or by crook, not through honest toil. Looking back on events, particularly my own fight against Shaw, I was naive to believe I would ever get a decision against one of the gangster's friends. There was no way the promoters were going to risk backing a fighter in a bout that would lose them money.

I was anxious to get into the ring and finally confront the man I then believed was the Guv'nor. Fights were breaking out in the crowd between the rival sets of supporters. People were calling for calm, others for the opposing fans' blood. Nosher Powell, a former boxer and stuntman who doubled for numerous celebrities in no less than 115 major films and TV programmes, was the MC. He stood in the ring amid the madness that reigned all around him and, clutching his microphone, appealed for calm. 'Ladies and gentlemen, your attention please. We have a man in the house tonight who wants to challenge the Guv'nor. Could Lew "Wild Thing" Yates please come into the ring?'

The crowd took a break from fighting and hurling insults at one another to look at what they thought would be Shaw's latest sacrificial lamb. As I made my way to the ring, I could see the Guv'nor sitting, staring at me. I glared back at him, my eyes fixed on his. The crowd began to applaud me, and people were shouting, 'Go on, my son, have him! Kill him! Kill him!'

When I climbed into the ring, Nosher Powell bellowed into the microphone, 'Please welcome the man who is challenging Roy "Pretty Boy" Shaw. Ladies and gentlemen, Liverpool's hardest man, Lew "Wild Thing" Yates.' Despite the fact that I wasn't from Liverpool, I enjoyed the moment. Everyone was on his or her feet clapping and cheering me. I looked across to where Shaw had been sitting, but he had gone. The public had witnessed my challenge. Roy, a man of honour, would now have to face me in the ring. The dream was finally back on course.

In the days that followed, I was expecting a flurry of activity. The date would have to be fixed, a venue found and tickets printed, but nothing happened. Every time I saw Peter Koster, I asked him if he had heard anything from Shaw's people, but the reply was always the same: 'Nothing, Lew. All they say is we will get back to you.' After a couple of months I accepted that Shaw was not going to fight me. He and his manager had used the excuse that I hadn't got the £10,000 stake money, but now that I had produced it, they had been struck deaf and dumb.

If I couldn't have Shaw, I decided to go for what people advised me was the next best thing: Lenny McLean. I knew Lenny was a big powerful man, but he had plenty of flaws. His head was always held high, making it easy to hit. He couldn't box that well and, as Shaw had proved, you could land plenty of punches on him. Don't get me wrong, McLean was no mug, but I knew that I possessed the speed and boxing ability to defeat him. Peter Koster contacted McLean's people, and the fight was arranged to take place at the Rainbow Theatre in Finsbury Park on 10 July 1978. Now that I had a fight to look forward to, I started a programme of intense training. In no time at all I was weighing in at 17.5 st., my body was ripped, huge slabs of muscle hanging on my frame, and I was loaded with menace. I had never tasted the canvas in a competitive bout, and I was confident that Lenny McLean wouldn't be the first to make me do so.

I was driving home from the Room at the Top after work one night when I passed a parked police car on the opposite side of the road. I glanced down at my speedometer and, to my dismay, saw that I was travelling at 60 mph in a 30-mph zone. It was the early hours of the morning and the roads were deserted. I hadn't considered my speed until I saw the police car. I knew that if I slowed down, the police might see my brake lights come on, realise I had been speeding and pull me over. The alternative was to carry on as I was and hope they hadn't noticed me. Keeping watch in my rear-view mirror, I saw the lights of the police car come on. It then turned in the road, the blue light and sirens were activated and the car came hurtling after me. I wasn't drunk, but I'd had three pints, so I didn't want to risk being breathalysed. The police car was quite a distance behind, so I too accelerated. I'd had a good start on the police, so it was unlikely they would catch me, but I knew they would radio ahead and ask their colleagues to either block my route or join in the pursuit.

Wanstead Flats is a large open space complete with football pitches, a wooded area and several lakes. It was nearby, so I decided to pull in there until the police grew tired of looking for me. As soon as I parked, I turned off the engine and my lights and got out of the car. I could hear the wailing police siren approaching, so I hid near a small outbuilding at the far end of the car park. The pursuing car flashed past, showering the hedgerow in gravel. The driver hadn't even slowed down to check out my parked car, but I guessed that he would be back before too long. I decided to walk home across the football pitches and pick up my car in the morning. I took off my bow tie, wrapped it around my keys and hid them near a set of goalposts. As I walked in the darkness, I could see a figure ahead ducking and zigzagging as it made its way towards me. I wasn't sure who or what it was. Wanstead Flats at that time of night is inhabited by all sorts of perverts, monsters and beasts who come to peep at fornicating couples and groups. Many of the local inhabitants were conceived on the back seat of a car in the parking area. Some people have even been known to play sport and walk dogs there too. Whoever or whatever it was that was approaching me appeared to be trying to avoid detection, so I assumed its intentions were not good. I walked to the goalpost at the other end of the pitch from where I had hidden my keys and began to urinate. Night was suddenly transformed into day as several high-powered searchlights were switched on and trained on me.

'Put your hands in the air,' an amplified voice ordered. 'This is the police!' I was pleased to learn that I hadn't wandered onto the set of some sort of perverted dogging movie, but I was concerned that they wanted me to raise my hands. Surely that indicated they thought I was armed? The only weapon I had in my hand was hardly dangerous. I looked to my left and to my right, but the blinding white lights prevented me from seeing anything. The voice became more hostile. 'Put your hands in the air or we shall release the dogs.'

My heart went cold – perhaps it was a group of weirdoes making a perverted movie after all? 'Look, mate,' I called back, 'if you are the police, release the dogs if you wish, but I'm only having a piss up a goalpost. Is all of this really necessary? It's hardly a hanging offence.' It was faint at first, but soon the sound of rapidly advancing panting dogs became too close for comfort. 'Come on, come on, good boys!' I shouted as I turned to see two Alsatians bearing down on me. One ran around me in circles yapping and the other jumped up playfully and let me stroke him. I had kept and bred dogs all of my life, so I knew they wouldn't attack me if they could not sense danger, anxiety or fear.

When I looked up, a group of ten or twelve puzzled and embarrassed police officers had surrounded me. 'Put your hands in the air!' one of them shouted.

'Haven't we been through that one, mate?' I replied. 'What on earth do you think I've been doing out here?'

A sergeant stepped forward, gripped my arm and said, 'A

robbery. Now get your hands in the air so I can . . .'

Before he had finished talking, I had sent him sprawling across the goalmouth. 'Keep your fucking hands off me, and that goes for all of you,' I said. I walked towards the tallest officer. 'I have done no wrong. Respect that fact and I will come with you and sort this out.'

The officer looked at his sergeant, who was brushing himself down. 'Sarge, is it OK?' he asked meekly.

'Get on with it, man,' the sergeant replied. 'Just get him in the van and down the station.'

When we pulled away, some of the younger officers were sniggering amongst themselves. 'Don't ever repeat this to our sergeant, mate,' one of them said, 'but you've made our day. He's had that coming for a long time.'

At the police station I was asked to empty out my pockets and take off my coat. 'Bloody hell,' the desk sergeant said, 'you've got some muscle. Do you do a bit of sport?'

'Yes,' I replied drily, 'I play fucking ping-pong.'

Half an hour later I was sat in an interview room opposite two detectives, who quickly accepted that I was on my way home from work and not from a robbery. 'You still may be able to help us, though, Lew,' one said.

'If you think I am going to train those useless dogs of yours, you're mistaken,' I replied laughing.

The detectives ignored my sarcasm and said that they knew I worked at the Room at the Top and it was common knowledge that it attracted some of east London's most notorious villains. 'You could be our eyes and ears,' they said. 'We will certainly make it worth your while.'

'Can I go now?' I replied. 'I am no gangster or crook, but I am not an informant either.' Ten minutes later I was back out on the street and hailing a taxi to take me home.

A new nightclub called Ripples opened in the West End, and I was asked to work there. I didn't want to leave the Room at the Top, but I did fancy a change, so I agreed to work an occasional shift there. The club was situated near Trafalgar Square and soon became a magnet for visiting football hooligans who had spent their day consuming vast amounts of alcohol, fighting on the terraces and throwing each other into the nearby fountains. They would turn up at the door dripping with beer, vomit and water, expecting to be let in. Being the self-proclaimed hardest man in Barnsley, Scunthorpe or Brighton cut little ice with the door staff, but we were nevertheless subjected to their threats every Saturday night. Freddie Botham and I manned the front door, and six others policed the inside of the club. Freddie was 5 ft 9 in., 15 st., very thickset and an extremely powerful man. Freddie and Neville Sheen are undoubtedly the two handiest doormen I have ever worked with. As an amateur boxer Freddie never lost a fight on home soil. It was only when he fought in internationals that he first tasted defeat. Forget the shit about fighting that so-called hard men write about in their autobiographies; when Freddie Botham hit you, the next face you usually saw belonged to a member of the ambulance service.

Trouble at Ripples didn't come exclusively from football hooligans; the West End provided combatants from all four corners of the globe. Two Greek guys with a serious attitude problem turned up one night. They were loud, abusive and improperly dressed, so we refused them entry. Instead of walking away, they stood right next to Freddie and began mimicking him. He jabbed one of the men in the head, sending him flying across the pavement into a parked car. I punched the other in the mouth, and he slumped to the floor. I grabbed the man I had struck and dragged him over the road to a pub, where I left him propping up a wall. His friend had recovered from Freddie's jab and started shouting about being a karate expert and how we were now both going to die. The man began prancing about in front of us, waving his arms and making whooping noises. He then threw a kick at me. I feigned a block, and when he responded by lunging forward, I knocked him to the ground with a right hook. 'Get up, you useless cunt,' I said. 'You aren't going to kill anybody but yourself.' The man jumped up and ran down the street screaming threats and insults. I chased him, and when he noticed that I was in hot pursuit, he lay on the ground and crawled under a parked car. There was quite a lengthy queue of people waiting to get into a nearby cinema, and they were all laughing at the man. When I went to one side of the car, he would drag himself to the other to avoid me. I could have crawled underneath the vehicle and caught him, but I didn't fancy getting covered in muck for a fool. Tired of the game, I eventually walked back to the club. My hand was extremely swollen, so I attended the local accident-and-emergency department after work to have it X-rayed. Every time I bent my hand towards or away from me, a sharp needle of pain shot up my arm. The X-ray results confirmed my worst fears; I had a hairline fracture of the hand. My fight with McLean, which was only a few weeks away, had been placed in jeopardy.

In my heart I knew it couldn't go ahead, but others told me that the fracture would heal in time for the fight. In the end it didn't matter who was right and who was wrong, because shortly afterwards my volatile temper destroyed any hope of the fight taking place. While I was working at the Room at the Top one evening, a swarthy-looking man kept staring intently at me. He was tall, stocky, in his late 20s and had a badly broken nose. His battered features gave away the fact that he was certainly no stranger to violence. I pointed the man out to Peter and said that if he kept staring at me, I was going to clump him. The man smirked at me, wandered over to the bar and deliberately pushed into a group of customers who were waiting to be served. The people who'd been shoved out of the way quite rightly took exception to the man's behaviour and began calling to staff to intervene. I saw no point in debating the moron's actions with him. It was clear that he had come into the club looking for trouble, and I was all for giving the customers what they wanted. One of the other doormen got to the man first and tried to calm the situation down. His pleas fell on deaf ears, so he asked the man to leave. For a moment the man stood motionless, but then he lashed out. A large ring that he was wearing caught the unsuspecting doorman and cut him deeply under his eye. I spun the man around to face me and smashed my head into his nose as hard as I could. Blood splashed across his face before he fell to the floor. Seeing the damage he had inflicted on a colleague, I decided to educate him about the use of unnecessary violence. I picked his limp body up and smashed it against a wall before dragging him away from the bar and into the manager's office. Once inside I sat astride the man and battered his face with my fists. Gordon, the assistant manager, came in and tried to drag me off him, but I was insane with rage.

When I had finished, I stood up and saw that the walls of the office were spattered with blood and my bandaged hand was also soaked in it. 'You've fucking killed him, Lew,' one of the door staff said. 'He's fucking dead.' Having calmed down, panic set in. The man lay awkwardly on the floor. His face, a mask of blood, was unrecognisable. I too thought that I might have killed him. I unwrapped the blood-soaked bandage from my hand, disposed of it in a bin and then hid in a storeroom at the rear of the main bar. The music in the club had been turned off, and I could hear people saying that an ambulance had arrived. I knew it would only be a matter of time before the police were

**Lew depicted in the ring with Roy Shaw seconds
before their fight was stopped** (© Sue Adler)

**Roy Shaw feeling the pain
and the strain versus Lew**
(© Sue Adler)

Murder victim Brynmor Lindop (left) with actor Ray Winstone

Lew's parents, William and
Gwen (both deceased)

Lew Yates aged seventeen (back row, third from left) with his trainer George Gilbody Snr (back row, fourth from left) and George Gilbody Jnr (front row, third from left), who went on to be ABA champion five times and Olympic British boxing team captain in Moscow, 1980

Lew's wife Jean with their daughter Joanne and son Glynn

Lew circa 1976,
when he first came to
London to fight
Roy Shaw

*Left to right:* Lew Yates, Alan 'Boom Boom'
Minter, WBC and WBA middleweight champion
1980, and Billy Aird, whom Lew was fighting
when he got disqualified and later banned from
boxing after attacking the referee

Dave Armstrong (left) and Lew. They worked at Stringfellows
nightclub together. Shortly afterwards Dave was shot
in the head and back whilst sitting in his car.
Miraculously he survived

Lew, aged 21, with his
firstborn, son Glynn

Lew with Charlie Magri (British flyweight
champion 1976, European flyweight
champion 1979, 1980, 1981, 1982, world
boxing flyweight champion 1983, 1985)

Lew with Dave 'Boy' Green (British light welterweight champion 1976,
European light welterweight champion 1976, 1979)

*Left to right*: Lew's son Billy, Neville Sheen, Lew and Lew's son Lewis, whose wife Alison was convicted of murder after intervening in a fight involving Lewis

This photograph was taken at Peter Koster's wedding in the late '70s. Lew is the bearded guy second from right with outstretched fists/hands. Peter Koster is in the centre wearing a red rose and a blue tie with white circles and holding a beer and a glass of champagne

Unlicensed fight fans, more familiar to viewers of *Crimewatch* than *Grandstand*, get in the mood

*Left to right*: Bernard O'Mahoney's son Vinney, Lew Yates and Bernard enjoying a night out in Basildon, Essex, during the writing of this book

Roy Shaw (right) taking punishment from Lenny McLean in their second fight

Nosher Powell, MC at many of the big unlicensed fights

The true Guv'nor of the unlicensed ring: hard cash!

*Left to right*: Carlton Leach, Nigel Benn and murdered Essex Boys gang boss Tony Tucker

informed of the incident and they too would appear on the scene, no doubt looking for somebody to arrest. After a few minutes I heard police officers instructing one another to search everywhere. I assumed that they had established that a doorman was involved and that he might still be on the premises, so I got out of the storeroom, opened a fire-exit door, walked to Ilford High Street and hailed the first taxi that I saw.

That night I received numerous calls from people telling me that the man had suffered brain damage, was in a coma or dead. I know from experience that people are prone to exaggeration, but it was fair to assume the guy was at least seriously injured. There was no point going on the run – I had the children's welfare to consider. I would have to front it out and hope that the man pulled through. I went to bed, but I didn't sleep much that night. The following morning Peter telephoned and asked me to meet him. 'It's nothing to do with me, Lew,' he said, 'but that guy is in a bad way and the club owner Mr Bednash has said he cannot allow you back in as either a customer or an employee.' I knew the police would give the management grief if they tried to defend my actions, so out of respect for my fellow doormen and Mr Bednash, who had helped me in my time of need, I said I would comply with anything that was asked of me.

Peter said that he had warned Mr Bednash that if my exclusion was permanent, all of the villains and riff-raff that I had ejected and barred from the club would return. Before I had started work at the venue, there had been a lot of undesirables going in causing trouble, and little had been done about it. I had weeded most of them out and restored order. To highlight his point, Peter reminded Mr Bednash of an incident involving Roy Shaw. One night Shaw had gone into the club, and the manager, who was aware of his reputation, had said he wanted him to leave.

The door staff were reluctant to ask Shaw to go, so the police were called. In fairness to Shaw he hadn't done anything wrong; he had merely popped into the club to socialise. The police, also aware of Shaw's reputation, turned up in force. When they marched into the club, Shaw was at the bar sipping a coke. The officers lined up in front of Shaw and asked him to leave. 'Fuck off, I'll leave when I've finished,' Shaw replied.

A senior officer stepped forward and told his men that he would deal with the situation. 'I'm asking you to leave,' he said to Shaw in his sternest voice.

'And I'm telling you to fuck off and get back in line,' Shaw replied.

The officer looked nervously at Shaw and said to his men, 'We will give him a few minutes to finish his drink.' Shaw started laughing and began walking around the club. The officers followed him in single file, but not one dared to touch him. Everybody in the club was laughing, except for the police. Eventually Shaw got bored of the game, finished his drink and walked out.

Upon reflection Mr Bednash decided that my exile would not be permanent. I could, he said, return to the club when the dust had settled concerning the badly injured man. The following day I was told by a reliable source that the man had suffered swelling of the brain and remained in a comatose state. I was pleased that some of the earlier, more dramatic, reports were wrong. I was also informed that the police were looking for me so it would be in my best interests to keep a low profile.

I drove to a hospital in east London and had my hand, which was by now extremely swollen and painful, X-rayed again. The hairline fracture I had sustained fighting the Greeks at Ripples had now become almost a clean break. There was no way I could fight McLean in this condition, so, after consulting his manager, it was agreed that the fight would be postponed until a later date. Two weeks after I had knocked the man out at the Room at the Top he regained consciousness. Fortunately he suffered from temporary memory loss and told police that he did not wish to complain or make a statement as he had no recollection of the incident. It turned out that he was a Portuguese merchant seaman whose ship had been docked at Custom House near Canning Town. The ship had since left without him. Thankfully he too left the country as soon as he was well enough to travel and I never saw him again.

The venue had been booked, the publicity posters had been printed and nearly all of the tickets had been sold for the McLean fight, so they had to find a replacement opponent to fight him. Solly Francis, a Geordie who worked with me at the Room at the Top, claimed he had beaten McLean in a bar-room brawl a few years earlier. Francis was about 15 st., well built, loud, brash and cocky. He wasn't a bad doorman, but he certainly couldn't box. I didn't know if Francis was being honest about the outcome of any altercation with McLean, but there had definitely been some sort of problem between the two, and the black blood of animosity had continued to flow.

McLean's people approached Francis and offered him the opportunity to fight their man in my place. Francis had already been booked to fight at the Rainbow on the same bill as me and so was already in training. 'I'll fight the mug,' Francis said as he accepted the challenge. He then started boasting to people about how he was going to punish McLean.

When I next met Francis, he started messing about, sparring with me and saying he could beat McLean and me together. I threw a half-hearted jab back at him and, to my amazement, his legs buckled. Everyone was laughing, saying don't put any money on Francis, he hasn't got a chance. When Peter and I went to watch the fight, there were no surprises. Sitting on a raised stage just three rows back from the ring, I said to Peter, 'When McLean hits him on the chin, it's over.' As soon as the bell rang, Francis head-butted McLean, which cut his eye. He then brought his knee up between McLean's legs and the giant doubled over in pain. To my amazement Francis stepped back and started laughing, taunting his formidable opponent. When McLean raised his head, he had murder in his eyes. I knew Francis was doomed. McLean roared like a wounded beast and bulldozed Francis back into the ropes. Seconds later Francis lay motionless on the canvas. McLean raised his foot above his head as if he were going to stamp on him, but then shook his head and walked away. That was the last time I ever saw Francis; he never came back to work or showed his face around the clubs again.

To make up for the nights I had lost at the Room at the Top, I went to work full-time at Ripples. I was pleased to get away from Ilford. I had enjoyed my time there, but I was in need of a change of scenery. Familiarity and boredom make you less aware of who and what is going on around you. Working on the door in that frame of mind is bound to get you imprisoned, badly injured or killed. I knew that it was time for me to move on, sharpen myself up both physically and mentally and drop any bad habits I had adopted. I knew I could always return if things didn't work out elsewhere.

# ROUND EIGHT

AFTER HIS VICTORY OVER MCLEAN ROY SHAW KNEW THAT PEOPLE WERE unlikely to place a bet on him losing the rematch, so he wagered approximately £12,000 of his own money on Lenny McLean beating him. The much-hyped second fight was staged at the same venue as the first, Cinatras in Croydon. McLean entered the ring looking sharper and much fitter than he had at his first fight with Shaw. When the bell went to signal the start of round one, McLean steamed into Shaw, hammering him to the canvas. Shaw got to his feet, only to be knocked down again. McLean, who appeared to lose control, began stamping on Shaw's head. Dazed but unbeaten, Shaw got to his feet, only to be knocked clean through the ropes into row B of the audience, where he remained. Shaw later told Jon Hotten that McLean hadn't knocked him out of the ring; he had in fact fallen out and remained in row B so that he could collect his winnings. 'He hit me, I went down and he was jumping on me,' Shaw said. 'I got up and my corner rang the bell, made the round short. He hit me again and I fell out the ring, so I let him have that one. Got about twenty-four grand.'

After two very lucrative encounters, both fighters had swelled their bank accounts and scored a victory. Neither could claim they were better than the other. There was only one course of action open to them: a third, even more lucrative decider would have to be arranged to find out who really was the Guv'nor. A date was set, a venue was arranged – The Rainbow in Finsbury Park, north London – and fans of unlicensed fighting lapped up the hype that Joe Pyle and others created around it. Tickets for the fight were in great demand and sold out within hours of going on sale. Graphic descriptions given by both boxers of what they intended to do to each other appeared in the newspapers and on television. On the black market the tickets began to exchange hands for three times their face value. No wonder the promoters of the fight were laughing and joking as the boxers made their way to the ring.

Shaw, who had told reporters prior to the second fight with McLean that he was retiring, looked drunk when he entered the ring. He later claimed that he had overdosed on ginseng, but it looked to me like he had been celebrating the financial success of the bout with champagne. Whatever it was he had taken or drunk, Shaw certainly didn't look like the man I had challenged five years previously. When the bell rang, McLean launched himself at Shaw, unleashing a flurry of devastating blows. Shaw tried to move around the ring to avoid punishment, but McLean continued to club him with his giant fists until Shaw fell to the canvas and remained there. I am not sure how hard McLean hit Shaw that night, but when Shaw came around to writing his autobiography *Pretty Boy* in 2003, he had either deliberately overlooked their third and final bout or suffered a total memory loss. Whatever his reason, he failed to mention the defeat.

It looked as if Shaw's career as a fighter was over and I had been robbed of my chance to fight him. I knew that even if we did get it on, his reluctance to accept my challenge at his peak had cost me the title of Guv'nor. I have absolutely no doubt in my mind that I could have defeated McLean and Shaw, who were, at best, poor boxers. That is not only my opinion of their boxing ability; it is McLean's manager Frank Warren's and Shaw's too. When asked about McLean, Frank Warren replied, 'Lenny was related to me. He was a big guy, funny and colourful, but he was also a bully and tried to intimidate people and like most bullies couldn't take it back. He was beaten by average ex-fighters such as Cliff Fields, and definitely would not have made it as a pro.' When asked about taking on professional boxers, Shaw is quoted in Jon Hotten's book as saying he and McLean 'ain't in their class'. If he knew that when he spoke to Hotten in 1998, he must have known it when I challenged him in 1981. Shaw knew he was coming to the end of his money-making days in the ring, so it was important he suffered no more humiliating defeats like the one handed out by his arch-rival McLean. Nobody was going to pay good money to watch a guaranteed loser, so I reckoned that Shaw would try to win future contests by any means available.

Peter Koster told me that there was a possibility of arranging a lucrative fight with a guy named Cliff Fields. I had heard a lot about Fields. Unlike McLean and Shaw, Fields was an ex-professional boxer rather than a bar-room brawler. He was a big, strong, powerful puncher who was known during his boxing career as the 'Iron Man'. He had boxed as a heavyweight against the likes of Richard Dunn, Billy Aird, Jack Cotes and Dick Reeves. He'd had fifteen professional fights, of which he'd won eleven and lost just four. Fields had fought McLean twice in unlicensed bouts and defeated him both times – a fact McLean forgot to mention in his autobiography *The Guv'nor*. Shaw had refused to even get in the ring with him. 'I wouldn't fight him,' he is reported as saying, 'because I knew he would have mullered me.'

It is beyond doubt that those in the unlicensed fight game were well below par when put in front of traditional experienced boxers. In their autobiographies, written years after the event, they boast about being the best but in private they know they are talking nonsense. I was a powerful heavyweight boxer, so I had no fear of Fields, who had lost against Billy Aird, whom I too had fought. I'd given quite a good account of myself but, as I've said, lost after being disqualified for head-butting. No disrespect to Cliff Fields, but it's fair to say that when he took up unlicensed fighting and was beating the best fighters it could offer, he was way past his prime. I felt sure that I could and would defeat him.

It was agreed that all concerned would meet in a pub at Cockfosters, north London. When Peter Koster and I arrived, we were invited to sit around a table with Fields and his manager. Fields had dark hair, narrow eyes and a typical boxer's nose that had been flattened across his face. I stared straight at him throughout the meeting, but he wouldn't look at me. He came across as a real Neanderthal man, because he wouldn't speak or even acknowledge people who were talking to him. When we left the meeting, I told Peter that I had already beaten Fields. 'He wouldn't look me in the eye,' I said. 'His bottle has gone before we have even put the gloves on.'

I didn't know it at the time, but Fields was an extremely shy reserved guy who never looked anybody in the eye or made conversation. In fact he was such a private person, nobody knew anything about him: where he worked, lived or even if he was married or had children. For reasons unknown to me the fight never did go ahead, despite numerous attempts by Peter to arrange it. 'We will get back to you,' Peter was told, but, like Shaw's camp, they never did. Many years later Cliff Fields was set upon by a gang of travellers and his eyesight was severely impaired. He was forced to retire from boxing and, like so many fighters before him and since, he sadly sought solace in the bottle.

I wasn't happy working at Ripples nightclub. It wasn't the guys

I worked with or the job I was doing; I was fed up of spending hours in traffic driving to and from the West End and then having the additional burden of finding an outrageously overpriced parking space. Feeding the meter every night was more expensive than feeding three kids. The logistics of commuting were certainly more stressful than bouncing drunks around and out of nightclubs.

My six months in exile from the Room at the Top had ended, so I asked Peter if it would be OK for me to return. Mr Bednash, still quite rightly concerned about the police's reactions to whom he employed, said I could return so long as I shaved my distinctive beard off. It seemed a small price to pay, so I agreed but left myself with a Mexican-style moustache.

The first night I walked back into the club, I was beckoned to the bar by two men in suits. 'Police, Mr Martindale,' they said. 'You can shave what you want off, but you can't hide those bloody big shoulders. You are extremely fortunate that the Portuguese gentleman didn't press charges. Let's keep it low-key in the future, eh?'

They were obviously not going to arrest me, so I replied 'OK' and walked away to prevent any further discussion. My card had been marked; I knew that things were never going to be quite the same at the club. Out of respect for Mr Bednash and a desire to keep my liberty, I tended to treat miscreants more lightly, and trivial misdemeanours were ignored. I was trying to be the gentle guy that pleased the police and the owner, but the gentle guy was losing the respect of the wannabe villains, who were getting away with taking liberties. Doing my job half-heartedly wasn't me – I was fooling myself – so I started looking for alternative employment.

I was approached by a man who said that he would like me to become the security manager at a new club in Harrow Weald called the Middlesex and Herts Country Club. The man was concerned that heavy criminal firms and faces would frequent the venue and scare away the more refined clientele he was hoping to attract. I was looking for a new job that didn't involve appeasing arseholes, a torturous journey to get there or the need to take a bank loan out for parking fees, so I agreed to start work on a trial basis.

The Middlesex and Herts Country Club was a vast complex. When you entered the grounds via a large set of gates, you followed a long winding road that went over a kidney-shaped swimming pool and ended at a very grand glass-fronted reception. The club had squash, badminton and tennis courts, a flying club and golf and equestrian facilities. In the garden bar George the pianist would play requests on a huge white grand piano. To ensure the ambience was just so, George would always be dressed in a white tuxedo, white top hat and a white pair of gloves. There was also a restaurant, cocktail bar, balcony bar, buffet bar and discotheque.

On the opening night I worked on my own, which is not the most sensible thing to do if you're a nightclub bouncer. Fortunately the customers were, in the main, celebrities, their fans, or guests and friends of the owners and so the night passed off without incident. However, I made it clear to my employers that several additional door staff would have to be employed if they wanted to keep good order on the premises. The following night a door team that couldn't have fought boredom, let alone agitated punters if the going got rough, met me. I sacked half of them and brought men in that I knew and could rely upon.

I hadn't been working at the club long when a coachload of rugby players decided to visit. After knocking back large quantities of alcohol, they began to scrum down on the dance floor. I went over to them and explained that they would have to calm down or leave. They apologised for their behaviour, but as soon as I turned my back they all started to laugh and got back into a scrum. I told a doorman to watch my back because I was going to knock the biggest guy in the rugby party out. 'You've got to go,' I said, looking up at a mountain of a man, 'and take your mates with you.'

'Do you want to fight me, then?' the giant said, laughing.

'OK,' I replied before driving my right fist into his chin.

I dragged him off the dance floor and into the reception area, where I kicked him in the head a few times. Nigel the manager was shouting 'Not in here, not in here!' but I wasn't listening. When I had finished beating the man, there was blood everywhere. The man's friends came into the reception area, picked him up and carried him outside. A taxi driver who had just pulled up refused to let them get into his vehicle because of the blood, so they began shouting abuse and kicking his car.

I went outside to assist the driver. The rugby players saw me coming and ran to the far end of the car park. Eventually two vehicles arrived to pick them up and they departed, hurling abuse and threats out of the windows. The manager warned me about my future conduct and I knew then that I wouldn't be leaving his employment with a gold watch for a lifetime of service.

Everybody in London had heard of Mickey Green, or the Pimpernel, as he was known. Throughout the 1950s and 1960s in north London he was a 'face' amongst the criminal fraternity. Faces were feared ruthless men who earned their wealth committing robberies, long-firm frauds or collecting protection money. Brandishing a sawn-off shotgun to fund a spell in sawn-off jeans on a Spanish beach was the mindset. In 1970 Green's luck ran out when he was sentenced to 18 years' imprisonment for his part in a robbery at Barclays Bank in Ilford, Essex. On 26 March 1979 he was released from prison, having served just half of his sentence.

Green had been telling the landlord of his local pub that he had heard a good night out was to be had at the Middlesex and Herts Country Club. 'I think I will take the missus and a few of the boys down there,' he said. Unbeknown to Green, the landlord was acquainted with the manager of the club, and he telephoned to warn him of Green's intended visit. 'You will regret letting him in,' the landlord advised. 'He will flood the place with villains and scare all your punters away. If he doesn't, his missus will. She is the widow of Jack "The Hat" McVitie, the geezer that the Kray brothers murdered.'

The Krays and their associates had never been very welcome in north London, so, understandably, visions of gang warfare taking place in the club flashed through the manager's mind. 'If a guy called Mickey Green comes here, Lew, don't let him in,' the manager said. Then, almost as an afterthought, he whispered, 'And if he asks to speak to the manager, say that I have gone out.'

That night Mickey Green and his entourage of flat-nosed friends and glamorous girls walked into the club. 'Hello, boys,' he said. 'Where do I pay?'

'Unfortunately you don't,' I replied. 'It's a members-only club, and you're not a member.'

Green glared at me. 'So how much do you want for a membership then, mate?'

I told Green that I wasn't his mate, memberships were not on sale and even if they were he couldn't have one because the management didn't want him in there.

'Is that fucking so?' Green said. 'Is the manager about?'

I told him that he wasn't and asked him to leave. For a moment Green hesitated, but then he walked out of the door without saying another word. The following evening the manager told me that Green had been in touch with him. He said I was to allow him and his friends into the club in future as they now had memberships. I had nothing against Green or his friends, but I was outraged that after telling them they couldn't come in I now had to eat humble pie and welcome them with open arms. 'They will think I'm some sort of fucking mug!' I shouted at the manager. 'They're hardly going to take any notice of me in the future, are they?' The manager, clearly embarrassed, didn't answer and walked away.

They arrived mob-handed that night: Green, about a dozen heavies and their female partners. 'Hello, boys,' Green said, smiling, as he walked through the door. 'I've cleared that little misunderstanding with your boss.'

I knew Green was trying to wind me up, but I decided to bide my time. 'Keep it sweet, boys,' I replied. 'I throw members out who misbehave too.'

After the champagne began to flow, two of their group began to argue amongst themselves. A half-hearted punch was thrown, and their friends pulled them apart. I had been waiting for something like this to happen all evening. It had been a mistake to let them in. I went over and said to Green that if his friends continued to fuck about, I'd throw him and them out. Green stepped towards me and sneered, 'I don't think you realise what you're up against. There are thirteen of us.'

I told him that I didn't give a fuck how many people there were, it was him who was doing the underestimating. Green's friends picked up their glasses and looked at him, waiting for the signal to attack. I stood my ground, staring at each of them in turn. 'If you want it, you can fucking have it, boys,' I said, 'but more than one of you will come with me.'

Green hesitated and then replied, 'You'd die for this place, wouldn't you?' I told him I wouldn't, but I would die for my self-respect. What happened next would be up to Green and his friends. I'd had my say and stood my ground; it was their move. 'Shall we drink up and go then, lads?' Green said to his friends. They looked at me, muttered, cursed, drank their drinks and left.

Shortly afterwards I read that Green had gone on the run as he was wanted in connection with a multi-million-pound VAT fraud that involved smuggling gold into the UK. Green later surfaced in Spain, where he set up a drug-trafficking cartel with one of my former friends, Great Train Robber Charlie Wilson. Since then Green has become one of Europe's most hunted criminals. He has been wanted in Holland, France, Spain, Ireland, Belgium and Britain and is on the target list of every customs and police force in Europe, South America and the United States. (Green was living in singer Rod Stewart's former Beverly Hills home when FBI agents arrested him as he lounged by the pool, but after being interviewed he was released without charge.) Today Green lives in a luxury villa in Marbella, Spain. Supergrass Michael Michael, who disappeared off the face of the earth into the witness-protection programme after betraying colleagues in a drug-smuggling gang, once owned the property. After Michael fled, Green had simply moved into the villa and declared it as his own. 'Well that bastard is hardly likely to come back and ask me to leave, is he?' Green reportedly told a neighbour. If you have front, I suppose you can get away with anything. Unless, of course, you encounter somebody with more front than yourself.

As soon as one hero left the scene at the Middlesex and Herts Country Club, he was inevitably replaced by another. Harry Boyd, as I'll call him, was about 35 years old, 6 ft 6 in. tall, with big broad shoulders and an equally big mouth. The minute he set foot in the club, I just knew he was going to cause grief. I shouldn't have let him in, but the other doorman seemed to know him, so I didn't wish to appear rude by excluding him for no reason. If I had barred everybody I didn't like the look of, there wouldn't have been too many females in the club and certainly no men. With a heavy heart I welcomed Boyd in, and once he had disappeared inside I asked the door staff what they knew about him. They told me that Boyd was an unlicensed fighter, a keep-fit fanatic and, despite his supposed fighting ability, he had a reputation for carrying and using a blade. Two hours later the head waitress called me to an incident at the balcony bar. When I arrived, she said that a big man had been touching the other waitresses' backsides. This was a distasteful but not uncommon occurrence in the club, as the female staff all wore very short skirts as part of their uniform. I asked the waitress to point out the guilty party, and she led me to Harry Boyd. When I told him he would be ejected if he touched another member of staff, he denied laying his hands on anybody. I explained that I wasn't sitting in judgement of him, I was telling him plain and simple that if he did it again, he would be out. Boyd looked at me, put his hand out to shake mine and said, 'I will apologise to the waitress and it won't happen again.' I ignored the offer to shake his hand and called the waitress over. 'I'm sorry for offending you,' Boyd said when she arrived. The waitress acknowledged his apology and went about her business.

'Drink your drink,' I said. 'You're going out now.'

'But you said that if I did it again, I'd be out,' Boyd replied.

'I know, but now I'm just saying get out, so leave,' I said, pointing to the door. Boyd got up and walked out of the club without saying another word.

The following week I was standing near the bar and saw Boyd walking towards me. 'Am I all right to come in?' he said when he reached me.

'You're in, so you must be,' I replied. 'But if you misbehave, you'll soon be put out.'

'You fancy yourself, don't you?' Boyd said.

'Let's just say I'm confident,' I replied. 'If you want to have a go, son, we can go outside.'

Boyd declined my offer and walked away. I kept my eye on him throughout the evening, but he sat quietly at a table without troubling anybody. A couple of nights later Boyd came to the club with two other guys. Both were muscle-bound bodybuilders and over 6 ft tall. The door staff manning the front door wouldn't let them in because they refused to be searched. The manager asked me to tell the men to leave the premises as things were getting rather heated. When I got to the front door, I told the men they were wasting their time arguing as they were not going to be allowed in. Boyd started shouting abuse, so I walked towards him. One of his friends grabbed a doorman around the neck from behind, so I punched him in the face. He released the doorman and staggered backwards before crashing into a set of double glass doors. The third man ran at me, but I head-butted him in the face before he had a chance to assault me, and he went down. Turning to Boyd, I said, 'You have caused all this, you piece of shit.' Unbeknown to me, Boyd had a knife strapped to his forearm in a sheath that was hidden by his shirt. As he tried to release the knife and let it slip into his hand, I punched him twice in quick succession. Boyd fell awkwardly, tried to get up but collapsed in a heap. By this time the first man that I had struck had got to his feet and was aiming karate kicks at me. I ran at him, but he turned and fled outside into the garden. I gave chase, kicked his legs from under him and he fell over.

As I stood over him, he began shouting, 'Help, no! Help, no!' I kicked and stamped on him until he fell silent. I then walked back inside as Boyd was getting to his feet. I punched him as hard as I could. The sound of his cheekbone snapping made others in the vicinity grimace and turn their heads. I knew it wouldn't be long before an ambulance and the police arrived, so I made myself scarce.

The following day I telephoned the manager and was assured that the police had taken very little interest in the incident. 'Boyd and his mates were carted away in an ambulance,' he said. 'The police scribbled down a few notes and then left. I haven't seen or heard from them since.'

I returned to work the following night, and no more was said. Then, six weeks later, I was upstairs in the balcony-bar area when the manager approached me. 'It's the police, Lew,' he said. 'They are downstairs and wish to talk to you.'

As I walked into reception, four detectives in cheap suits approached me, asked me to confirm my identity and then arrested me for assaulting Boyd and his two friends. 'Can I take my car?' I asked as we walked onto the car park. 'It will save you bringing me back when this is cleared up.' To my surprise, the detectives agreed, but I had to make the journey to Harrow police station sandwiched between their vehicles. When we arrived, I was taken into a room and interviewed. I couldn't believe that Boyd, a knife-wielding bully, and his equally violent friends had made a complaint and the police were taking it seriously. I was charged later that night with three counts of causing actual bodily harm. Over the next few weeks and months I made several appearances at Harrow Magistrates' Court until finally the day of my trial arrived. When Boyd was called to give his evidence, the magistrate gasped and remarked, 'I thought the defendant was an exceptionally large man, but Mr Boyd is, if he will excuse my saying so, enormous.' Everybody in the court laughed politely, except for me. I was thinking it was a pity they didn't know how big his mouth was.

Boyd claimed that he had suffered a wound to the back of his head when I had struck him with a metal cosh or iron bar. I had then beaten him around the face with it, which had resulted in him suffering a broken jaw. When his two friends were called in to give their evidence, they supported his story and said they too had been beaten up by me. I could see the magistrate looking at me and then looking at these three giants. I was doing my best to make myself look as small as possible in the witness box. My head was half-buried in my hunched-up shoulders, and I slipped so far down the bench my knees were only inches from the floor. At one point during the proceedings he asked the prosecution if they were sure that I was the only person involved in allegedly assaulting the three men. When the prosecution stated that was indeed the case, the magistrate remarked that he found that very hard to believe. Various witnesses from the club gave evidence and confirmed that no weapon had been used by me at any time during the incident. After deliberating for no more than a few minutes, the magistrate found me not guilty and awarded me the costs that I had incurred as a result of the prosecution.

I continued to work at the Middlesex and Herts Country Club, but I had done my job so well that the troublemakers stayed away and it become boring. I felt like I needed a fresh challenge, so I began looking for another club to run. I started working occasional nights on the door of a hotel in Greenford, west London. This place was rough, really fucking rough. Even the cockroaches that infested the place wore steel-toecapped boots. Neville Sheen, Dave Young and I had been asked to work there because the previous door team had lost control of the place. It attracted so much trouble that the police made a point of coming in to survey the carnage every 30 minutes. For reasons known only to himself, Charlie Wilson, the former Great Train Robber, used to drink in there. I liked Charlie a lot. Nothing fazed the guy. He would sit at the bar drinking his drink while glasses and furniture flew all around him, and he wouldn't appear even to notice.

A man dressed in a ridiculous-looking white-fur full-length coat came to the door one night and said, 'I don't pay, boys. I am down to Charlie Wilson.'

The man had the manners of a pig, and I told him so, adding, 'I'm no boy, and I don't give a fuck who you are down to.'

The man was a shit gangster but a fantastic actor. He knew all of the poses to strike and all of his lines. 'You don't understand, sonny,' he said through gritted teeth. 'I'm coming in, I'm not paying and you're not going to stop me.'

I don't know if the puddle he landed in ruined his white fur coat, but judging by the amount of blood he lost I am fairly certain his nose was badly broken. When I told Charlie about the altercation with his friend, he asked me to describe him, and as soon as I mentioned the polar-bear coat, he howled with laughter. 'Nice one, Lew,' he said. 'Let me buy you a drink.'

I stood at the bar enjoying a drink with Charlie, but after a few minutes I was called to the front door. One of the biggest men I have ever encountered stood outside with a tarty-looking blonde. The guy was 6 ft 8 in. and very well built. I was standing in the reception doorway, he was standing two steps below me and I was still looking up at him. 'I'm with Charlie,' he said.

'Don't tell me. You don't pay to get in,' I replied.

The man looked at me as if asking him to pay to get in was a crime. 'I don't pay to get in anywhere,' he said, 'especially shitholes like this.'

'It's OK,' I replied. 'On second thoughts you don't have to hand over any money.'

The man grinned at his air-headed girlfriend and put his foot on the step. I asked him where he thought he was going. 'In the hotel,' he replied. 'You said I didn't have to pay.'

'What I actually said was you don't have to hand over any money. The reason you don't have to hand over any money is that you're not coming in.'

The man put his hand in his pocket, so I hit him with a beautiful left hook under the jaw. I was expecting him to shake his head, roar and start throwing punches at me and the other doormen. Instead this giant of a man went down like a felled oak tree. I wasn't keen on letting him get up, so I began kicking him in the head. His girlfriend started screaming and the other doormen tried pulling me off him, but I just kept kicking him. The man's blood was spattered all over the walls, his girlfriend's dress and over me and the other doormen. He continued struggling and I continued hitting him until he lay motionless.

When I was satisfied that he was not going to get up, I dragged him across the car park and left him lying behind his car. As I walked back towards the hotel, the man got up from the ground and started shouting abuse at me. When I turned around, I saw that he was propping himself up on the back of a white Vauxhall. 'Wanker!' he shouted. 'Fucking wanker! Come and have another go.' I didn't need a second invitation. I ran over to the man and unloaded a barrage of punches that left him sprawled on the car. I grabbed him by the hair and kept banging his head until the back window was covered with his blood. When I released him, he slipped to the floor and, despite efforts from his girlfriend, he remained there for 20 minutes. When he eventually did regain consciousness, he was unable to walk. I watched him crawl on all fours to his car while his girlfriend gripped him by the collar of his shirt. It looked as if she was taking a rather large dog for a walk. When they reached his car, his girlfriend opened the passenger door, he crawled in and then she got in the driver's seat and sped away.

The police were due to make their 30-minute visit at any

second. There was blood splashed all around the car park and all over a couple of cars. I asked one of the bar staff to fetch buckets of hot soapy water and flush all evidence of the altercation away. Just as he finished, a police car pulled up. 'Everything OK, lads?' one of the officers asked.

'Certainly,' I replied. 'Somebody was sick, that's all. The bar staff have washed it away.' The police officers laughed, wished us well and drove away. I was relieved to see them go, but little did I know I would be even more relieved to see them return before the night was out. Just before closing time a fight broke out at the bar. To be honest, I would have been more alarmed if one hadn't. The grudges, menacing stares and threats that were routinely exchanged between customers would fester throughout the evening and generally come to a head when the bar closed. Neville and Dave said that they would go and break it up, so I remained at the front door.

The shouting, screaming and sounds of furniture and glasses being smashed would generally subside after a minute or two, but this night it just got louder and louder. I ran inside and saw that everybody in the main room appeared to be fighting. Dave was lying on the floor unconscious, the remnants of a wooden table all around his head. Neville's face was unrecognisable; he had been glassed, and all I could see were his eyes and bloodstained teeth. The main aggressors appeared to be three stocky guys who were throwing punches, glasses and furniture at everything and everybody. As I moved towards them, one picked up a stool and charged at me, but he fell over a body on the floor and landed at my feet. After stamping his head into the beer- and blood-soaked carpet, I went after his two friends. I began fighting with them and a girl joined in, jumping on my back, scratching my face and pulling my hair. We were all pushed forward, and suddenly there seemed to be police everywhere. I could hear the barman shouting, 'The doormen have been squirting people with ammonia! The doormen have got weapons!' I later learnt that he was an ex-policeman.

After talking to the barman, the police arrested Neville and put him in an ambulance. I went to the rear of the vehicle and through the open doors asked him if there was anything he wanted me to do. Neville threw his head forward and began rocking back and forth, while moaning loudly.

'Are you OK?' the policeman asked him.

'It's just stomach cramp. I get it all the time. It will pass.'

Assured that Neville was in no danger, the policeman became less interested in his prisoner and began writing notes in his pocket book. I stood in front of Neville and tried to reassure him about the injuries to his face. The policeman no longer had a clear view, so Neville slipped a handgun, a bottle of ammonia and a knuckleduster from his coat under the ambulance seat, leaned back and breathed a sigh of relief. I had guessed he was up to something because I had never known him to have stomach cramps. When the police officer wasn't looking, I grabbed the weapons, put them in my coat and walked away. I wiped the weapons clean of fingerprints and hid them near the delivery bay at the rear of the hotel before going back inside. We arranged to have them picked up the following day.

Several of the customers had been badly injured, and the police were making themselves busy trying to arrest anybody who may have been involved in the trouble. Dave Young had come to by this time and, after seeing Neville being arrested, slipped away into the night. I knew they would eventually seek me out, so I asked the landlord to lock me in a room upstairs. Two hours later, when everybody had left, I telephoned a taxi and asked the driver to take me to Stratford, in east London. From there I would walk home. I knew that if I had asked him to take me to my house, he may have passed on my address to the police. During the journey the driver said, 'That was some battle in there tonight. It's been on the local radio. A few of the lads said the bouncers who used to work there came back to attack the new ones. Big Lurch went down to sort it out first, but they bashed him up.' I asked the driver who Big Lurch was. 'He runs everything around here,' he replied. 'He's about 6 ft 8 in., a real good friend of the train robber Charlie Wilson.' I couldn't answer as I was trying not to laugh. It's surprising that Charlie and I ever got on, as it seemed every friend he ever had I either upset or bashed. I guess Charlie never kept good company.

In April 1990 Charlie Wilson's choice of company got him murdered. Charlie was shot dead beside his swimming pool in Marbella. He had been hosing down the path around the pool when his wife, Patricia, answered their front door. A man with a cockney accent asked if Charlie was home. Patricia called Charlie to the door, and the two men walked back out to the pool. At her husband's inquest Patricia said, 'I heard the man say, "I am a friend of Eamonn's." I had a feeling there were two people there, although I couldn't say why. I heard two very loud bangs and at first I thought it was from the building site next door, but then I heard the dog screaming.

'Charlie was lying at the side of the pool face down. The man had gone and the gate was open. I saw blood coming from his mouth, and Charlie did a sort of press-up and gestured in the direction the man had gone.'

Nobody has ever been charged in relation to Charlie's murder, and from what I hear, nobody ever will be. Charlie had become immersed in the drug world with Mickey Green. After a botched drug importation into the UK, Charlie's friend James Rose stood trial at Chelmsford Crown Court. He received a reduced prison sentence after pointing the finger at a man named Roy Adkins as the kingpin in the importation – a move that had been endorsed by Charlie. Charlie clearly had no fear of Adkins and thought nothing of using him to help his friend Rose. Not surprisingly Adkins wasn't happy. He knew all about Charlie's reputation and the company he kept, but he refused to take their betrayal on the chin. Instead Adkins paid to have Charlie executed. Five months later Roy Adkins was himself gunned down in the bar of the American Hotel in Amsterdam. It wasn't Charlie's friends that had pulled the trigger. Adkins had taken liberties with two Colombians who had been involved with him in the sale of several stolen parcels of emeralds. It doesn't matter who you think you are or who you know; if you front people up and try to take a liberty, there will always be somebody bigger and better to put you in your place.

I didn't return to the hotel in Greenford. The thought of featuring in another court case so soon after the Harry Boyd fiasco was undoubtedly a major factor in my decision to seek employment elsewhere. I decided to leave the Middlesex and Herts Country Club too. I felt that I should make a clean break from that part of London and head for pastures new, preferably nearer my home.

# ROUND NINE

WHEN THE WORLD-FAMOUS NIGHTCLUB STRINGFELLOWS FIRST OPENED IN London – as a disco, rather than the table-dancing club it would later become – Elton John's former minder John Smith was appointed head doorman. I knew John; he had worked for me at Boobs nightclub in Croydon, where I ran the door for a while. He claimed to be some sort of judo expert, but I never witnessed him displaying any sort of expertise in anything. One evening he was manning the front door at Boobs when he got into a confrontation with three men who had been ejected earlier that evening. They were demanding to be let back in, and I had already said that they shouldn't be readmitted under any circumstances. I had always had personal doubts about John's ability as a doorman, so, rather than intervene, I watched to see how he would handle the situation. The men became more vocal, and one tried to push past him. Turning towards me, his face filled with terror, John pleaded, 'Can you help me, Lew?'

I grabbed John by the scruff of the neck and flung him out of the way. I punched the biggest man of the trio, knocking him to the floor. I then hit his two friends, who joined him face down on the pavement. Turning to John, I said, 'Get your coat and fuck off home. You're useless!'

I heard that an old friend of mine named David Smith (who is no relation to John) had started work at Stringfellows, and, as I wasn't working, I popped into the club to see him. When I walked in, John Smith, whom I hadn't seen since making him redundant in Croydon, asked if he could have a word with me. When we were out of earshot of the other door staff, John said, 'It's got nothing to do with me, Lew, but Peter Stringfellow and his general manager Roger don't want you in here. They say that bodybuilders and big men intimidate the customers.' I asked John where Stringfellow was because I wanted to talk to him. 'He's locked himself in the office with Roger,' John replied. 'They won't come out while you are here.' I don't know if Stringfellow or Roger even knew I was on the premises or if John was just saying that to get rid of me, but, out of respect for my friend David Smith, I decided to leave rather than cause a scene. I made my reasons clear to the judo expert before departing, because I didn't want him to start thinking that he had been the reason I'd chosen to walk out.

Several weeks later John Smith and the other members of the door team walked out of the club following a dispute. Only David Smith remained. He telephoned me and asked if I could get a couple of guys to go to the club to help him out. I contacted Dave Armstrong, a reliable, no-nonsense doorman. Neither of us were working at that time, so he agreed to join me and we drove up to Stringfellows together.

When Dave and I walked in, Roger approached us and introduced himself. 'Lew Yates?' he said. 'I think I recognise you.' I could see that he was embarrassed. On my last visit he and his boss were supposed to have objected to my presence, but now that the shit had hit the fan, they were welcoming me with open arms. Dave Smith was standing behind Roger pulling faces, smirking and obviously enjoying hearing him squirm.

To save Roger any further embarrassment, I quickly changed the subject. 'If you show us around the club, we can familiarise ourselves with the layout and get on with the job,' I said.

Roger smiled and gave us a guided tour of the premises before letting us get on with what we knew best. We worked at Stringfellows for almost a year until eventually our friend Neville Sheen was given control of the door. It was a really enjoyable place to work. The club was packed every night with celebrities and well-behaved revellers out to enjoy themselves rather than cause trouble.

After leaving Stringfellows, Dave Armstrong and his business partner got involved with a gang who made their money importing cocaine. There was some sort of falling out, and threats were exchanged. Dave's business partner went missing shortly afterwards but eventually turned up dead in Scotland with half of his head missing. He had been badly beaten and had suffered multiple gunshot wounds.

Two weeks later Dave was visiting his former wife's home on the Isle of Dogs in east London. After saying goodbye to her, he got in his car, closed the door and leant forward to put the key in the ignition. There was a loud bang, then blood began to pour out of his nose, ears and mouth. Dave heard a second loud bang and then the sound of footsteps, as his assailant made his escape. When Dave tried to open the car door, he realised he couldn't move. He had been shot twice. The first bullet had entered the back of his head behind the ear. It had destroyed his eardrum, smashed the upper palate of his mouth and continued to travel down, breaking gums and teeth. The second bullet had entered the top of his neck and lodged in his spine. When the police examined the scene, they discovered the front tyre of his car had been deflated. Fortunately Dave had not noticed this. Had he done so, he would have been bending down changing the wheel when the gunman struck. This would have allowed the assassin to empty the gun into Dave's head with ease. Despite his appalling injuries, Dave is fortunate that he is able to continue living a reasonably normal life. He does, however, carry a constant reminder of the day he nearly died. The bullet that lodged in his spine is still there, because surgeons fear he may be permanently paralysed if they try to remove it. I and many others are pleased that Dave survived this cowardly attack. He has always been there for me when I have needed him; he's a true friend.

Big Freddie Botham contacted me and asked if I would look after the clubhouse door of an amateur football club in Essex. No disrespect to this particular football club, but I wasn't aware they were having problems with crowds of people at their games. As far as I knew, they had never attracted a large crowd, never mind had trouble. Essex isn't what I would call a football-mad county, Colchester United and Southend United being the only two league teams. Freddie explained that the offer of work related to the social club, rather than policing the matches. 'It's fucking rough, Lew,' he warned. 'These boys aren't like the lads you've been bouncing around that Country Club.'

I'd been looking for a fresh challenge nearer home, and Freddie's offer ticked both boxes. 'I'll do it, Freddie,' I said. 'When can I start?'

The club resembled most working men's clubs: there was a long bar and a large function room. The only difference was that this was overrun by drug-dealing and drug-taking delinquents every Sunday night. I'm no saint, and nor do I think I am in a position to look down on others, but this place had been conquered by invading scum. The first night I worked there,

I watched more than 100 unwashed yobs bully and intimidate the handful of decent people who had dared to enter the place. Within a month I had beaten every one of the main faces, kicked their hangers-on out and rid the place of drugs. When word got around that the 100 losers who had previously inhabited the club were gone, 500 decent people whose only intention was to have a good time replaced them. I had worked long enough in clubs to know that the drug-dealers wouldn't just walk away. Their pride had been hurt, their reputations rubbished. They would come back at me in force and with a vengeance.

It started as a scuffle in the middle of the dance floor. At first I thought the two young guys were pretending to wrestle one another. No punches were being thrown. When I went to break it up, I saw that they were doing nothing more than grappling with one another. 'Leave it out, lads,' I said. 'You know the score. Any more bother and you'll both have to leave.'

As I turned to walk away, they started grappling with each other again, so I grabbed the largest of the two. He was about 26, a fairly big lad with broad shoulders. He began to struggle, and I slipped over in a puddle of beer that had been spilt on the floor. 'Kill the cunt! Kill the cunt!' the broad-shouldered lad started shouting. Approximately ten of his friends came out of the crowd and began to attack me. I managed to get to my feet and hit those closest to me. I wanted the lad who had started this, so I pushed, punched and shoved people out of the way until I reached him.

His friends were still hitting me, but I had decided that if I was going to go down, he was going with me. I roared when I finally managed to grab his head, and this seemed to startle some of his friends. During that momentary lapse in the attack on me I managed to get the lad in a headlock and start running. People jumped and were forced out of the way as I charged towards a set of double glass doors that were hidden by a pair of full-length velvet curtains. The sound of splintering wood, breaking glass and screaming filled the air as I continued running, taking the curtain pole, curtains, doors and the offending customer with me. The lad whose head I had used to demolish the doors lay on the floor drenched in his own blood. It seemed pointless punishing him further, so I ran back inside shouting, 'Who wants it? Who wants it?' The others who had attacked me were almost clambering over one another in their efforts to get through the front door first. An ambulance was called for the person who had exited via the doors, and once he had been taken away, things returned to normal. I was fairly certain that neither he nor his friends would be returning for a while.

On the way home I called into a club called Mr Jim's on the Romford Road in Ilford. I was friends with the proprietor. He didn't employ door staff, but if I was passing at closing time I would always stop by to ensure things were OK. I stayed at Mr Jim's for approximately an hour, and then I went home. As soon as I walked in and took my jacket off, Margaret said, 'Oh my God, Lew. What has happened?' I had no idea what Margaret was talking about until she told me to remove my blood-soaked shirt. I then realised that during the fight I had been stabbed in the back. I genuinely didn't feel any pain – until the following day, that is. When I awoke, I was barely able to stand and walking was agony. When I went to the hospital, I was told that I had suffered an inch-and-a-half-deep wound that was dangerously close to my spine. It took me more than three weeks to recover, and even then I still suffered occasional discomfort. I never did find out which one of the little bastards stabbed me.

Over the years my relationship with Margaret had gone from strength to strength and we had eventually ended up living as man and wife, but after my painful experience with Jean, the subject of marriage or having children had never been raised. Her father, an old-fashioned Irishman, wasn't very happy about the fact we were 'living in sin', but, apart from the odd comment, he did nothing to prevent us from being together. Everybody could see that Margaret and I adored each other, my children were happy and so it was hard, if not impossible, for people to criticise our union. Girls in the East End were brought up to be homemakers, and Margaret thrived on being the perfect housewife. That may sound derogatory in this day and age, but it's the way things were back then. A stable, clean, happy home was far more important to many women than a career at the office and coming home to a hubby dressed in a pinafore serving up microwave chips.

Shortly after I had been stabbed, Margaret announced that she had fallen pregnant. We decided that, rather than have a child born out of wedlock, we would do what was considered to be the decent thing and marry. We exchanged vows at East Ham Registry office and became Mr and Mrs Martindale. For some time Margaret had been asking me to give up working on the doors. Now that we were man and wife with a baby on the way, the pressure to get a proper job increased tenfold. I knew that working the doors was riddled with risk, but I was being paid £250 per night when most men were not earning that in a week in their 'normal' nine-to-five jobs. I have to admit, as well as the money, I was enjoying the different challenges that each night offered. I told Margaret that I would consider giving up working on the doors, but deep down I knew it wasn't going to happen just yet. I had other unfinished business that I wanted to resolve before settling down to what most consider to be a normal life.

I had never forgotten Roy Shaw and the fight that I longed for, but I had come to accept that it was unlikely ever to take place.

While the slightest hope remained of it happening, though, I was prepared to pursue it. I went to a club called the Circus Tavern in Purfleet, Essex, one night. As I walked in, the door staff mentioned that Shaw was sitting at a table with his friends in the main room. 'Oh, is he?' I replied. 'I had better go and say hello, or he will think I'm rude.' A cabaret act were coming to the end of their performance as I approached Shaw's table. I could see Joe Pyle laughing and big Ginger Ted sitting next to him. Shaw had his back to me. I walked around the table and stood directly in front of Shaw, who immediately looked up at me. 'Do you mind? I can't see the show,' he said.

'Hello, Roy,' I replied. 'Are you ready for me yet? Are you going to fight me or are you going to keep running away from me?' Shaw jumped to his feet and was immediately restrained by his friends. I laughed at him, hoping I could taunt him into fighting me. 'Let him go. Let him go,' I said. 'Let's have it now.'

Ginger Ted, a man I respect, said, 'Come on now, Lew. Not here. We are on a night out. You've had your fun. Turn it in.'

Shaw was still struggling, but I knew he wasn't trying hard enough to break free. 'Any time you want it, Shaw, you know where to find me,' I said before walking away.

Shortly after this incident Shaw's manager Joe Carrington contacted Peter Koster and arranged for us all to meet at the William the Conqueror pub in Manor Park. When we arrived, Carrington was present, but Shaw was absent. 'Do you still want to fight Roy?' Carrington asked when we all sat down.

'He knows I do,' I replied. 'I've been asking him for the last five years.'

Carrington said that the fight could definitely go ahead, but there was a condition: 'Roy's getting fed up of you insulting him in public. He wants this to happen sooner rather than later. You fight in six weeks or you don't fight at all.'

I nearly fell off my stool laughing. 'Six weeks to prepare for a fight? Are you mad?' I asked. 'Any decent fighter needs at least four to six months to get fit for a fight. I have an umbilical hernia from working out when I shouldn't have been, I am overweight, out of shape and recovering from being stabbed.'

'We know all that,' Carrington replied, 'but that's our final offer: six weeks or nothing.'

My heart ruled my head that day. I should have said no, got box fit and challenged him again, but there had been so many challenges, so many disappointments, that I stuck my hand out and said, 'Fuck it. You're on.'

I was asked to go to an unlicensed fight that was being staged at a nightclub in Ilford to make the challenge in public. When I arrived, I joined Peter Koster and several other friends at the bar. Peter told me that Shaw was ringside. He had been given the job of operating the bell to signal the beginning and end of each round. 'I have spoken to Carrington,' Peter said. 'You will be called into the ring after the final bout to challenge Shaw.'

At the end of the evening the MC called me into the ring. The crowd, excited by the prospect of violence, were stamping their feet and cheering. As the MC announced the now all-too-familiar forthcoming contest between Lew 'Wild Thing' Yates and Roy 'Pretty Boy' Shaw, I looked over at Shaw and saw that he was staring at me. I really wanted to fight him there and then. 'Get up here now!' I shouted. 'Let's fucking do it now!' The crowd, who couldn't hear my words but knew I was gesticulating, goading Shaw to fight me, began to roar encouragement. Shaw remained out of the ring, gazing blankly through me.

Joe Carrington came over to me and asked me to calm down. 'For fuck's sake, Lew,' he said. 'Take it easy.'

'He's never going to fucking fight me, is he?' I shouted. 'Get him up here now!'

Carrington's head came into contact with mine. I don't know if he had intended to do it or not, but I pushed him away. 'It's only gamesmanship, Lew,' Carrington said. 'Don't be like that. Behave yourself.' The ring, to me, has always been a place where two men fight, not act. It sounded as if I was expected to take part in some sort of staged farce rather than a blood-and-guts boxing contest. As Carrington stepped towards me, I head-butted him in the face and sent him flying across the ring into the ropes.

Ginger Ted put his arms around me in an effort to stop any further violence. 'Calm down, Lew,' Ted kept saying. 'Just leave it.'

Two men outside the ring grabbed my leg and tried pulling me to the canvas. I bent down and attempted to punch one of the men, and Ted ended up hanging almost upside down on my back. Shaw jumped into the ring; at last he had come to fight me. I stood up. By now the ring was crowded with people. 'Come on then, Shaw!' I shouted. 'Let's do it here and now!' Shaw ignored me and went to the aid of his manager, who was clutching his mouth. There was no point in provoking Shaw further; he was clearly not interested in having it with me.

Eventually I was ushered out of the ring by Peter and others. As I was climbing out, an extremely overweight lady began shouting, 'You bully! You bloody bully! Who do you think you are?' I didn't reply.

Carrington and Shaw came to the ropes and looked down at me. I turned and called out, 'Come down here now. I will fight you both.' The pair just stood motionless, staring at me. They were not going to come. I walked over to the bar. I was shaking with temper, and adrenalin was surging through my veins. Lenny McLean was standing next to a cigarette machine, drinking a glass of lemonade. 'Let me buy you a pint, Lew,' he said. 'I loved that.'

My anger instantly subsided, and we both started laughing. I spoke to Lenny for a few minutes, and then Peter Koster joined us. 'It's going to go off in here,' he said. 'Shaw's mob have got the hump over your little outburst. We had better make ourselves scarce.'

Lenny looked at me, trying to gauge a reaction. I looked back at him and laughed. 'Fuck it, Peter,' I said. 'We are staying for a drink.'

Nothing did happen that night, but I knew I had given Shaw's people the needle. They were never going to forgive me for embarrassing them in public, and they were going to ensure that I was made to pay one way or another. I had been down this road so many times with Shaw that I still wasn't convinced the fight was ever going to happen.

All the talk of fighting, hearing the crowd cheer when I was in the ring, albeit to challenge Shaw, made me want to box again. I wasn't fit enough to do so, but I thought that if I sharpened myself up against mediocre opponents and spent more time in the gym, I definitely had a few good fights left in me.

Eddie Richardson, the infamous south-London gangster, had recently got involved in the unlicensed fight game. Eddie was managing a doorman from Eltham named Harry Starbuck. In his autobiography *The Last Word* Eddie concedes that most unlicensed fights were decided long before the fighters had even entered the ring. There was simply too much of a risk for ambitious gangsters to wager the money they had thieved and robbed on a guy who might have had a glass jaw. If a fighter had lost two or three consecutive fights, it was highly unlikely that anybody would pay his stake money or bet on him, so he would become a worthless nonentity. The name of the game for a fighter was either to take a substantial backhander from an opponent's manager to lose, which would enhance the other fighter's worth as a crowd puller, or to avoid any opponent that looked capable of beating him, which would result in prolonging his lucrative but short career. Clocking up a respectable tally of victories in the ring would mean the bookies would offer very good odds against the fighter being defeated. Therefore, when the fighter thought he was reaching the end of his career, he would ask family and friends to place substantial bets against him winning his next contest. At some stage during the fight he would allow himself to be caught with a sucker punch, hit the canvas and remain there, dreaming of all the money he had just earned while waiting for the count to ten to end. Many of these unlicensed boxers and promoters alike certainly knew what they were doing. The punters were being entertained and the cast were making a living.

Desperate to get back into the ring, I decided to go to one of Eddie Richardson's unlicensed boxing nights at a place called Harvey's in Charlton Road, south London. It was my intention to challenge Eddie's man, Harry Starbuck. I considered Starbuck to be an average fighter at the end of his career – just the type of opponent I needed to sharpen myself up on. When I arrived, I noticed that Roy Shaw was in the audience. He was sitting at the end of an aisle with Joe Carrington. When Shaw saw me, he walked over, greeted me and asked me what I was doing there. 'I have come here to challenge Starbuck,' I replied.

Shaw looked puzzled. 'I'm here for him too.'

'If Starbuck accepts your challenge rather than mine, you ought to knock him out in the first minute of the fight or there's something wrong with you,' I said.

Shaw glared at me, shook his head and walked away. I watched the fight, which Starbuck won comfortably by knocking his opponent out. As the MC was announcing the result of the contest, I made my way down to the ring so that I could issue my challenge. I couldn't see Shaw, so I assumed he had changed his mind about offering to fight Starbuck. To my surprise, the MC announced that Starbuck's next opponent was going to be Roy Shaw. The fight had obviously been arranged between Eddie Richardson, Starbuck, Shaw and his camp without the customary public challenge having to be made. I decided to attend the fight so I could look for Shaw's strengths and weaknesses in the ring. It was important that I knew everything about the man I was due to face.

The fight was held at Dartford Football Club in Kent and attracted a crowd of 4,000 people. As I had predicted, Starbuck didn't even last a round. Shaw ended the mismatched encounter without even breaking into a sweat. After the bout the MC, a huge black guy, called me into the ring. Shaw was bouncing around, arms aloft, celebrating his victory as I reached the ropes. Although I had already challenged Shaw, I assumed that the opportunity to hype the fight in front of such a large crowd was one the promoters did not wish to miss. Before I managed to climb into the ring, though, the MC announced that I would be Shaw's next opponent. I was, to say the least, surprised that I wasn't allowed to publicly challenge Shaw, but not as surprised as I would be when I heard the absolute rubbish that he spouted afterwards. Describing me as a 'stocky little geezer', Shaw claimed I had in fact got in the ring and challenged him after the Starbuck fight.

'He had challenged me and McLean about five times,' Shaw said. 'We told him to put the money up and we would have it with him. Yates borrowed the money off a geezer named Terry Hollingsworth [Shaw is wrong about this], who I had already fought and knocked out in the first round of a winner-takes-all bout. So I decided to take Hollingsworth's money twice and shut Lew Yates up at the same time. That's why I accepted the fight, just to shut him up.'

Something didn't seem right to me about the way Shaw's last few fights were being hyped. Nearly everything he and his camp were telling the media was false or grossly exaggerated. Only now, with the benefit of hindsight, can I deduce that the fights were well-orchestrated events that his management were ensuring he could not lose. Not only were they ensuring victory in the ring by any means, they were building Shaw up for their next money-spinner: lucrative media deals covering his boxing achievements.

In my opinion the men behind Shaw realised that his days of making money in the ring were over, so they decided to sell the myth they had created to make even more money. Footage of Shaw's fights against Donny Adams, Paddy Mullins and Lenny McLean was turned into a short film titled *The Guv'nor*, produced by Bob Brown (who went on to form Purple Rose Films with actor Jeff Daniels). On the front cover of a glossy Australian martial-arts magazine Shaw was described as the king of the unlicensed ring and the Guv'nor. As I read the feature in the magazine, the claims and boasts regarding Shaw just got more and more ridiculous. As an amateur Shaw was said to have had over one hundred and fifty fights, one of which was at the schoolboy championships of Great Britain. Another of these amateur fights was said to have been in the ABA final. The most ridiculous claim was that Shaw had fought ten professional fights and was managed by Mickey Duff. I say ridiculous because the BBBC have no records of these fights, Mickey Duff strenuously denies ever managing Shaw and, by Shaw's own admission, he wouldn't have stood a chance against a professional fighter.

When the Shaw camp were asked to explain the flaws in the stories about his past that were given to promote his new media career, they were equally creative. Shaw claimed his boxing record was erased from the BBBC records because his decision to set up unlicensed boxing bouts with Joe Pyle had 'pissed them off'. It's a feeble explanation, but an explanation all the same. Unfortunately it doesn't stand up to scrutiny as far as I am concerned because several other fighters such as Cliff Fields, Kevin Paddock and Johnny Waldron fought unlicensed fights and their professional boxing records remain intact with the BBBC.

Shaw claims that Mickey Duff's denial was made for much the same reason: 'Duff was employed by the BBBC. It would have therefore been suicidal for him to admit to managing unlicensed boxing's most famous fighter.'

This excuse does not hold water for me either. Frank Warren works with the BBBC and has never felt the need to deny his extensive involvement with unlicensed fighting during the early days of his career. *Time Out* magazine was invited by the Shaw camp to cover the fight with me. Don Atyeo, the journalist sent by the magazine to write the article, was given a story that enhanced Shaw's reputation further. Atyeo was told that Shaw had lost the two fights against McLean because the first time he had overdosed on ginseng and on the second occasion he had overdosed on Vitamin E. 'I take nothing but honey now,' Shaw remarked in an effort to bolster his explanation.

'But if you have lost, Roy,' Atyeo replied, 'you can hardly claim to be the Guv'nor, can you?'

Shaw thought for a moment and then said, 'Well, that's what it's got to be down to, ain't it? Now it's between him and me.'

Nobody quite knew what Shaw meant, and, surprisingly for a journalist, Atyeo didn't ask him to explain further. Shaw spent a lot of time in Atyeo's company before his fight with me. They visited the Seven Kings pub in Ilford, where the pair watched several unlicensed bouts and enjoyed dinner with Joe Carrington. Little wonder that Atyeo ridiculed me, giving a distorted account of my fight with Shaw and describing Shaw as 'London's hardest man' in the article he eventually wrote. The result of all the hype ensured that talk of books and feature films about Shaw filled numerous column inches in the media. The cash cow that was once the fighter Roy Shaw was turning into a far more lucrative product, and nobody, including me, was going to be allowed to get in the way.

In order to prepare myself for the Shaw fight, I began training at a gym near the Green Man pub at Plashet Grove, East Ham. George Walker, the proprietor, was related to Billy Walker, a legend in the ring who had fought Henry Cooper, Jack Bodell and Johnny Prescott. George was a really pleasant man, in his mid-40s but still very fit. I told him that I was in training to fight Roy Shaw, and George encouraged me to train hard for the fight. I was running three and a half miles per day and sparring with Neville and a man named Pat Thompson, but I couldn't do sit-ups or allow my sparring partner to hit me in the stomach because of the umbilical hernia. Furthermore I couldn't duck or weave very well because of the stab wound in my back, and the excessive weight I was carrying drained my energy. On and on, though, like a demented runaway train, I went, hurtling towards physical targets that I was never going to hit within six weeks. I knew that and so did Shaw. I started telling myself that if I caught him with a good left or right hook it would all be over. It was hardly a viable strategy, and there was certainly no plan B. Three or four days before the fight I had to start tapering off my training. I only did a quarter of the programme I had set for myself. The day before the fight I went for a long walk, had a short jog, did a bit of shadow-boxing and then spent the evening relaxing. When I went to bed that night, my mind was awash with thoughts of the bout I had waited five long years for. This time tomorrow, I kept thinking, I will be in the ring with Shaw; this time tomorrow I will finally achieve my goal.

I should have remembered the prophetic words of one of the greatest fighters that has ever lived before I closed my eyes that night. Muhammad Ali once said, 'The fight is won or lost far away from witnesses, behind the lines, in the gym and out there on the road, long before I dance under those lights.' I assume that when Ali uttered the words 'long before', he meant more than six weeks. Despite my lack of physical fitness, though, Roy Shaw knows he avoided a humiliating defeat that night for two reasons: he was out on his feet in the second round and his associates had the bell rung early to save him; then, after being subjected to such severe punishment, his corner men realised he was never going to go the distance with me, so they had the referee stop the fight. According to the various journalists that Shaw and his management spoke to later, I was 'slumped on one knee against the bottom rope, [my] face covered in blood, one red gorgon's eye staring balefully out at the roaring crowd'. All I can say to that is photographs, unlike Shaw's entourage, don't lie.

When I walked out of the Ilford Palais, Barry Dalton was waiting for me. 'You was fucking robbed, Lew!' he shouted.

'I know, I know,' I said. 'They were never going to let me beat him fair and square, Barry. His people had too much money riding on him.'

Barry put his arm around my shoulder and told me to forget it. 'Come to the Room at the Top with me and we will have a few pints.'

To be honest, I didn't fancy going anywhere, but I didn't want to melt away into the background and look as if I had accepted defeat. 'Fuck it, Barry, let's go,' I said. 'Let's show the bastards Lew Yates is far from beaten.'

Barry laughed and we walked up the road together talking about the fight and a future rematch. I'd first met Barry when he'd appeared on the bill of an unlicensed prizefight that was being held on a disused barge moored on the River Thames. In the dark sweaty cargo hold, a ring had been erected that was illuminated by fluorescent light strips that hung precariously from a chain secured to the underside of the barge's deck. As soon as Barry leapt into the ring, three-quarters of the crowd were stomping their feet and cheering him. The adoration wasn't really for Barry; it was for the fact that he was a white man about to do mortal combat with a black fighter. The East End and south London villains who were present didn't attempt to hide the fact that they were racist. When Barry's opponent, a Jamaican guy from Tulse Hill, south London, climbed into the ring, he was greeted by jeers and monkey chants. Approximately 50 people were there to support him, and they made it clear they were not happy about their man being racially abused. As soon as the fight started, I could see that Barry was going to do well to survive three rounds. The black guy was dancing around, unloading punches and jabbing Barry at his leisure. Beer cans began to rain down on the fighters as the crowd sensed Barry was only one decent punch away from defeat. At the end of the first round Barry too knew that he was in trouble, so he walked across to his opponent's corner and head-butted him as hard as he could in the face. The man fell, clutching a broken nose, which began pumping blood all over the canvas. Barry began to dance around the ring with his arms aloft in a victory pose. Those supporting him were screaming with delight; those supporting his bloody opponent were screaming in anger. Barry, undoubtedly revelling in his new-found infamy, picked up his corner stool, ran across the ring and threw it into the section of the crowd that was jeering him. The place erupted. Black against white. A pitched battle raged both in and out of the ring, and in the middle of it stood Barry Dalton laughing like a lunatic. Whatever he did, Barry never failed to make me laugh.

I needed cheering up after being robbed of victory at the Shaw fight. I think that's why I agreed to go for a drink with Barry afterwards. When we arrived at the Room at the Top, a loud cheer greeted us. People were patting me on the back and offering their support. As I was standing at the bar with Barry, three black guys approached me and said they had been at the fight. 'You were beating him, big guy,' one of them said. 'That fight should never have been stopped.'

'Thanks for that, mate,' I said. 'I just hope everybody else saw it that way.' I extended my hand and said, 'My name is Lew Yates, by the way. I'm pleased to meet you.'

'I know your name, Lew. Everybody in this club knows you. My name is Nigel, Nigel Benn,' the man said, smiling, 'and I am pleased to meet you.'

It was to be another six years before Nigel was to turn professional, but I could see he had something about him. He looked fit, sharp, lean and very, very mean. Nigel told me that he had recently joined the 1st Battalion of the Royal Regiment of Fusiliers but he was currently on leave. He said he had grown tired of life in Ilford and wanted a change. It was the first time that I had met Nigel. He seemed to be a decent all-round good young guy. He said that he often came to the Room at the Top for a night out with his friends. In fact he had been sneaking in there since he was a teenager. I hadn't noticed him previously, but I told him I would be keeping an eye on him in the future. We both laughed, but I didn't realise then just how true that statement would turn out to be. For almost a decade I followed

Nigel Benn's outstanding boxing career, and during that period we met up several times.

Danny, one of his six brothers, used to go to a club called Stop Outs, which was also in Ilford. I went in there one night to see a friend. As I made my way through the crowd, I heard somebody shouting, 'Yo! Big Lewie!'

I turned around and saw a black guy beckoning me towards him with his hand. 'Do I know you?' I asked.

'I'm Danny, Nigel's brother. You know Nigel,' he said.

There are thousands of Nigels in the world, so the vague details Danny gave me were not much help. 'I still don't know you, mate,' I replied. 'Who's Nigel?'

'The boxer, Nigel Benn,' Danny said.

The penny finally dropped. 'I didn't recognise you,' I said, shaking his hand. 'You have changed since I last saw you. How is Nigel?'

Danny said that his brother was in Atlantic City, training for his WBO world middleweight title fight with Doug DeWitt. I sat down with Danny talking about Nigel's prospects concerning the fight until it was time to leave. Danny then asked me if I would give him a lift to his parents' home. It wasn't far away, so I agreed. When we arrived, Danny said, 'Wait here a minute, Lew,' before disappearing into the house. Moments later he had returned to my car. 'Nigel would want you to have this,' he said.

Danny handed me a framed photograph of his brother. I thanked him for it, placed it on the passenger seat and drove home. I hadn't been able to have a good look at it in the car as it was dark, but when I got it home I had to laugh. The photograph depicted Nigel in action at the Royal Albert Hall during his Commonwealth (British Empire) middleweight title fight against Michael Chilambe. In the bottom right-hand corner

Nigel had signed the photo with the words 'With love to Mum and Dad from Nigel'. Despite Danny's admirable intentions, I have a feeling that the photograph was never intended for me.

When Nigel returned from America after defeating DeWitt, I called around to his house to see him. The area was in darkness when I arrived, because the street lighting had failed. As I went to get out of my car, I saw Nigel cross the road and go into a corner shop. I restarted my engine, put my headlights on full beam and waited. Moments later Nigel came bounding out of the shop and into the road. 'Benn, Nigel Benn,' I shouted in a menacing voice.

Nigel turned and shielded his eyes from the bright headlights. 'Who's that?' he said. 'Who wants me?'

I turned the engine off and got out of the car laughing. 'It's Lew,' I called out.

Nigel came over, stood behind me and said, 'There's only one man with shoulders like that: big Lew Yates.'

Nigel invited me into his home and introduced me to his family. We talked about his recent success, and when it was time to leave, he gave me a bag of baseball caps and other merchandise for the children. We continued to see each other fairly regularly until Nigel moved out of the area. Few fighters in the history of boxing have had the aggression Nigel showed in the ring and the compassion, warmth and integrity he has shown out of it. He is undoubtedly a credit to boxing, unlike some of the other fighters I met while in London.

# ROUND TEN

WHEN THE CLUB FINALLY CLOSED, BARRY AND I WALKED BACK TO MY CAR. MY ribs were playing me up, so Barry suggested that I go to the hospital and have them checked out, but I just wanted to get home. 'Do you want a lift, Barry?' I asked.

'Not fucking likely, Lew,' he replied. 'I'm off to find another watering hole.'

We shook hands and wished each other well. I stood watching Barry as he bowled down the street. He looked as if he didn't have a care in the world. Poor soul. If only I'd known just how many problems he did have, I would certainly have tried to help. Barry was always good to me, but another side of him existed that I knew little about. As well as prizefighting Barry indulged in setting up protection rackets and drug-dealing to make a living. He had consequently taken so much punishment both in and out of the ring over the years that his face was completely battered flat. Furthermore he was from inner-city Dublin and, although not involved himself, had several friends who had been active members of the IRA during the 1970s and '80s. Anybody who met him was left in no doubt that his chosen profession was violence.

His boxing signature tune was somewhat ironic: Bobby Darin's 'Baby Face'. Barry Dalton's face, far from being that of a baby, was in fact his greatest misfortune. At one stage Barry was sparring with 22-st. Lenny McLean, who took things too far one day. What was essentially a training session ended up being a bloodbath, with Barry on the receiving end. Everybody present was laughing as McLean smashed Barry around the ring; he even held him up rather than let him go to the canvas, just so that he could punish him further. As Barry was helped to his feet, he saw that people, inspired by McLean's treatment, were ridiculing him and swore bloody revenge. The following week he went around to McLean's home and knocked on the door. McLean appeared wearing just a bath-towel and said to Barry, 'What the fuck do you want?'

Barry didn't answer. He pulled out a double-barrelled shotgun, cocked both hammers and fired at McLean, who was by this time fleeing up the stairs. 'Don't ever try and fucking mug me off again!' Barry shouted, before putting the gun back in his coat and calmly strolling away.

Blood poured down McLean's legs and started to soak into the carpet. The lead shot had hit him in the backside, leaving a gaping hole and causing massive blood loss. He couldn't see the wound, but McLean knew it was serious and he knew he had to get help as soon as possible. Running out into the road, McLean hailed a taxi and demanded the driver take him to hospital. 'You can't get in my cab,' the driver said. 'You're covered in blood.' Fearing he may be bleeding to death, McLean told the driver he would kneel on the seat rather than sit on it and pay to have the taxi cleaned. By the time McLean reached hospital, he was beginning to feel dizzy and faint because of the amount of blood he had lost. When staff in the accident and emergency department saw the extent of his injuries, McLean was laid on a trolley and rushed to the operating theatre, where his backside was stitched back together. The following day McLean awoke to find police officers sitting at his bedside. 'We have been waiting to take a statement from you,' they said.

McLean, a scholar from the old school, replied, 'You're going to have a long wait then. I don't talk to you people. I'm saying nothing, so you may as well bugger off.'

The officers told McLean they would return in a few days, when he had been able to appreciate the severity of the attack against him. After three days the police reappeared, but McLean still refused to assist them.

When Barry Dalton heard that he was going to get away with the shooting, he couldn't stop laughing. Anyone else would have feared for their life after shooting McLean, but Barry was so 'can't give a fuck' arrogant that he refused to show concern about McLean's fearsome reputation. Barry knew that McLean would fight any man and, more often than not, come out on top, but he also knew McLean wouldn't resort to using guns or committing murder. McLean knew it too. Instead of telling people that Barry had shot him, he told those who asked that a couple of crackheads had taken a pot shot at him when he was working on the door.

Some time later Barry appeared on the same bill as McLean to fight at a venue in Woodford, Essex. People warned Barry not to go because McLean had vowed revenge, but Barry told them, 'If he hurts me again, I will shoot him again. He will get tired of being shot before I get fed up of being punched.'

As Barry sat in his dressing-room preparing himself for the bout ahead that night, he heard somebody trying to open the door, which he had locked. Moments later there was an almighty crash, and McLean stood growling in the splintered doorway. He stepped forward, grabbed Barry by the ears and smashed his head against a metal locker. 'You mug!' McLean shouted at Barry. 'You were big enough with a gun in your hand, now look at you shaking!'

Barry's bravado had disappeared. He thought that McLean had flipped and was going to pull him apart with his bare hands. 'Please, Lenny,' Barry begged, 'let me explain. I was on the gear. I was on drugs . . . I didn't know what I was doing.'

McLean threw Barry to the floor and raised his foot as if to stamp on him. 'Let me apologise, Lenny!' Barry shouted. 'Don't do this. Just let me apologise and shake your hand.'

'Shake my hand?' McLean replied. 'I'll shake your hand to say it's over, Barry, but I want you dressed and out of here in two minutes. Forget your fight tonight. Just get as far away from me as possible.'

Barry got to his feet, shook McLean's hand and started to get dressed. He knew that, despite having to grovel to McLean in private, he had scored a moral victory. He could openly walk the streets and drink in his old haunts, and people would know he had shot McLean and nothing had been done about it. Regardless of what McLean told people, Barry still appeared to have put him in his place. The incident set a very dangerous precedent for Barry. He now believed he could shoot or threaten to shoot people and, like McLean, they would back down.

Unfortunately for Barry a lot of villains in the East End of London are more than happy to arm themselves if threatened, and they are equally happy to use those arms. Around the same time as the incident in Woodford, Barry had unwittingly fallen foul of one of east London's most powerful families. Barry, backed by a firm from west London, had been putting the frighteners on a gang of scaffolders who had just secured a lucrative contract on Canary Wharf. His intention was to take the contract from them and sell it on to another company. Unfortunately for Barry the owner of the scaffolding company had connections in the underworld, and a very heavy east London crime family became involved.

As Barry sat in a pub in Canning Town, two brothers from the family approached him. One sat to Barry's left; the other to his right. 'All right, boys,' Barry said, eyeing the men nervously.

The man to his right stood up, took a sawn-off shotgun from his coat and pointed it at the landlord, who was talking to half a dozen customers gathered around the bar. 'You lot, carry on fucking talking but don't turn around!' the man shouted. Nobody argued. The landlord and customers turned to face the opposite wall. Their feet were rooted firmly to the floor. None of them dared to turn around or pass comment to the gunmen. The man to Barry's left produced a handgun and pushed it hard against Barry's temple. 'See you, cunt. Are you ready to die?' he hissed.

'No, don't do it. Don't do it,' Barry pleaded.

The man removed the gun from Barry's temple then pressed it against his throat. 'Leave off the people in Canary Wharf. Do you understand who and what I am referring to?' Barry, unable to speak, nodded frantically. 'So we understand each other, cunt?' Barry nodded again. The two men put their guns away and strolled back out of the pub. Barry had been warned.

Some time after Barry had been spoken to by the two brothers, he contacted them and said he had a bit of business they might be interested in. Barry had kept his word about not troubling the scaffolding gang, so the brothers had no reason not to listen to any proposal Barry might have had. A meeting was arranged to take place at the pub where the men had first 'met' in Canning Town. 'Do you remember the place?' one of the brothers asked.

'Remember it?' Barry laughed. 'I'm still having fucking nightmares about it.'

When they arrived at the pub, Barry told the brothers that through his contacts in Dublin he had been told that the IRA had confiscated 500 kilos of cannabis from dealers in County Cork. Not wanting to damage their public image in Ireland by being caught with illicit drugs, the IRA had made it known that they wanted to offload the heist outside the Irish Republic. Any top-drawer villain knows that a deal with a terrorist organisation like the IRA can be invaluable. A favour done is a favour owed, and when it came to assassinations and losing bodies, the IRA were the world's best. The brothers thought it would be good to have such powerful allies, so they agreed that their family would buy all of the cannabis. Before doing so, they wanted to make their position clear not only to Barry but also to his IRA friends: nobody who wasn't directly involved with the deal could know of the transaction, and further enquiries from potential buyers could no longer be considered, regardless of the amount of money offered. A deal had been struck, and they were not interested in entering into any sort of ongoing auction. Everybody concerned agreed to abide by the conditions of the deal, so plans to import the drugs into the UK were put into operation.

Despite Barry agreeing not to talk about the deal, as soon as he started to celebrate clinching it, he couldn't control his tongue. Believing it was the start of a lucrative relationship with not only the IRA but also the brothers and their family, Barry began to act as if he were now invincible. He threatened people using the names of his new 'partners', and despite the agreement he had entered into, he offered the shipment of drugs that had as yet not arrived to villains that he thought might be interested. Word soon got back to the brothers and the IRA men, and neither party was happy.

One evening Barry turned up at a minicab office he had been demanding protection money from. 'Things have changed, mate,' he told the proprietor. 'Instead of £200, your rent's £500 a week now. I've got two new heavy partners, and they also need a cut.' The man said that he couldn't afford £500 per week, so Barry spelt out exactly who his new partners were in an effort to terrify the man. It worked. Barry certainly did unnerve the man. Unfortunately he scared him so much that the man ran to the police for protection. Unknown to Barry the police installed various recording devices in the man's cab office and set up an observation point in a first-floor flat directly opposite it. As soon as Barry walked into the cab office and demanded his protection money, the police swooped. Barry was charged with several offences and remanded in custody to await trial.

Silly Barry – I wish he had stayed in prison. If he had, he might still be alive today, but it wasn't to be. Barry applied for bail and was back on the streets within two weeks. The brothers had already discussed Barry's future with the IRA members involved in the drug deal and the conclusion reached was that Barry Dalton had no future. He was going to be terminated.

During his brief spell in prison Barry had become friends with a villain named Del Croxson, who was serving five years for threatening a man with a gun. The pair became close because of their mutual interest in bodybuilding. Del was a powerful stocky man who worked the door at Antics nightclub in Bromley-by-Bow, east London. After Croxson was released from prison, his friendship with Barry continued. They would train together, and whenever Barry had a prizefight Del would be Barry's corner man.

Friendship was not the only thing the two men shared. Barry and Del both had heroin habits, which began to affect their judgement as their craving for the drug intensified. Not only did this addiction affect them mentally, it also affected them physically. Their once muscular frames were soon reduced in size dramatically. Barry not only used heroin, he also sold it and made a comfortable living from doing so. Del, on the other hand, struggled to finance his habit, and before long relations between the two men began to deteriorate. Barry, not the most tactful person I've ever met, would taunt Del in front of people, asking him if he needed ten pence for a cup of tea or loose change for a meal. Although the pair never came to blows, it was obvious that Barry had nothing but contempt for Del and that Del now despised Barry. Heroin was the only thing they had left in common, and their need for it kept them bonded together. Knowing Del Croxson not only hated Barry but was always short of money and willing to do anything to earn it, the brothers approached him with a proposition. 'Barry was involved in a bit of business with us, Del,' they explained, 'but his mouth's too big. If you do a job for us, you can have his rather substantial cut.'

'And what may that job be?' Del enquired.

'Top him,' came the reply. 'Erase Barry Dalton from your life and everybody else's.'

'Say no more,' Del replied. 'I've waited a long time for this opportunity. The cunt's history.'

Del telephoned Barry and told him that he had been offered a bit of work but he wouldn't be able to handle it himself. 'It's a big job, Barry,' he said. 'I would need not only help but backup in case it went tits up. I've heard you have major backup these days.'

Getting into character, Barry boasted that he was prepared to help, but any help would involve his people being paid too. 'No problem,' Del assured him. 'You tell me the price and we have a deal.' As both men replaced the receiver, both smiled.

Barry thought he was going to be mugging Del off on a deal, and Del had just laid the bait that would lure the man he hated to his death. Later that week Barry parked his car near the Alexandra Palace entertainment complex in Wood Green, north London. When his friend Del walked up to the car, got in and greeted him, he had no idea that he was in any danger. 'Just drive, Barry,' Del said. 'I think I am being followed.'

Barry slipped the car into gear and pulled away, eyeing his rear-view mirror nervously. Del took a sawn-off shotgun from inside his coat, pointed it at Barry's head and fired both barrels. Barry's car, which hadn't yet gathered speed, left the road and crashed into a wall. He was later found dead, slumped across the front seats. Barry Dalton was 35 years old when he died and married with five children.

I learnt of Barry's murder through another doorman. I can only say how I felt: absolutely gutted. I had little knowledge of the murky world in which he had immersed himself. I knew Barry loved to fight and regularly got into trouble with the police for doing so, but the news that he was involved in heroin and extortion to feed his habit shocked me. Under normal circumstances I would have attended his funeral, but I have always hated drugs and the world they represent, so I stayed away and said my goodbyes in a prayer for him. I have never taken a hard drug, a steroid or a so-called soft drug in my life. One minute those who do take them are your best friends; the next they want to stab you in the back. A drugged body has a drugged brain controlling it. It's a fucked-up world to inhabit and not one that I even wish to visit.

In his confused and poisoned mind Del Croxson thought that snuffing out Barry had turned him into a fully fledged gangland enforcer. Instead of lying low, he began asking people if they wanted anybody else sorted. Villains are always on the lookout for lunatics or losers to do their dirty work, so it wasn't too long before he secured another grisly task. Del agreed to slash with a knife a man who was suspected of being a police informant. The man lived in Lincoln, and the agreed fee for disfiguring him was £2,000.

For the job Del recruited two other men, whom he agreed to pay £500 each. When the trio arrived at the man's house, things went horribly wrong. Instead of the suspected informant answering the door, an old lady opened it. 'Can I help you?' she asked. The trio asked if the man they wanted was home, but before the lady could answer, their intended victim put his head out of an upstairs window and asked them what they wanted. In a moment of desperation or frustration Del pulled out a 9-mm automatic handgun and fired a shot at the man. Del, who was certainly no marksman, got lucky; his intended target not so. The bullet struck the man in the head, but miraculously the wound was not fatal. Unfortunately for Del and his henchmen the police had the house under surveillance, and when they became aware of the gunfire, they immediately called for backup. A frightening car chase ensued, with Del hanging out of a window firing shots at any police vehicle that dared to come near. Just outside the city Del leapt from the car and made his escape on foot. His two companions were caught shortly afterwards in a police roadblock.

When Del arrived back in London, he went into hiding, but within a week the police found out his address and arrested him. Del was charged with attempted murder and remanded in custody. While awaiting trial in HMP Belmarsh, heroin was smuggled in to him by 'friends' who knew of his addiction to the vile drug. Del was extremely grateful and eagerly injected the heroin that he had been craving without knowing it was pure. Nobody knew for sure if Del was going to talk about who employed him to attack the man in Lincoln or to carry out the Dalton murder, but it was decided he was never going to be given the opportunity. Del Croxson died within minutes of injecting the drug. He was 32 years old. He had a wife who was pregnant at the time of his death and three children. Two men dead, two families destroyed, numerous others injured: did anybody really win in the end?

I have been offered the chance to get involved in the lucrative drug trade on several occasions. The misery it causes, which I have witnessed, would never allow me even to be tempted. Anybody reading this who is involved or even thinking about getting involved should look at those they love and think again.

A new nightclub opened in Dagenham, Essex, called Lautrec's. Because it was in a rough area, Kenny Lynwood, the manager, knew it would attract trouble, so he asked me to work there. 'How much do you want a night, Lew?' he said confidently. 'I'll pay you well to run the door for me.'

I thought for a moment and replied, 'Two hundred and fifty pounds a shift will cover it.'

Kenny nearly fell out of his chair. 'Two-fifty? I can't afford that,' he said.

'Good luck with your club then,' I replied, 'because you obviously can't afford me.'

I walked out of Kenny's office and was getting into my car when I heard him call me. 'Two-fifty it is then, Lew,' he said, 'but for fuck's sake don't tell any of the other doormen, or they will all want ridiculous wages.'

I assured him that I wouldn't and drove home. I would be unable to work at the football club and Lautrec's, so I gave my friend Dave Armstrong the football-club door. If he ever needed backup, I was only a phone call and a short drive away.

I'm not sure if the proprietor was trying to import some much needed culture into Dagenham or if he was taking the piss when he chose the name Lautrec's for the club. Henri de Toulouse-Lautrec was a famous French painter in the late 1800s. He stayed in the Montmartre section of Paris, the centre of the cabaret-entertainment and bohemian life that he loved to paint. Circuses, dance halls, nightclubs – all these social activities were brought to life on his canvas. Toulouse-Lautrec would sit at a crowded nightclub table, laughing and drinking, and at the same time he would make swift sketches of people and events going on around him. The following day he would use the sketches to produce his now famous paintings.

I couldn't see the link between Lautrec's paintings and Dagenham, so I assumed it had to be the man's appearance and lifestyle. Many of the customers who staggered into the premises certainly behaved and looked like Toulouse-Lautrec. As a child Lautrec was extremely delicate and more often than not sick. At the age of 12 he broke his left leg and at 14 his right leg. Lautrec's bones did not heal properly, and the limbs ceased to grow. The painter reached maturity with a body trunk of normal size but with abnormally short legs. He was only 4.5 ft. Unable to live what most would consider to be a normal life, he drank heavily. By the 1890s the drinking started to affect his health. Eventually he was confined to a mental institution, but he could not overcome his alcohol addiction and died in 1901. That, I concluded, had to be the link between him and the customers we had to deal with at Lautrec's. Most were drunk out of their minds by 10 p.m., ranting and raving like lunatics by midnight and suffering from physical abnormalities after being kicked around the streets at closing time.

Kenny got good value for his money when he paid me £250 each night. Lautrec's had its fair share of heroes, but the door staff I picked to work there were solid. They dealt with trouble firmly and efficiently. One bouncer was a guy named Paul Dobson.

Through him I was introduced to two lads in their early 20s who said they were looking for door work. Johnny Butler and Carlton Leach were friends who had earned a bit of a reputation amongst their own age group causing havoc around the East End and at football matches. On Paul's recommendation, I gave them both a job. They turned out to be decent lads who did whatever I asked of them and were always there when needed.

There were several incidents each night at Lautrec's. Some were minor; others far more sinister. There was one guy who used to come in with three of his friends. They were always courteous and always offered to buy the door staff a drink. One evening he pulled me to one side and said, 'If a big blond lad comes here, don't let him in. He is my son. He is on drugs, and he is a nightmare. I don't want him allowed in anywhere where he can hurt himself, others or get into trouble.'

I assured him I would look out for his son, but the problem was there were plenty of big blond lads in Essex.

I had forgotten all about the 'big blond lad' when, a few months later, he came to the door asking for Kenty. I told him that no such person worked at the club, but he refused to listen. 'I want to see Kenty,' he shouted, 'and I want to fucking see him now!'

I repeated what I had already told the man and added, 'Even if there was such a person, you couldn't come in, because it's nearly closing time.'

The man became abusive, so I advised him to walk away while he still could. He glared at me, walked five or six paces away and then pulled out a handgun, which he aimed at my head. 'You're going to die, you bastard!' he screamed. 'You're going to fucking die!'

The man wasn't drunk, but he did appear to be on something, which I guessed was making him brave. 'Am I going to die?' I said, laughing at him. 'Pull the fucking trigger then, you mug.' I gripped the push bars on either side of the fire doors and began to swing back and forth. 'If you're going to shoot me, then fucking do it.' The man pulled out a magazine of bullets, banged it into the butt of the gun, spun the weapon cowboy-style on his finger and pointed it back at me. 'You fucking fool,' I said, 'it's you who is going to die.' I had gained quite a bit of momentum swinging back and forth on the doors. I knew that he would only get one shot off before I could grab him. If he failed to pull the trigger or missed, he was mine. 'This is stupid,' I said. 'Put the gun away, and come in and have a drink.'

'Fuck you,' he replied. 'I don't trust you. If you try anything, I swear I will blow your head off.'

I assured the man I didn't want any trouble. 'You're armed. What on earth could I do if you came into the club?'

He fell for it. As soon as he took a few paces forward, I let go of the doors and flew at him. I hit him as hard as I could with a left hook, which shattered his jaw. I grabbed the gun and smashed him repeatedly over the head with it. His forehead split open and began pouring with blood. I stood up, grabbed his arm and dragged his lifeless body around the side of the building, where I left him. I went into the club and said to Kenny, 'I have got a present for you.'

'What's that?' he asked.

'Somebody outside who thinks your name is Kenty wanted to give you this,' I replied as I handed him the gun.

Kenny's face drained. 'You are joking, aren't you? Tell me you're fucking joking, Lew.'

When I walked back out to the front door, I was confronted by a large group of armed police, who demanded to know who had a gun. I pointed towards Kenny, and moments later they were dragging him outside. All of the door staff were laughing.

I was tempted to let the police take Kenny away. He was looking at me with terror in his eyes, pleading with me to intervene. I eventually explained to the police what had happened and they released Kenny, before taking the still unconscious gunman away.

A year later I was subpoenaed to attend court to give evidence against the man, but, out of respect for his long-suffering father, I refused to go. I have no idea of the outcome of the case and never saw father or son again.

The owner of Lautrec's purchased another nightclub called Moonlights in Stratford, east London. The venue had been open for a number of years, was tainted with a fairly bad reputation but was controlled by a group of half-decent doormen. As I had done a good job of controlling the hooligan element at Lautrec's, I was asked to run the door at Moonlights. I agreed to do so but saw no reason to change the door staff. They had done their job in the past, and they knew who to let in and who to refuse entry to. I decided to leave them in place and pay sporadic visits to the club to ensure that everything was running smoothly.

Within days of the club changing hands, a mob stormed in, smashing furniture, beating the doormen and stabbing one who had the audacity to fight back. The following day I was asked to supply a completely new door team. Carlton and Johnny were from the Stratford area, knew all the local faces and had a reputation amongst them, so I sent them to go and work at Moonlights. Around midnight I decided to leave Lautrec's and visit Carlton and Johnny to see how they were getting on. When I arrived at the club, only Johnny Butler was standing on the door. I asked him where Carlton was, and he motioned upstairs with his eyes. I went up, looked around the bar but couldn't see him. Then, out of the corner of my eye, I saw this familiar face bouncing around the dance floor looking happy as Larry. 'No, it can't be,' I said to myself. 'Surely fucking not?' But I was wrong; it was Carlton. He was raving on the dance floor, pilled out of his head with all the other revellers, having the time of his life. 'For fuck's sake, Carlton,' I said when I'd fought through the crowd to reach him. 'You can't leave your friend on the door while you dance.'

Carlton apologised and reluctantly left the dance floor to continue his work. I made my way to the manager's office to reassure him that everything was in order. He shook my hand, greeted me warmly, made me a cup of coffee and then we sat talking about nothing in particular. Behind the manager's head was a CCTV screen that showed various images from inside the club. 'That Carlton's a decent lad,' the manager said. 'He seems keen. I wish there were a few more like him.'

I spat my coffee out to prevent myself from choking on it. As the manager had been talking, Carlton's face, with a huge moronic grin, had appeared on the screen. He was back on the dance floor giving it loads. 'Yes, top bloke,' I said, trying to hold back my laughter. 'I'm sorry, really got to go – dodgy curry.'

I flew down the stairs and onto the dance floor. Carlton saw me coming and froze in his dance tracks. I had to pretend that I was annoyed, because it was my job to ensure that the door staff remained on their toes – that is, on the look out for trouble, not throwing shapes on the dance floor. I bollocked Carlton, and he went back to work. In later years Carlton employed his own door teams to run some of the most prestigious nightclubs in London. A film titled *Rise of the Foot Soldier* is currently being made about his very eventful life. In his book *Muscle* he says some very complimentary things about me and the way I went about my business. I thank him for that and hope he doesn't mind me revealing a story from his apprenticeship that he probably wanted to forget.

I needed some spare parts for my car, so a friend suggested that I go and see a man named Brynmor Lindop, who owned a scrapyard just a short walk from my flat. When I arrived at the scrapyard, I eventually located an office that was tucked away under an old railway arch. Outside were parked various old military vehicles that appeared to be guarding the door. I guessed that I was about to meet some sort of army-barmy anorak. When I walked into the office, I saw that the proprietor had stuck machetes in his desk, imitation firearms hung from one wall and another had been strafed by a machine gun.

A Welshman about 30 years old, 6 ft 1 in. with an enormous frame, stood up from behind the desk and said, 'Hello, my name is Bryn. What can I do for you?' I explained that a mutual friend had sent me and I needed some car parts. 'No problem,' Bryn said. I don't know what it was, but Bryn and I clicked, and from that day on we became good friends. He would call round to my flat in the day for coffee and a chat and to offer me the cheap stolen contraband he always had on offer. Bryn was quite deep. He didn't say too much about the business he was involved in, but he did tell me that he had a serious problem with 'some people' from Stratford. I offered to help him out, but he was adamant that he could sort the matter himself. A few days later Bryn drove over to Stratford and shot the ringleader of these people in the leg. The bullet smashed through the man's thigh bone, causing it to protrude through the skin. The problem, Bryn calmly announced, had been resolved.

# ROUND ELEVEN

I WAS WORKING ON MY CAR ONE DAY, AND MY SON BILLY, WHO WAS THEN aged about eight, was riding his bike nearby on the forecourt outside our flat. I heard a woman shouting, 'If you come past my window again, you little cunt, I'll cut your fucking head off!'

Not quite believing what I had just heard, I got from underneath my car, stood up and looked around. I saw that a bleached blonde woman was screaming at Billy from outside her front door. I jumped over a low wire fence that divided the gardens and when I reached the woman I said, 'Excuse me, you'll do what to my son? Cut his fucking head off, will you?'

Instead of being intimidated by me, the woman shouted in my face, 'You big useless bastard, my husband will fucking kill you!'

It was apparent to me that this foul-mouthed trollop had skipped finishing school and opted to be educated in the gutter, so I saw no point in debating the issue further. 'Send your husband around,' I said. 'I'm home until 8.45. I must warn you, though. If he does come to my front door, don't expect him to come home, because you will lose him.'

I picked up my son's bicycle and told him that he would have to come home with me. I was fuming, but I thought it best to let the situation calm down, as we all lived in the same street and I didn't relish the thought of enduring unnecessary neighbourly disputes. The rest of the day passed without incident, so by the time I was ready to go to work I assumed the row had been forgotten. I had, after all, no reason to expect a visit from the foul-mouthed woman or her husband. It was her appalling behaviour that had caused the incident, not mine. To be on the safe side, I told Margaret not to open the door if anybody was to knock on it. Margaret, a woman who hated any sort of trouble, assured me that she would telephone either me or the police if anybody came near the house.

While at work, I was tempted to ring Margaret, but I decided against doing so. The children would have been in bed, and I would only have made Margaret more anxious. By 1.30 a.m. I had not heard anything from home, so I assumed that the matter was over. The club closed at 2 a.m. and the last punters were generally out by 2.30 a.m., so it must have been around 3 a.m. when I finally pulled up outside my home. I opened my car door, got out, bent down to remove the keys from the ignition and was struck over the head with a metal bar.

Blood poured down my neck and face. I turned and punched my assailant as he went to take another swing at me with the bar. He fell backwards into the car but swung the weapon again, striking me in the side of the head. I grabbed him by the throat, head-butted him three times as hard as I could in the face and he fell to the floor, releasing his grip on the bar as he did so. I bent down, held my assailant's head with both of my hands and repeatedly smashed it into the paving stones. I totally lost control. When his body went limp, I stuck my index finger in his eye and gouged it out of its socket, leaving it hanging on his cheek. As I went to stand up, I felt a blow to the back of my head. I instinctively turned around and saw that the mouthy woman from earlier was attacking me with a house brick. After hitting me with it two or three times, she dropped it and then kicked me in the eye, which started to bleed profusely. Clearly intending to cause me serious injury, the deranged woman then took her stiletto shoe off and began beating me with the heel. I was still not standing fully upright, so I pushed the woman over and, in an act of spiteful revenge, continued pounding her husband's head on the pavement.

As this was going on, a white transit van entered the road and the woman ran in front of it, screaming, 'He's killed my husband! He's killed my fucking husband!' The van screeched to a halt, and the woman began shouting at the driver, 'Get the police! My husband has been murdered!' The woman ran into her home, and the van driver accelerated off down the road. I stood up and looked down at the man, whom I was convinced I had killed.

Moments later the sound of sirens filled the air and blue flashing lights cast eerie shadows around the street. A police officer approached me and asked me what had happened. I gave him my version of events and was then ushered into my flat. A petite blonde WPC came in a short while later and said, 'The man outside in the street is not dead. His wife is distressed and thought the worst. He is in a bad way and has been taken to hospital.'

Rather foolishly I blurted out, 'I don't care if he is fucking dead. In fact I wish I had've killed the cunt.'

I went outside and saw that the police had erected bright lights, which illuminated the scene. I was advised by a police officer to go to the nearest hospital and get my wounds attended to. I was still in shock, so instead of going to the hospital, I went to see my friend Ray Todd in Stratford.

'Fucking hell, Lew. What's happened to you?' Ray said when he answered his door. My hair and clothing were matted and drenched in thick congealed blood. I told Ray about the fight, and he urged me to attend the hospital. I said I would once I had been home to check that Margaret and the kids were OK. I don't know why I wanted to return to my home, because I had only just left it. The only explanation I can give is that I may have been in shock.

As soon as I drove into the road where I lived and got out of my car, three unmarked police cars sped towards me and screeched to a halt, blocking my path. Eight or nine officers jumped out of the cars and began shouting, 'Stand still! Stand still!' I remained where I was and seconds later was informed that I was being arrested for Section 18: wounding with intent. The officer asked me to remain calm. 'This may end up as a murder enquiry,' he said. 'A man is currently under observation in the critical care unit and may have a blood clot on his brain.'

At Forest Gate police station my clothing was taken from me and I was given a white paper suit to wear. A doctor was called to examine me, and he said that I was suffering from concussion and should be taken to hospital immediately. After various tests were conducted at the hospital, I was stitched up, given the all clear and returned to the police station later that morning. Around lunchtime I was taken out of the cells to be interviewed. I was informed that the man had suffered various lacerations, a broken nose, a broken jaw, a broken cheekbone, a fractured skull and had lost an eye.

I gave a frank and fairly honest account of what had happened. I told the police I regretted that the man had suffered such serious injuries but I was, after all, literally fighting for my life after a totally unprovoked attack. The officers reminded me that I had said that I wished I'd killed him, before returning me to the cells. 'We will talk to you later when we have an update on his condition,' they said, before slamming the door.

After an hour or two I became desperate to urinate, but there was no toilet. I pressed the cell bell, but nobody came to see me, so I began kicking the door and shouting, 'I need to use the toilet!'

Eventually an officer did come to my aid, and I was moved to a cell that had a toilet in it. When the officer left the cell block, I heard a man shouting, 'Lew? Is that Lew Yates?'

'Who the fuck is that?' I called back.

'It's Bryn, Brynmor Lindop,' the man replied.

Bryn asked what I was locked up for, and I said, 'I can't discuss it. You know those cunts eavesdrop on prisoners' conversations.'

Bryn said he understood, and I heard no more from him until later that day, when he shouted out to me, 'Goodbye, Lew.'

I assumed he was being released, so I called out, 'Goodbye and good luck, Bryn. Have a pint for me.'

Two days later I was charged with Section 18 wounding and released on bail. When the matter came before the courts, I was rightfully acquitted.

As soon as I got out, I telephoned Bryn to see if he was OK and to explain what had happened to me. Bryn laughed and said he had been arrested for a similar matter. 'Your attacker picked on the wrong guy, and I did too, Lew,' he said.

Bryn explained that a man had been hassling his wife, and after making extensive enquiries, he had been given his address. Bryn had driven around to the man's home armed with a baseball bat. He had got out of his car, walked up to the front door, knocked and waited for the man to answer. Crack! As soon as the door had opened, Bryn struck the man in the mouth with the bat. He then continued to club the man as he lay on the floor screaming and spitting out teeth. Having made his point, Bryn then got into his car and drove away. The man was later found unconscious in a pool of his own blood and taken to hospital. A neighbour had taken the number of Bryn's car, and he was subsequently arrested. Bryn, as usual, denied everything and was bailed. It turned out that the man Bryn was really after lived next door to the man he had assaulted. When the intended victim heard what had happened to his innocent neighbour, he left the area without even taking the contents of his house with him.

Bryn was jack of all trades but, sadly, master of none. He worked the door at various clubs, collected debts, sold firearms and got himself involved in any scam that was going. In later years he acquired a yard in Docklands, which he took me to see. He showed me where he had several different guns, complete with ammunition, hidden away. Bryn explained that he had recently got involved in a new venture: stealing plant and machinery and exporting it to Africa and the Republic of Ireland. Sadly, Bryn's home life was affected by his unorthodox way of earning a living, and his long-suffering wife eventually divorced him. The divorce settlement, which strongly favoured his wife, resulted in Bryn being declared bankrupt. In an effort to rebuild his life and modernise his business, Bryn enrolled on an unemployed person's computer course at Ilford and got involved in dubious deals, taking more risks than he normally would have considered taking. I warned him to be careful, but he was never going to listen.

When Margaret gave birth to our son Lewis, her pleas for me to give up working on the doors became even more persistent.

I argued it was the only profession I knew and it paid well. 'You won't be able to do it forever,' Margaret replied. 'Time will ensure that.' I knew Margaret was right, but how could I walk away from a job that paid so well without having anything to fall back on? Like Brynmor the unorthodox lifestyle I was leading was destroying my relationship with the woman I loved. Walking away meant, in my mind, that all of the villains I had ejected and barred would come back into the club. They would think they had won, and defeat was something I didn't wish to contemplate.

I gave Lautrec's doorman Paul Dobson a lift to his girlfriend's one night after work and, after dropping him off, headed home via Wanstead Flats. It was approximately 3.30 a.m. as I passed the City of London Cemetery and turned right to drive up Capel Road. Just after the Golden Fleece pub there are several sleeping policemen in the road, so I slowed down to drive over them. These particular traffic-calming devices are exceptionally high, so I was forced to select first gear in order to pass over them safely. As I reached the second sleeping policeman, the window immediately behind my head exploded, and a split second later the opposite window blew out. To my right was a line of trees, and I saw a figure with what appeared to be a rifle to his shoulder. I put my foot down on the accelerator and sped away from the scene. Some bastard had just tried to murder me.

I drove to my home to pick up a .303 rifle that I had stored there. Margaret got out of bed to find out what I was up to, and when she saw me grab the gun, she began to shout and scream. 'For God's sake, Lew, what on earth do you think you're doing?' she cried. 'This is madness, absolute madness! Please don't leave the house with that.'

My temper was preventing me from listening to or seeing sense. I barged past Margaret, who was trying to stop me from leaving, jumped in my car and headed back to Capel Road. I ran around Wanstead Flats, ducking, diving and charging towards bushes like some sort of deranged war hero. 'I'll kill you! I will fucking kill you!' I shouted at the darkness. God knows what the Wanstead Flats perverts thought of the madman running around the park with a rifle.

When I returned home, Margaret was sitting in the lounge. 'This has got to stop,' she said. 'The children and I cannot live like this any more.' I knew Margaret was right. I was either going to lose her, get locked up or get murdered if I didn't change the way I was living my life. I sat down with my wife, and we talked about the future for hours. Margaret was terrified that the person who had tried to shoot me would return and succeed on the second attempt. I assured her that wouldn't happen. When you work on the doors around London and Essex, there is always some nutcase prepared to blow you away for saying the wrong thing or looking at them the wrong way. The following day they have usually calmed down, sobered up or come down from a drug-induced high, and the matter is forgotten. I had no idea who had tried to shoot me or why, and despite making numerous enquiries I never did find out.

I eventually agreed to give up working on the doors, but I told Margaret that I couldn't do it overnight. We decided that we would leave London and I would start up my own business – doing what, I wasn't sure, but I was confident that I could come up with something. In the meantime I would continue to work on the doors. We needed an income to sustain ourselves and to secure a mortgage for a new home. Within a month we had found and purchased a home in a village called Manea, in Cambridgeshire. It felt as if a great weight had been lifted from my shoulders. Margaret was happy, I was happy and the children were overjoyed. There was no way we would have ever allowed them to play unsupervised on the streets of the East End, but here in Manea we could open the front door and let them play in the nearby fields without having to worry. It felt so right being away from London and the dangers that inner-city life poses.

I was still working at Lautrec's, but I had begun to look at the possibility of breeding dogs for a living or selling mail-order boxing equipment. Before I could do either, disaster struck. It started while I was weight training. Sweat was pouring out of me, and I felt incredibly weak. My initial thought was that I may have contracted a flu-type virus, but as the day went on, my condition deteriorated. I went into work, but I spent the night huddled around a radiator, sweating, shivering and unable to focus on anything. When I got home, I was so weak I had to crawl up the stairs to bed using just my hands. I had no idea what was wrong with me, and the doctors were unable to diagnose my problem. I diagnosed the illness myself by chance. I was watching a programme about round-the-world yachtswoman Clare Francis. She said that she had suffered from an illness called myalgic encephalomyelitis (ME, or 'yuppie flu'). She explained that it caused her severe disabling fatigue that had not been relieved by rest. Other symptoms she described included debilitatingly low energy levels, painful muscles and joints, disordered sleep, gastric disturbances, poor memory and concentration, neuropsychological complaints and painful lymph nodes. 'That's what I have got,' I said to Margaret.

The doctor was called the following day, and after several tests were done, my suspicions were proved to be correct. I went from being an extremely powerful man to somebody who had to drag himself across the floor because he was too weak to stand up. With no income I was forced to tell Margaret to sell everything we owned in order to keep the wolf from the door. It was two long years before I was well enough to return to work. Our worldly possessions consisted of the beds we slept in, the chairs we sat on and a tatty old Sherpa van that we had been forced to keep because we lived in such a remote area. The vehicle was in such a state that members of the travelling community used to wave at me, thinking I was one of them. I didn't care where I worked, but I knew I had to do something to bring some sort of quality of life back to our home. I telephoned everybody I knew, and soon afterwards I was offered a job, back on the doors.

Twins Gary and Barry Day said that they were opening a nightclub near the Ford car plant in Dagenham and asked me if I would run the door. After two years at home I knew I was far from fit and returning to work on the door was a gamble. My fighting technique had obviously not been affected by my illness, though, and I knew I would soon regain my strength once I started training, so I accepted their offer. Margaret, while appreciating the severity of our financial situation, was not so happy but agreed the job would suffice until I found an alternative. The club was called B.G.'s and initially attracted a good crowd. Success in the Essex badlands, however, tends to attract the criminal fraternity, who are eager to have a share of anybody's hard-earned cash.

I was in the office one evening when I was told about 'eight big geezers asking for protection money'.

'Good evening, fellas,' I said when I reached the front door. 'How can I help?' One of the men stepped towards me, and his friend held his arm. They had clearly rehearsed their routine. I was meant to be scared of the prick who was being held back. 'Let his arm go,' I said to his friend. 'Let's see how good he is.'

One of the men pulled out a bottle of ammonia and squirted one of my fellow doormen, who fell to his knees clutching his face. I ran to the reception desk and picked up a machete I kept there for emergencies. When I ran back towards the men, they had fled through the door. I chased the one who had squirted my colleague. He took the ammonia out of his jacket as he ran and squirted me in the left eye. The pain was excruciating, and I found myself narrowly missing a bollard as I continued to try to run blind. Realising pursuit was pointless, I returned to the club, threw down the machete and laid into the other men, who were still hanging around the car park.

By the time I had finished, a bone in my hand was dislocated. I forced it back into place and ordered one of the door staff to fetch a car. I picked up the machete, then Barry Day and I jumped into the vehicle. We roared down the A13 in the hope of finding the man who had used the ammonia. We eventually caught up with him running up a side road. Hurtling towards the man, we watched as he disappeared up a nearby garden path and into a house.

Smash! Smash! Smash! The sound of breaking glass and splintering wood broke the late-night silence as I destroyed the door and all of the downstairs windows with the machete. When the front door eventually came off its hinges, I could see the man hiding behind a mature male who was in the hallway wielding a pickaxe handle. 'Stay back, you lunatic,' the man said. 'If you come in my house, I will kill you.'

I could hear other people screaming in another part of the house. It sounded as if at least one of them was female, so I decided against entering the property. 'You'll fucking get yours,' I said, pointing the machete at the man who had squirted the ammonia. 'This is far from over.' Hiding behind the older guy, the man didn't answer.

'Get in the motor,' Barry shouted, 'the Old Bill are coming!'

I too could hear sirens approaching, so I jumped in the car and Barry accelerated away. Every window frame and every pane of glass in the front of the house on the ground floor was smashed. The front door had been hacked, stamped on and eventually broken in half. I was expecting a visit from the police, but I was fairly certain we wouldn't be getting any more demands for protection money. The police did arrive at the club the following morning. Barry was told that the identity of the doorman who caused the damage was known, but the family whose home it was had refused to make a complaint. 'Tell him to be careful because these people have been linked to a murder in the past,' the officer said. 'They are very dangerous people.'

I had made my own enquiries and knew that the man who had squirted me had been arrested for stabbing three people outside a nightclub in Dagenham. One of the men had subsequently died from his injuries. Police enquiries were met with a wall of silence, and nobody was ever charged in relation to the death. I decided to keep my eyes and ears open regarding these people, but I never did see them again. The house remained boarded up for six months, and after that the occupants moved.

Despite the best efforts of Barry, Gary and the door staff, the club continued to attract trouble. On more than one occasion I was asked to stay overnight in the office with a loaded pump-action shotgun because of threats to firebomb the building. Two years on Barry and Gary reluctantly decided to close the club and later sold it to my old friend Dave Maxwell.

The money I'd earned while working at B.G.'s had allowed Margaret and me to restore some sort of normality back to our lives. Our relationship had gone from strength to strength, and we'd had another child together, a beautiful daughter named Sarah. When B.G.'s closed, Margaret and I feared that we would soon slip back into the financial black hole that we had just escaped from, so I took the first job that was offered to me. Much to Margaret's dismay the job, unsurprisingly, was on the door of yet another nightclub. 'You promised you would give up that way of life years ago,' she said. 'I know we need the money, Lew, but if you don't find a normal job soon, I am leaving.'

I knew I had to honour my promise, but I could never have foreseen the terrible illness I'd been struck down by and the problems that had caused. 'This will be the last door job,' I promised. 'I will look into starting my own business as soon as our financial situation is stable again.'

The Dickens in Wickford, Essex, was run by a former doorman whom I'll call Sid. He was a big burly guy who tipped the scales at around 19.5 st. The door team consisted of me, Johnny Wacker and a really handy guy named Ian Jones. Despite the Dickens being located in a relatively small village, it attracted a lot of its custom from neighbouring towns such as Basildon, Billericay and Chelmsford. We soon got to know who was who and weeded out the troublemakers.

As the popularity of the venue increased, it began to attract coaches full of revellers on stag nights from London, whose traditional destination had always been Southend. I was called upstairs one evening to ask a group of lads on a stag night to calm down, as they were giving the bar staff grief. 'Any more nonsense and you're out,' I said. 'Does everybody understand?' One of the men tried to answer back, but his friends told him to shut up, promised me there wouldn't be any further problems and walked away. I went back downstairs to join the other doormen. The remainder of the evening passed off peacefully in the club, but as the lads on the stag night were leaving, they became rowdy and abusive. 'Keep on walking,' I said to them as they stepped outside. 'You really don't want trouble with us, boys.'

One of the group, an extremely tall well-built guy in his mid-20s, replied, 'It's you who should avoid trouble with us, wanker.'

I walked out onto the car park and urged the man to shut up and go home, but he was never going to listen. The first punch put him on his knees. He was grasping at the handle of a car, trying to get back up, when I hit him a second and then a third time. 'Pick this lump of shit up and take it home with you,' I called out to his friends. At first they began shouting and advancing towards me, but when I stood my ground, they halted in their tracks. As far as I was concerned, the incident was over, so I walked back in to the club. When I closed the door, every single window in the reception area seemed to explode. Garden tables, chairs, bottles and bricks were all being used as missiles, and the door staff were the intended targets.

The manager dialled 999, and within minutes a police car swept onto the car park. Instead of restoring order, the police presence seemed to antagonise the baying mob further. A man brandishing a large carving knife appeared to be leading the 50-strong mob, and when a WPC went to disarm him, he knocked her out with one punch. Her colleague, fearing for his safety, called for backup, and soon officers with dogs and several other vans arrived. The mob showered the police with volley after volley of missiles and at one stage charged the thin blue line. The police retreated and the mob responded by turning a police car over and leaving it on its roof. More and more police reinforcements arrived until eventually the mob scattered. Some arrests were made, but many of the men involved in the incident escaped.

Sid the manager was so scared of a reprisal attack he asked me to sleep at the club, which I did for three consecutive nights. The club was never the same after that incident. People simply stayed away. 'Can you take a drop in money?' Sid said to me one evening. 'I can't afford to pay your wages any more. When the club gets busy again, I will revert your wages to the old rate and repay you what I have deducted.' I knew the club was struggling, I knew I had promised Margaret it was to be my last door job and I knew I had no alternative employment lined up, so I agreed. It wasn't a dramatic wage cut; I had been earning £250 per night and Sid cut it to £200, so I was hardly going to starve.

Three months after I had agreed to a reduction in wages, Sid announced that he was going abroad on holiday. He left without telling anybody where he was going, but when I heard he was sunning himself on some foreign beach, I wasn't very happy. I thought that if he could afford a holiday, he could afford to pay me the money he owed me. I decided to pull him about it on his return. 'I'll sort your money out in a week or two,' Sid said when our paths finally crossed. A week or two turned into a month, so I approached Sid again about my money. 'Tomorrow, tomorrow,' he said, but I just knew tomorrow was never going to arrive.

The following night Sid was drinking at the bar surrounded by a large group of hangers-on. 'Play the game, Sid,' I said. 'This is getting silly. Just pay me what you owe me.'

Everybody fell silent as Sid got off his stool and glared at me. 'I am not bothered about you,' he replied. 'You'll get your money when I am ready.'

Perhaps he had spent too long on the beach in that hot foreign climate and the sun had affected his brain. Sid had certainly never tried to mug me off before. I waded into him, delivering blow after blow to his head and body. All of his friends were shouting but doing nothing to stop me as I knocked him through tables and chairs. Sid was on his knees, unable to stand up, and I could hear his wife screaming. I punched him in the head, and as he fell to the floor, I punched him repeatedly in the kidneys. His wife jumped on my back, pleading with me to stop, so I stood up and stepped back. Sid remained on the floor. I left the club and drove home.

I was told that Sid had suffered a broken cheekbone and spent five days in hospital. I had never wanted to fall out with him, but I felt he was treating my kindness as if it were a weakness. I did bump into him some time later at a mutual friend's funeral. After the service the mourners gathered at a nearby pub. I was at the bar when Sid spotted me. He glanced once, took a second look and then turned his back in the hope I hadn't noticed him. Having been served, he sat a table with his friends. When it was time for me to leave, I walked over to Sid, who still had his back to me. 'I will see you all later,' I said, putting my hands on his shoulders. 'It's been good seeing you all again.' Sid didn't even move. He sat staring at the wall in front of him. He knows he was wrong. We all make mistakes. It's a pity he wasn't prepared to say so.

'You haven't forgotten your promise,' Margaret said when I told her it was possible I might have lost my job after beating up my manager.

'No, I haven't forgotten,' I replied, 'and it's unlikely I will be going back there to work, so I shall start looking for something new to do.'

I have to admit it, I missed the danger of working on the doors and I missed the friendship of the guys I faced that danger with. However, living what most people would consider to be a normal life also had its advantages. I was able to spend a lot more time with Margaret and the children and enjoy the simple but memorable things that family life provides.

Ever since I was a young boy, I had kept dogs. In the 1980s Rottweilers, bull terriers and other similar breeds were becoming popular, so I decided to set up a business selling them. The property we lived in was some distance from other homes, had plenty of space for kennels and so was ideal for this purpose. I bred English mastiffs, Staffordshire bull terriers, Rottweilers, Dobermanns and Jack Russells. The demand for these dogs in the south-east of England at that time could not be met. The success of the business took both Margaret and me by surprise. A stress-free job and financial security brought about domestic bliss. Margaret and I were, for the first time in what seemed like an age, happy again.

In June 1986 Margaret gave birth to our second daughter, Danielle. Life for us seemed to be getting better and better. But, as always in my life, highs were inevitably followed by lows. The more dogs I sold, the more dog-breeding businesses I noticed appearing. People I had supplied dogs to over a long period of time were beginning to use them to set up their own businesses. Bad publicity about unprovoked attacks on people by the breeds of dogs I sold also had a negative effect on my business. As my sales figures plummeted, I was forced to concede that I would have to look elsewhere to bolster my ever-decreasing income.

Through advertisements in the *Boxing News* magazine, I started to sell skipping ropes and something I had invented called the Martindale Reflex Ball. This device was a tennis ball attached to headgear by a long piece of rubber tubing. A fighter would punch and jab the ball, which would fly forward and back, assisting them with improving their hand and eye coordination. A lot of people initially scoffed at the idea, but I sold thousands of them. Robin Read, the WBF super-middleweight champion, who was also known as the Grim Reaper, purchased several, as did many other well-known professionals. The money I made from selling boxing equipment and breeding dogs was never going to make us rich, but we did manage to live what most would consider to be a fairly comfortable lifestyle.

In April 1988 my father died. Over the years he'd had two relatively minor scares involving his heart, and doctors had advised him to give up smoking, but Dad had refused. My father started smoking during the Second World War, after he had volunteered to join the army aged just 17. After six and a half years' service he left but retained the smoking habit that would later claim his life. My thoughts on both of my parents are too painful to commit to paper. I am just grateful that neither of them suffered at the end. My parents were on holiday in Spain and were dancing together when Dad's heart failed. He was rushed to hospital, but he passed away shortly after arriving. Mum came home alone, and Dad's body was flown home a week later. Margaret, the children and I all attended the funeral, which I don't mind admitting broke my heart. My father was a top-class fellow, a real man's man. If I have grown into being half of the guy he was, I will die a happy man. Even though Dad retired at the age of 59, he used to leave the house every morning and carry out voluntary work for the elderly within his community. I only found out when some of the people he had helped turned up at his funeral. My mother struggled to carry on after losing my father. Her health deteriorated, and her once-vibrant never-say-die personality diminished. In August 1991, while visiting Bournemouth on a coach trip, Mum's heart failed and she died. Like my father, Mum was a remarkable person. In her youth she had been the Northern Counties sprint champion and insisted on her children living a clean, healthy lifestyle. My mother was cremated, and I placed her ashes on my father's grave. Despite the pain I still feel after losing them, I take great comfort from the fact that they are once more together and forever will be.

# ROUND TWELVE

THE BIBLE CLAIMS THAT THE GOOD LORD GIVES AND THE GOOD LORD TAKES away. In July 1994, just three years after the death of my mother, Margaret gave birth to our fourth child and my seventh, a daughter named Sarah-Jane. Three years may seem like a long time, but in my heart my beloved mother's passing still felt like yesterday on the day that Sarah-Jane was born. I'm not a religious man, but Sarah-Jane's arrival into the world brought me inner peace and helped heal the pain caused by my loss. The birth of my children and the passing of my parents undoubtedly made me more mature and – let's not get carried away here with sentiment – 'slightly' more responsible! Ideas about returning to work in nightclubs were no more, and I genuinely did my best – although I concede my idea of success may be considered to be failure by others – to be a good husband and father at home.

Jimmy Sheridan and I first met when I was working at Lautrec's. I had been involved in an altercation with three men, and I ended up knocking one of them out and hurling the other two through the door and out onto the car park. When it was over, Jimmy walked up to me and introduced himself. He was laughing and said that he had never seen any man being hit so hard in his life. Everybody in London knows Irish Jimmy Sheridan. If there's money to be made, you'll find Jimmy somewhere amongst it. Jimmy has a son named Jason, who was living in Basildon, Essex, during the early '90s. He was friends with some of the men who later became known as the Essex Boys firm. For reasons known only to Jason, he purchased a revolver from one of them. However, he didn't have all of the required fee, so the gun was stored in a false ceiling in the reception area of Raquel's nightclub, where the man worked. Jason was told that he could have the gun when he came up with the rest of the money. A few days later Jason went into Raquel's and asked his friend for the gun, promising he would pay whatever was owed at the weekend. The man relented and handed him the gun and ammunition.

Within hours this act of charity was proved to be an act of stupidity. The doorman was called up to the dance floor because Jason had put the gun to a reveller's head and threatened to shoot him. Nobody knows if the man's dance steps or dress sense had provoked Jason, but he was clearly upset. The club manager, who was called to the incident, demanded to know how a man had got into the club carrying a loaded gun. Pausing momentarily, trying desperately to think of an excuse, the doorman eventually replied, 'You've got it wrong, mate. Wait here.' He grabbed Jason by the arm and escorted him from the building. When he returned, he said to the manager, 'What's the problem?'

The manager, almost choking in disbelief, replied, 'Problem? What's my problem? He put a loaded gun to a man's head!'

The doorman began to laugh. 'That wasn't a loaded gun, you fool. He's been to a fancy-dress party. The gun was an imitation.'

The manager looked more shocked by the blatant lies the

doorman was telling him than by the fact that somebody had nearly been executed on the dance floor. 'You think I'm stupid,' he said. 'The gun's no longer on the premises, so I cannot prove it was real. Make sure it and your deranged friend never darken the doors of this building again.' The manager walked away shaking his head and mumbling to himself. The doorman raised his hand and the DJ drowned out his laughter by putting on another record.

The following week Jason was forced to go to another nightclub because he had been informed about his lifetime ban from Raquel's. Jason and his friend Simon Wally washed up at a venue called Time, which was just across the road from Raquel's. During the evening a girl accused Jason of pinching her backside and demanded an apology. Jason denied doing any such thing and told the girl to fuck off. The girl, who was by this time extremely irate, stormed off saying that she was going to fetch her cousin, who would sort Jason out.

Simon and Jason thought the girl was either drunk, mistaken or both, so they continued socialising without thinking any more about the incident. About an hour later Jason went to the bar to get himself and Simon a drink. As he turned to walk away after being served, a man head-butted him in the nose and a fight broke out. The girl's cousin had found Jason, but he was soon wishing that he hadn't bothered. Jason wrestled the man to the floor, sat astride him and began to give him a lesson in the art of fighting that he was unlikely to forget. The door staff intervened, but instead of pulling the men apart, they began to attack Jason. He fought back but was overpowered and ejected from the club. 'Wankers! Wankers!' he screamed as he got to his feet. 'I'll be back for all of you!'

Simon ushered his friend into a taxi and the pair left the scene. They told the taxi driver to take them to Jason's house, which was less than a mile away. Throughout the journey Jason was saying that he was going to get a gun and shoot the people who had assaulted him. Simon was trying to calm Jason down, but he had totally lost control and was having none of it. He told the taxi driver to wait outside his house, ran inside and returned a few minutes later. 'Take me back to Time,' he ordered the driver, 'and don't hang about.'

When they got out of the taxi, Simon was still pleading with Jason to calm down, but his pleas fell on deaf ears. Jason walked with purpose to the club entrance, flung the doors open, pulled out his gun, identified the men who had assaulted him amongst those in the packed reception area and began to fire. One man raised his arm to protect his head and a bullet struck him in the elbow, travelled up his arm and exited through his wrist. Another was struck in the ankle as he fled. People were screaming and running everywhere. Jason had made his point, so he turned and walked away. He was later arrested, charged with attempted murder and sentenced to 12 years' imprisonment.

Jimmy, like any father, was concerned about the company and way of life his son had become immersed in. What was done was history. Jimmy knew that he couldn't change the past, but he hoped that he could guide his son Jason towards a brighter trouble-free future for when he got out of jail. 'Come with me and see him,' he said to me. 'I need people to tell him he can't live his life like that. He might listen to a big guy like you, Lew.'

I didn't know if Jason would listen to me, or anybody else for that matter, but if I think I can help somebody, I will always try. A few days later I found myself heading down the M2 with Jimmy. Our destination was HMP Maidstone, where Jason was serving his sentence. Maidstone prison looked quite daunting as we pulled up in a pub car park across the road from it. The high stone walls and ancient gatehouse seemed to scream out 'abandon hope, all those who enter here'. I didn't mind visiting one of the 600 souls it housed, but I wouldn't want to spend the night in there.

Jimmy said that he always smuggled Jason in a few forbidden creature comforts to make his time inside a little easier. These illicit gifts included cash, which is not allowed in prison but is worth double its value on the black market inside, whisky, which is also forbidden but much sought after, and tobacco, which is allowed but expensive when purchased on a prisoner's meagre wages. Jimmy and I bought a bottle of whisky and filled up two plastic Lucozade bottles with it. Jimmy explained that he used Lucozade bottles because the lids and the bottle were made of plastic, which could not be detected when officers used metal detectors to search us. Jimmy and I secreted the bottles down our trousers and then entered the prison. We were told to sit in a large waiting room before being called through to an adjacent room one at a time. 'Anything metal put it in that box,' the prison officer said as I entered the room. 'Have you got anything you shouldn't have?' he asked.

'Mounting bills and a bad back,' I replied. The prison officer waved the metal detector around my body, asked me to pick up my possessions and then told his colleague that I was clear to go through.

As I sat in another room with Jimmy, awaiting final clearance to go into the visiting room, a bald-headed man wearing dark glasses and a long Crombie coat walked in. Moments later he was joined by a man I immediately recognised as Charlie Kray. I had met Charlie in several nightclubs where I had worked, so we exchanged pleasantries. As we were talking, a prison officer entered the room and asked us all to follow him to the visiting area. When we eventually sat down with Jason, Jimmy and I talked to him about the past, the present and what the future might hold. He appeared to be listening, but I don't think he was taking in much of our advice. When everybody in the visiting room appeared to have settled, we purchased several cans of Coke from the canteen, drank half of each can and then, after checking that nobody was watching us, topped them up with whisky, which we gave Jason to drink.

Shortly afterwards a female prison officer with a full figure stopped at our table and said that she could smell alcohol. We naturally denied having any in our possession. The officer then accused Jason, who was clearly pissed, of drinking. I stood up and asked her if her poorly paid job was really worth all the trouble she was about to cause. After looking me up and down, she leaned forward, whispered, 'Don't ever take the piss out of me again,' and walked away.

The confrontation, despite no voices being raised, had been noticed by a lot of people in the visiting room. I saw that Charlie Kray, the man in the glasses and others at their table were looking over and laughing. When they saw me looking back, one of the men got up and walked over to our table. 'Reg Kray,' he said, offering his hand. 'Are those bastards giving you grief?'

Reg Kray, one half of the infamous Kray twins, was much shorter than I had imagined he would be. In his prime Reg had been a competent boxer who could have done well in the ring if he hadn't turned to crime. I noticed he was wearing a gold boxing glove on a chain around his neck, so he was obviously still a fight fan. Jason knew Reg well because he was housed in the cell next door to him. He introduced us all to Reg, who then sat down to talk to us for a while. Although we had never met, Reg said that he'd heard of me through his friends in Ilford and around the East End. He asked me to meet his friends, whom he had left sitting at the other table. I was introduced to his brother Charlie, whom I already knew, Freddie Foreman, a kid named Bradley Allardyce and the man in the dark glasses.

Unbeknown to me at the time, Allardyce, who was serving nine years for robbery, was Reg Kray's lover. Allardyce was released a couple of years after we were introduced, but in 2005 he was sent back to prison for life. Allardyce and two other men, Wayne Turner and Shane Porter, were found guilty of murder and conspiracy to murder. Their victim, David Fairburn, aged 26, was stabbed and beaten to death in Barking, Essex.

Freddie Foreman seemed like a decent guy. He told me that he too was a big boxing fan. Foreman was a major player in London's underworld during the 1960s. He had murdered a man named Ginger Marks and a prisoner who was on the run named Frank Mitchell. Foreman had also disposed of Jack 'The Hat' McVitie's body for his friends the Krays. I was sure Mickey Green's wife, the former Mrs McVitie, wouldn't have approved of the company I kept that day.

The man in the glasses stood up to shake my hand. 'Dave Courtney's the name,' he said. He pushed his glasses up onto his forehead and started to tell me all about himself. I knew I had seen this man somewhere before, but I couldn't quite place him. He reminded me of somebody I had slapped and ejected from Boobs nightclub in Croydon, but in all fairness I couldn't be sure. He knew a lot of people I knew and claimed they always spoke highly of me. Courtney has been involved in one or two controversial incidents since we met. As a result different people I know hold opposing views about him. All I can say is that, on the rare occasions that I have met him since, he has been humorous, polite and good company.

I continued to visit Jason with Jimmy on a regular basis. Regrettably, when Jason was released, it was clear that, as I'd assumed, he had chosen not to listen to anybody. His father Jimmy is a good well-meaning man who tried to help him. Jason repaid this kindness by attacking him whilst armed with a hammer following a heated argument about Jason's behaviour. They no longer talk, which is a terrible shame. At the time of writing Jason is back in jail. I hope that one day he reads this, contacts his father and they are both able to put the past behind them.

Not long after meeting Reg and Charlie Kray in Maidstone prison, I was contacted by Kate Kray, the former wife of Reggie's twin brother Ronnie. Kate said that she was writing a sequel to her book about the hardest men in Britain and my name had been put forward by several people for inclusion in it. I wasn't keen at first, because I had moved away from that lifestyle, and the people in the area in which I now lived knew nothing about my past. I was told that my friend Carlton Leach was going to be included in the book, and nobody in it was going to be portrayed in a distasteful light, so I eventually agreed.

When I met Kate, who turned out to be a charming lady, I was asked to give a brief history of my life and to answer the same 14 questions as the 23 other men in the book. Several did not really apply to me, as they referred to living a life of crime. The book, titled *Hard Bastards 2,* was published in 2001, but it wasn't the sort of thing I would read. I hadn't heard of half of the so-called hard bastards in it, and describing them as such was, in my opinion, stretching the truth a little.

After saying goodbye to Kate, I was asked to accompany an excellent photographer named Geoff Langan to Dagenham Dock in east London, so that he could take a few photographs of me. At first Geoff could not find a suitable location, but eventually he spotted a scrap-metal yard that he thought would capture the mood he sought. I could not believe it when I walked through the gates and saw a group of my old friends standing around talking. Little Joe, a doorman from the Room at the Top, Brynmor Lindop and various other old faces all called out and greeted me when they saw me. It had been a few years since we had seen each other, so we all had plenty of stories to tell. I asked them what they were doing in the scrapyard, and Little Joe said that it was his. Geoff was pleased by this news, as he wouldn't have to seek out the owner for permission to use the yard. Geoff and I excused ourselves and got on with taking the photographs, one of which was used for the cover of this book. After Geoff had finished, I remained in the yard talking to Bryn and Little Joe. The conversation eventually turned to work, and I explained that although I was keeping my head above water, I could do with some sort of new business venture.

'Sorted,' said Little Joe. 'I have just the thing for you here in the yard.'

Just the thing turned out to be a burger van in need of repair. Joe explained that the area was swarming with workers during the day, and a fast-food outlet couldn't fail to make money. Without giving it much thought, if indeed any, I stuck out my hand and agreed to purchase Little Joe's burger van.

Over the next two weeks I worked hard repairing the van until it was ready to open for trading. I parked it down Ripple Road, which is the main thoroughfare that runs through an industrial estate near the Thames river. Business was surprisingly brisk, and I was soon making a reasonable living out of it. Every day Bryn would come to my van to have a sandwich and a cup of tea and to talk about old times. We soon became very good friends again, doing odd jobs and favours for each other as we had done in the past. Bryn used to look after a man who owned a lot of land along the Thames waterfront. In later years it was developed and became known as Docklands. Back then it was run-down and occupied by in excess of 30 scrapyards, and competition amongst the metal merchants was fierce. Bryn was employed to keep the peace and collect the rent from those who rented the yards, of which 99 per cent were foreign nationals. One Jamaican man refused to pay his rent because his office kept getting burned out by rivals, so Bryn went to see him. When he arrived at the yard, he was confronted by a hostile group of the man's friends. Cool, calm and collected, Bryn pulled a revolver out from the inside of his jacket and fired just over the Jamaican man's head. The man fell to his knees and his friends ran away, screaming in terror. The man was begging Bryn not to shoot him. Bryn hesitated, cocked the weapon and fired a shot just in front of him. He then made the trembling and sobbing man beg for mercy and apologise. The man did so, paid the outstanding rent and was never seen again.

I was told that Bryn had got involved with a consortium of men who planned to import a large shipment of cocaine. The drugs were delivered on time and in good order, but members of the consortium fell out over the percentages of payment that were due, and threats were made by all parties.

One of the men Bryn had fallen out with owned a garage where cars were resprayed. Bryn broke into the garage one night, doused the place in petrol and set it on fire. Unfortunately for him the paint that was stored on the premises acted as an accelerant, and his escape route was quickly engulfed in flames. Fearing for his safety, he was forced to smash a window with his bare hands and climb out, cutting himself badly in the process. The following day he received numerous threatening phone calls from the garage proprietor, who accused him of being responsible for the blaze.

These calls became even more sinister when the garage owner told Bryn and others that there had been a large quantity of cocaine hidden in the boot of a car that had been parked in the garage at the time of the fire. The man told everybody that he had searched the burnt-out wreckage of the vehicle, but no trace of the sports bags that had contained the cocaine could be found. The implication was that Bryn had broken into the garage, stolen the cocaine and then firebombed the premises in the hope that people would believe the cocaine had been unwittingly burnt. Bryn told the man and his irate friends to go and fuck off because he wasn't responsible, but few believed him.

I went to the scrapyard once and found Bryn raking over a big pile of ashes. He was laughing, and when I asked what he was doing, he replied, 'I can't get rid of this bastard. I've burnt him. I keep raking him into the ground, but the cunt's teeth and jawbone won't break down.' I could clearly see large pieces of bone, but I have no idea if they were human or not. Nothing would surprise me when it involved Bryn. The bones probably belonged to one of the foreign scrap-metal merchants he was always trying to catch in the various mantraps he set up along his yard fence.

The police drove by one day while Bryn was standing at the burger van talking to me. As soon as they saw him, the car slowed down and the officers inside glared over at us. Bryn told me that he had a gun on him, which didn't come as a surprise to me, as he always carried one. 'Fuck me, they had a good look, Lew,' he said. 'If they come back and search me, I'm fucked.'

Fearing for my friend, I said, 'Give me the gun, Bryn.' When he handed it to me, I wrapped it in a tea towel and put it in one of the empty water-heater tanks. Moments later the police drove by at a snail's pace staring at Bryn until eventually they sped off.

Later that day Bryn was giving me a lift to the wholesalers in his Range Rover. We passed a police car containing the officers who had shown great interest in Bryn earlier. The car quickly turned around and began to follow us. Bryn, in a matter-of-fact manner, said, 'If they pull us over, you'll have to chin one and I'll deal with the other. There's something in this car I can't let them find.' Bryn did not elaborate and I did not ask. When we reached the next set of traffic lights, Bryn turned left into an industrial estate and fortunately the police car carried on straight ahead.

In December 2001 Bryn told me that he was tired of London and all of the grief he got himself involved in. 'I'm leaving, Lew,' he said. 'I have got an apartment in Tenerife and I am going there to retire in a few months.' He told me that he had recently paid for a boat to be built out there and couldn't wait to leave. To be honest, his news saddened me, as I was undoubtedly going to miss his wild antics, but I wished him well all the same.

On Saturday, 26 January 2002 I rang Bryn at about 8 a.m. to see how he was doing. He answered the phone, shouted 'Fuck off!' and slammed the receiver down on me.

I thought 'Fuck you too' and immediately rang him back. 'What do you think you are doing putting the phone down on me?' I asked when he answered.

Bryn said, 'I'm sorry, Lew. I didn't realise it was you. I will ring you a bit later.'

At about 10 a.m. Bryn called and said, 'All is OK with me. Don't worry. I was still half-asleep.'

I told Bryn that he seemed on edge, but he kept assuring me that he was OK. We said our goodbyes, but about an hour later he telephoned me again to ask if I had seen anybody down at the yard. I told him that I had only seen the usual faces; there had certainly been no strangers about. Something wasn't right; I just had a bad feeling about the way he was talking and behaving. The Bryn I knew would come roaring down the yard in his car and jump out guns blazing if there was a problem, but he seemed scared. I told myself that Bryn's problem had to involve the police, and that's why he was being cautious.

He turned up at the yard at around 4 p.m. Bryn usually had a cup of tea and a bacon sandwich, but on this particular day he said, 'No, leave it. I'll be back later. I'm going to get the front disc pads replaced on my Range Rover.' He still seemed very on edge, looking around as we spoke and staring at oncoming cars. I laughed and asked him if he was sure everything was OK. Bryn said, 'Yes, Lew, yes. I have told you I am fine,' but he never did stop looking around. I knew Bryn was troubled, but he wasn't going to tell me about it, so I let it drop.

The next morning Bryn's mate Dave Allen rang me and said, 'Brynmor's dead. He's been shot!'

'Don't fuck about, Dave,' I replied.

'I'm not. He was shot last night outside his flat in Goodmayes,' he said.

I later learnt that when I had seen Bryn the afternoon before, he had been visiting his yard in order to hide his guns in an old crane. He would normally keep them in his car, but as it was due to be worked on, he had removed the guns because he feared the mechanics might find them. After picking up his car from the garage, he drove to his flat and was talking on his mobile phone as he pulled up outside. Normally vigilant, Bryn was concentrating on the call and on parking his car, rather than observing what was going on around him. When he stepped out, he was still talking on the phone.

He failed to notice a man getting out of a dark-coloured

241

car, similar to a seven-seater Chrysler Voyager, with blacked-out windows. The man walked briskly towards him, pulled out a .45 automatic handgun and fired, but he missed his target and the bullet struck a car. Confused and in shock, Bryn ran back towards his own car, presumably thinking his guns were still in it. When he reached the vehicle, he remembered that he had removed the guns earlier and so ran towards his flat. The gunman opened fire again, and this time the bullet struck Bryn in the hip. As he fell to the floor, he knew he would have to get up and run or die where he lay, as the gunman was approaching him. With blood pouring from his wound, Bryn got to his feet and started to run towards his home. The gunman casually raised his arm and fired again. The bullet struck Bryn in the mouth, and he fell dying on the road. Bryn did get back onto his feet and managed to stagger a few yards towards his flat before collapsing again. When the paramedics arrived and began working on him, he must have thought he was being attacked again, because he grabbed one of the medical team and flung him across the street. Sadly Bryn died of his injuries four hours later in hospital.

When the gunman had sped away in the dark Chrysler-type vehicle, a BMW that had been parked nearby followed him. The Chrysler was later found abandoned. It had been wiped totally clean and the headrests had been removed. Detectives believe that a professional hit man had carried out the murder, because the cleaning of the motor and, more significantly, the removal of the headrests indicated that those responsible knew the police would have them tested for DNA traces. I was visited by the detectives investigating Bryn's murder on four occasions. They said that Bryn's phone records showed that he had been telephoning me throughout his final day, but I was unable to help them. I wish I could have been of more assistance. I was saddened by my friend Bryn's murder.

His funeral was surreal. Nobody present could quite believe that the big guy was dead. The police did tell me that had he not died, it was only a matter of time before he was going to be arrested. 'We can't elaborate,' the officer said, 'but we have been taking a keen interest in Mr Lindop's activities for some time.'

The police had always taken an interest in Bryn's business. In the 1990s he had been arrested for supplying firearms. When the serial numbers of the seized guns were checked, a lot of them turned out to be lost or stolen police firearms. Bryn's solicitor had warned him to expect a lengthy term of imprisonment, but he had replied, 'We shall see when they find out who lost or was in control of the guns.' When the matter came before the courts, Bryn was given a two-year sentence. He told me that he had been advised by the police to serve it in silence, whatever that meant.

When police searched Bryn's flat in the hope of finding clues that might give them a motive for his murder, they discovered a hidden camera in the wall of his bedroom. Tearing out the wall to look for more devices, they discovered that the camera was connected to a video recorder, alongside which was a pile of VHS tapes. When officers viewed the tapes, they found footage of Bryn and numerous different females having sex. The possibility that he had been murdered by a jealous boyfriend or husband was given additional weight when the identities of some of the females were established. At least three were major criminals' wives, and two were married to senior police officers.

Another motive that was pursued involved Bryn's son. He had been employed on Dagenham Dock as a nightwatchman. Shortly before Bryn's death a man described as looking and behaving like the character John Coffey from the film *The Green*

*Mile* pulled up at the Dock gate in a Mercedes and demanded entry. Bryn's son opened the locked gate to approach the car and explain to the man that entry was not permitted. As soon as he opened the gate to walk to the car, the man drove through. Bryn's son called to the man to stop. The Mercedes' brake lights came on and the huge man got out. Before the situation could escalate, an Asian man who also worked nights on the Docks appeared and explained that Bryn's son wasn't being rude, he was merely doing his job. The man called Bryn's son an arsehole, got back into his car and disappeared down the Dock in a cloud of dust. When Bryn heard about the incident the following day, he appeared to ignore it and get on with his work.

Around midday the Mercedes carrying the John Coffey lookalike pulled onto the Dock. Bryn took a 9-mm handgun out of his desk and walked outside. By this time the enormous man who had insulted Bryn's son had got out of his Mercedes and was talking on his phone. Bang! A shot rang out and the man dropped to the floor clutching his leg. 'You cheeky fucking nobody!' Bryn shouted at the man. 'Do you want to insult my boy again?' Before the man could answer, Bryn shot him again in the leg, kicked him in the head and walked back to his office. The man crawled to his car, pulled himself inside and sped away. Bryn continued with his work as if nothing had happened.

When the injured man was interviewed in relation to Bryn's murder, he had a cast-iron alibi and so was eliminated from the inquiry. Amongst the criminal fraternity loyalty is fickle. Feuds and greed divide gangs and leave festering sores that only revenge can heal. Thankfully a man closely linked to those who murdered Bryn has broken ranks after a dispute with them and given off-the-record information about the incident. Bryn's family are hoping that the man will find the courage to make a full and frank statement about his associates, so that they can eventually face justice.

I had noticed that Margaret was becoming increasingly unhappy and depressed. I asked her what was wrong, and she told me that she was homesick. 'I want to return to London,' she said. 'I used to like it out here in the countryside, but it's such a lonely place, I have grown to hate it.'

I wanted to remain in Manea, so, after a lot of tears, we agreed to live apart. There was no way I was going to ask my wife to live in a place she hated, but there was no way I was going to return to live in London. A compromise of sorts was eventually reached. Margaret agreed not to move to London, and I agreed that if I liked the area she chose to move to instead, I would join her.

Margaret and the children eventually moved to a house she had found in Chatteris, Cambridgeshire. Our eldest son, Lewis, insisted on remaining with me. The property Margaret moved to was only seven miles down the road from where we were already living, but she insisted that it was a change nevertheless and the children would be able to continue their education at the local school. Constructive negotiation descended into volatile debate, and when all lines of communication eventually broke down between us, divorce papers were served. A few weeks later, when tempers had calmed, Margaret and I agreed not to get divorced and to try to improve relations between us. At first things went well, but I should have known from past experiences that any period of happiness was usually the calm before a storm.

I was in the house one morning catching my breath after a 90-minute workout when I heard the dogs barking and jumping at the fence. I went out to the front garden and saw a large young man leaning against my fence holding a racing bike. For some unknown reason he was shouting at the dogs and taunting them. I called out to him and asked him what he thought he was up to. He looked at me and shouted, 'Fuck off, you wanker!' before jumping on his bike and cycling away.

I went into the house, collected my car keys and drove up the road to try to catch him. I soon pulled in front of him, jumped out of the car and asked, 'Who's a fucking wanker?' The man laid his bike on the road, rolled his sleeves up and squared up to me. I hit him with a left hook, which knocked him into a dyke. As he struggled to get back onto the road, I shouted, 'Get up, you mug, so I can knock you out!'

The man scrambled back onto the road, got to his feet and began to fight me. Eventually I knocked him down and, as he lay on the road, I opened his legs and stamped as hard as I could on his bollocks. He rolled over in agony, so I began to jump up and down on his back. I heard a loud crack and saw that his elbow had broken and the bone was now sticking out of his arm. The man was screaming, 'Please, no more! Please, no more! You're mad!'

I'm not sure if I was mad or just irate, but I had definitely lost my temper. When I stopped jumping up and down on the man, he tried to flag down a passing motorist. As the car slowed, I shouted at the driver, 'Fuck off and don't get involved!' Blood from a wound above my eye that had been caused by the man's large sovereign ring was running down my face and had covered my shirt. The driver of the car looked at me, put his foot on the accelerator and roared off. My opponent was clutching his arm and begging me not to touch him again. I got back into my car and drove home.

Nine days later a dozen police officers arrived at my home. I asked Margaret, who happened to be at my house that day, to tell them that I was in London. The officers didn't appear to believe her and said that they wanted to come into the house to look for me. The dogs were roaming free in the front garden and the police, reluctant to face them, asked Margaret to put them away. Quick thinking from Margaret granted me a temporary but much needed reprieve. 'Only my husband can control them,' she said. 'You will have to come back later when he is here.'

Clearly disappointed, one of the officers replied, 'Contact your husband and tell him we need to speak to him about a very serious matter.' Margaret said she would, and the police disappeared.

I contacted a solicitor, who arranged for me to hand myself in at the local police station. Upon my arrival I was arrested on suspicion of assault and interviewed three times. I was at best economical with the truth, and the interviewing officer was aware of that fact. After considering all of the evidence, he eventually charged me with Section 18 wounding. I was bailed and told to attend court the following week.

Before I left the police station, an inspector came to see me. He said that the man I had assaulted was a leading member of the travelling community in the area and I would be well advised to take my family and leave Cambridgeshire. I smirked at him and shook my head. 'Reputations have never impressed me. If the travellers want trouble, they can have it,' I said before walking away. After appearing numerous times at the magistrates' court, I was sent to Peterborough Crown Court for trial. The traveller I had fought, and who undoubtedly claims it is an unforgivable sin to inform on others, gave evidence against me and I was found guilty. Due to the seriousness of the charge, the judge told me to expect a custodial sentence, but because I was of previous good character, I received a suspended sentence of five years. I was also given 150 hours' community service to complete and had to pay £500 compensation to the victim.

When Margaret served divorce papers on me this time, they were not withdrawn, and a divorce was granted. I will never blame Margaret for the breakdown of our marriage. We simply grew apart and fell out of meaningful love. I do and always will love her, but I accept that we can never be more than friends, which I hope we will once more be one day in the future.

# EPILOGUE

SHORTLY AFTER OUR DIVORCE MARGARET AND THE CHILDREN RETURNED TO live in London. Relations between the two of us deteriorated, until we stopped talking altogether. After all we have endured together, it breaks my heart that people I love no longer wish to talk to me. Time, I hope, will heal the rift, so that we can at least talk in the future.

Lewis and I moved to a house in Ely. The divorce had unsettled Lewis. He would stay out late at night and oversleep in the mornings. He was working at a local garage as an apprentice mechanic at the time, and his employer warned him about his poor timekeeping. Lewis failed to take any notice of the warnings, and inevitably he lost his job. I did my best to try to help him, but he started getting into trouble. My home was searched by police on four occasions. In an effort to try to make him pull out of the downward spiral he was in, I told him that he would have to leave my home and live with his mother.

Lewis failed to settle in London, and within weeks he had returned to Cambridgeshire and rented a flat not too far from me in Wisbech. Here Lewis met a girl named Alison Walde, and shortly afterwards they set up home together. Like all couples Lewis and Alison had their ups and downs, but they appeared to be relatively happy. Alison had two children from a previous relationship and wanted to move away from Wisbech so that she could sever all ties with her former partner and start afresh with Lewis. London, they agreed, wasn't a suitable place to bring up children, so they decided to move to Littlehampton, a small picturesque coastal town in West Sussex, where Alison had originally come from.

They soon settled in, and Lewis became friends with a local man in his late 20s named Adrian Ede. At first relations between the two were good, but Ede was a domineering man by nature and soon he began to take liberties with Lewis. He would take his car for days on end without asking and then return it with hardly any petrol in the tank. He would borrow money and tools but never return either. Lewis told Ede that he didn't want him taking anything from him again, but Ede just laughed and ridiculed him. Shortly afterwards Ede took Lewis's car without his permission and refused to return it.

Not wanting to get involved in what would undoubtedly end in a violent confrontation, Lewis went to the police and explained what had happened. Adrian Ede was arrested as a result of this complaint, but for reasons known only to the police he wasn't charged. Ede thought he was above the law and began taunting Lewis, calling him a grass and a nobody.

I have since read numerous newspaper reports about similar situations that have ended in tragic circumstances. The inquiry that follows always concludes that if the police had done their job at the outset and put the aggressor before the courts, the innocent victim would not have been forced to react. This is exactly what happened in Lewis's case. Ede turned up in Parsons Close, where Alison and Lewis lived. Ede glared at Lewis, who happened to be on his way home from a local shop, and asked him if he had a problem. Lewis walked past and told him, 'If you've got a problem with me, you know where I live.'

Ede removed his sunglasses, caught up with Lewis and said, 'Come on then.'

More words of a threatening nature were exchanged, but Lewis just kept on walking. When he got home, Ede hung about outside his house. Hoping he would grow tired of his game, Lewis ignored Ede but eventually he decided that enough was enough. He didn't want trouble with Ede; he just wanted him to go away and leave him alone. Lewis picked up a carving knife and ran out of the house to scare him. 'Fuck you!' he shouted. 'Just go away and leave me and my family alone.'

Alison heard the commotion, looked out of the window, saw Lewis shouting at Ede and began shouting at him herself. Ede wasn't concerned by Lewis's threats or the fact he was armed with a knife. He fancied himself as a bit of a hard man, when he was in fact no more than a village bully. Instead of walking away from Lewis, Ede walked towards him laughing. Having no intention whatsoever to use the knife other than to scare Ede away, Lewis retreated back into his home.

Ede had stolen Lewis's car and escaped prosecution. He had now made an armed Lewis back down. The bully thought he was above the law and invincible. Two weeks later, as Lewis and Alison were getting on with their lives, Ede turned up again in Parsons Close. Lewis was standing in the garden smoking a cigarette and saw Ede pull up in his car. When Ede saw Lewis, he said, 'What's your fucking problem?' There was no point trying to hold any sort of civil conversation with this man. Lewis knew that the abuse and threats wouldn't end until he had granted Ede's wish and fought him. Reluctantly he walked over to his tormentor and a fight broke out.

Alison had been preparing a chicken curry in the kitchen when she heard the men start fighting. Without a moment's hesitation she ran barefoot out into the street still holding the knife she had been using to chop up chicken. As she reached Lewis and Ede, the two men separated but started fighting again after Ede struck Lewis. A friend of Ede's joined in the attack, and Alison tried to push them all apart. Ede punched Alison as hard as he could twice in the face, and she shouted, 'Fuck off and go home!' before pushing him away again.

Ede was heard shouting, 'Fuck you, you bitch!' and shortly afterwards Lewis and Alison went back into their home. Adrian Ede had sustained two stab wounds to his shoulder and regrettably died later in hospital. A post-mortem revealed that a 19-cm-deep wound had punctured his right lung, and this had proved fatal. Tests on his blood showed a high alcohol content, and there was also evidence of amphetamine and cannabis use. Despite this and the aggravating factors that led up to the incident, Alison, then aged just 21, and Lewis, also 21, were charged with 29-year-old Adrian Ede's murder. The charge against Lewis was later dropped, but in August 2005 Alison went on trial at Lewes Crown Court for murder. The jury refused to accept that she hadn't intended to stab Ede whilst trying to break up the fight; instead they believed that the stabbing was a deliberate act, and they found her guilty. Alison was sentenced to life imprisonment with a recommendation that she serve at least 12 years. Judge Anthony Scott-Gall told Alison, 'You deliberately armed yourself with a knife to go to the assistance of your partner, who was fighting with the deceased. This was a deliberate and cold-blooded stabbing in order to cause the deceased serious bodily harm. However, I believe it was never your intention to kill him.'

I could so easily have ended up in the same situation

following the intrusion onto my property by the traveller who was taunting my dogs. Farmer Tony Martin, who lives just 20 miles from me, was forced to endure a similar situation. He was charged with murder and sentenced to life imprisonment after shooting two burglars who were robbing his home. Martin's murder conviction was later reduced to manslaughter following an appeal, and he served four years' imprisonment before he was released. The laws in this country no longer favour the victim; they protect the aggressor, and in doing so mock those who have been wronged. Lewis and Alison wanted to live in peace with their children, but Ede intimidated and provoked them until matters came to a head on that tragic day.

In my opinion, so many things have changed for the worse over the years. Able-bodied men capable of controlling violent criminals in pubs and clubs have been replaced by steroid-enhanced fools armed with council badges because the former are no longer allowed to work if they have convictions. Violent criminals only understand one language, and that is violence. Trying to talk rationally to a man who is threatening to cut or shoot you will only get you cut or shot. Aggressive people have to be taken down, put in fear and made to understand that they cannot go about bullying and hurting people. The police and licensing authorities, in their infinite wisdom, decided to exclude the men the hooligan element respected and feared from working in the security industry. That is why today nightclubs and pubs are dangerous places to visit and drugs are openly on sale. When I see the cannon fodder they have standing on the doors of pubs and nightclubs these days, I am glad that I am no longer part of it.

As Glynn, Joanne and Billy grew older, they began to ask questions about their mother, Jean. I explained to them what had happened, and I did my best to explain the circumstances that might have led to Jean leaving. I was working away and Jean was at home alone with three children. It's hardly an excuse for the misery her departure caused, but they are the facts. Billy, who was broken by his mother's departure, decided that he wanted to find her. I knew where Jean's brother lived in Blackburn, so I gave Billy the address. Within minutes Billy had called directory enquiries and obtained the telephone number, which he rang. When Billy explained who he was and why he was looking for Jean, he was given her address in Somerset and a telephone number. I have no idea what Billy said to his mother, and I did not ask, because he still has a lot of issues that remain unresolved with her. I did learn that she is no longer with Paul Smith, the man she left her family for.

Shortly after Billy contacted Jean, she travelled to our daughter Joanne's home to meet the children. I wasn't aware of the meeting until Joanne rang me and said there was somebody there who wanted to say hello. Jean and I spoke, and these days we are friends once more. I hope that one day Margaret and I can also become friends again. There is too much animosity in this life, and not enough time for those we cherish.

I live alone in Cambridge these days. Older, and perhaps wiser, I try to be civil with all of those I have loved in my life, but it's not always easy. I still train at a local gym and offer advice to the young kids I meet in there. I don't mind admitting that seeing them work out fills me with envy and regret. If only I was younger; if only I had kept my cool against Billy Aird; if only Shaw had fought me when I first challenged him; if this, if that. Boxing has been my life, and I would love to be the same age as the kids I see down the gym so I could climb into the ring again and win what is rightfully mine.

There are many who will not be happy with the contents of this book. The reputations and grand titles these people have bestowed upon one another will be called into question. The truth does have a tendency to hurt. I am entitled to have my say after reading the drivel some of these people have written about me in their autobiographies. I grew up loving the sport of boxing. I was taught how to fight dirty, how to exploit my opponents' weaknesses, but never to fix fights or take part in a theatrical charade. I may have been naive to believe I would ever be given a fair opportunity to claim the unlicensed ring's coveted title of Guv'nor, but those who accepted my challenges in public and failed to organise the fights were not naive. They knew that if they'd got in the ring with me, they would have lost not only the fight, but their manufactured reputations and the opportunity to fix future lucrative fights. They are a disgrace to boxing and the many great men who have put on gloves and climbed into a ring in search of glory. They may have fooled many people, but no man can fool himself. They know they avoided me in my prime to avoid defeat, and they know they fixed the fight with me that after five years they were embarrassed into staging. They know who should hold the title of Guv'nor, and they know where to find me if they wish to dispute that fact.

# APPENDIX

## BY A UNANIMOUS DECISION, THE UNDISPUTED UNLICENSED KING, LEW YATES

# GEORGE GILBODY SNR
## Senior trainer at Lowe House ABC

I was a coach at Lowe House ABC, and when Lew joined, I became his main coach, sparring partner and friend. I've always kept pretty fit, so we had a great time against each other in the ring. In competition Lew was a raging-bull-type character: he would never give in and always give his best. He was probably at his fittest while he was with me and won numerous bouts against renowned boxers within the northern counties at that time. One bout springs to mind: when Lew fought Dave James, the Welsh international and soon-to-be ABA national coach. Lew was holding his own when, halfway through the contest, by a complete freak accident, Lew and James clashed heads and Lew's eyelid split open. Within a few seconds I threw in the towel and the referee stopped the contest. Lew went absolutely berserk, and for a moment I thought he was going to attack me. 'Why did you stop the fight?' he shouted. 'I would have beat him! I would have beat him!' That was always Lew's Achilles heel, his uncontrollable temper!

In 1970 Lew was present when my son George was boxing in Blackburn for Lancashire versus Wales. George was poor that night and lost on a tight decision to a guy named Chris Davies. This was George's 50th fight and turned out to be only his second defeat in a total of 67 contests. I felt that George had performed badly and was criticising him. George was naturally upset at losing and at having to listen to me have a go at him afterwards. As I was talking to him, Lew walked into the dressing-room. He didn't say anything at first, but a few minutes later he asked me if he could have a word with me outside. When I stepped out of the venue onto the car park, Lew picked me up by the scruff of the neck and pinned me to the wall. He had totally flipped and threatened to do me all kinds of unimaginable damage if he ever heard me talk badly about George again. I'm no coward, but I didn't retaliate because I realised how hurt Lew felt about George's defeat. I just agreed with everything Lew said until he finally calmed down. That's how much Lew loved boxing and how much winning meant to him.

I have met and fought some of the hardest men in the world of boxing, and I don't say this lightly: Lew is without doubt the hardest man I have ever known. Out of the ring Lew is a great friend and a gentleman. When my wife Joan and I celebrated our 70th birthdays, Lew secretly arranged to come and stay at the place we were having a meal. As we sat down to eat with our family, there was a loud knock at the dining-room door. When it was opened, Lew was standing there with a knife and fork in his hand and asked, 'Is there any room at the table for a little one?' I nearly fell off my chair. Lew had made a 400-mile round trip just to be with Joan and me for our birthdays. Lew Yates gets my vote any day!

# CARLTON LEACH
## Author of *Muscle*

Lew was the best doorman I've ever known – a proper gent of the old school, respected throughout the industry as hard, fair and effective. I saw him drop a troublemaker with a right-hand piledriver and the guy was unconscious before he had even hit the deck. For the next ten minutes he lay flat on his back with a silly grin on his face as though he was tucked up in bed in a five-star hotel. That's the way big Lew went about his business. Two warnings and you were out. The night he was forced to poleaxe the half-pissed troublemaker outside a Dagenham nightclub, he had been provoked by a stream of threats and abuse that would have challenged the patience of a saint. In the end Lew had no alternative. Bosh! The man had come looking for trouble, and we all did our best to please the customers.

I have seen dozens of chancers take on Lew. Not one of them came close to succeeding. And no one got through the door when Lew said no. What was different about the 22-st. northerner was that he had no malice whatsoever in what he did. He was old-fashioned muscle: smart suit and dicky bow, out to stop trouble, not start it. A true mark of Lew's style was that after he had knocked the troublemaker out at the club, he checked that he was not seriously hurt, then organised a cab to take him home, knowing that when he woke up, he would have a headache that he wouldn't forget as a souvenir of his meeting with the big fella and a reminder not to be so stupid again.

# BIG JACK HOLT
## Chairman of Bolton Olympic Wrestling Club, former bouncer at thirty-three clubs throughout the north-west of England

What can I say about Lew Yates other than he is the man? I have worked throughout Lancashire and the north-west and have encountered the hardest guys the area has to offer, but none are a patch on Lew. Don't get me wrong, being hard doesn't mean you have to behave like a thug. Lew is a gentleman and would die for anyone he cares about.

I have mainly humorous memories of the times I spent working with him at the Cavendish Club in Blackburn. This may be hard to believe, but one night we turned away three African guys complete with tribal scars, etc., because they were out of their heads on drugs. After closing the doors on them, we walked back into reception, but then heard thud, thud, thud! We looked at each other, gingerly opened the doors and found three spears sticking in them! I swear it's true. Lew pulled one of the spears out of the door and ran after these three guys shouting, 'Woo, woo, woo!' like a Red Indian. I wasn't sure what to do, so I grabbed myself a spear and followed Lew. We never did catch up with the guys, and I'm not sure what would have happened if we did. When we got back to the club, Lew and I spent the rest of the evening laughing. I have witnessed many strange events in and around nightclubs in my time, but being attacked with spears is something I shall never forget.

On another occasion Lew threw a guy out of the Cavendish for being drunk and misbehaving. Once outside the man, who was absolutely fuming, started shouting and being abusive. Lew was laughing at him, which made the man even more irate. Screaming at the top of his voice, the man tore his own jacket off to reveal a false arm that was made of cheap, hard, flesh-coloured plastic. He took the arm out of the leather straps that held it in place and hurled it at Lew. Still laughing, Lew picked it up and lobbed it over the wall of the multi-storey car park, and it shattered on the street three floors below. For the next five minutes we watched the guy staggering around the street, picking up the pieces of his false arm and cursing Lew.

I have been a good friend of Lew's for 35 years now. Wherever he may be, he always rings to ask how my family and I are getting on. I honestly cannot speak highly enough of him. When his wife left him, I will never forget how he dropped everything to bring up and care for his kids. That's what sticks in my mind the most about Lew Yates, his heart; it's bigger than those enormous shoulders of his, and that's saying something!

# NEVILLE SHEEN
## Former trainer with British karate team coach Ticky Donovan OBE

I remember clearly the first time I saw Lew. He was a new bouncer at my favourite nightclub, the Room at the Top. I walked over to where he was and there was some commotion going on. As I got near, I saw three big guys on the floor and a fourth was running away. I was wondering what gang had done these three, who it transpired were bouncers from another club nearby. Then I saw Lew. He looked like someone you see in a fairground mirror that shortens and widens them. The first thing I wanted to do when I met him was pat him on the shoulder to see just how much was jacket. Of course there was no padding; it was all Lew. He was a strange shape. He looked wider than he was tall. I started to speak to him, slightly nervously at first, but to my surprise he was funny and personable – nothing like any bouncer I had met, let alone one who was capable of such awesome power that he could despatch in seconds four big lads who were supposed to be local tough guys and worked on the door of a club.

Soon after this I became good friends with Lew. I was a black belt at a time when it was a very rare thing in the UK, and I was in a top karate team, one that was without a doubt the most successful club team in the UK. We went all over the country and won every open title. No matter what anyone says about martial arts being special techniques that need to be learnt over long periods of time, all the team members had their feet on the ground – meaning that we knew what was important in a street fight. What mattered was the ratio between speed, reflexes and power. We would train constantly to increase our ratio. The top fighters in the club, me included, would take doorman jobs just to get practice in the real uncontrolled situations you encounter in nightclub fights. What I'm trying to say here is I know what I'm talking about when it comes to fighting and those that fight.

Lew was without doubt the fastest and hardest-hitting heavyweight I ever saw. On most occasions when I was with Lew and there was trouble, you would have to be quick to see what happened. It was always over in seconds. A good example was at a club in Greenford. The manager had asked me to help him because he was being terrorised by the local gangsters, and he would pay big salaries for me and a crew to go and make the place safe for the general public. Most doormen I knew said they had heard of the goings on there and thought it was too risky. In the end only Lew and one other friend of ours, Dave Young, would do it. To be honest, we felt a bit like the Magnificent Seven, only four of the others didn't show up! The place was dark and depressing, and I remember thinking why would anybody come to such a place anyway, but by 11 it was buzzing. In those days anything dank, dingy, with loud music and a bar could make money so long as people could feel reasonably safe there.

The manager told us that the local gang had to be banned if the place was to survive, because they were terrorising everyone there. He said that the main problem lay with one individual in particular: a huge 6 ft 6 in. monster who would beat the shit out of anyone who as much as looked in his direction. He said that we would have a big problem with this one. A few nights later I was in the bar area and the assistant manager ran up to me in a complete panic, saying this monster man was at the door. I ran to the door immediately. As I got there, Lew was walking towards me. I told him that the big lump we were looking for was here. He said, 'Yes, I know,' and chuckled. As I looked over Lew's shoulder, I saw the Terror of Greenford, as we'd named him, sprawled on the floor.

Dave Young said, 'It's simple. The big guy gave Lew a bit of lip, and a few seconds later he was out.'

When Lew got going, it would be almost impossible to stop him. I saw the other doormen at the Room at the Top trying to hold him back when one of the most feared gangsters in east London was trying to push some people around. This guy smashed a pint mug onto Lew's head, but it didn't even slow him down. Big Lewie continued to try and shake all the other doormen off of him, seemingly unaware his head had been split open. The other doormen were sure that these gangsters would have come back shooting if Lew had got his hands on this one, as he would have surely sent him to hospital for a long time. Lew always hated bullies and gave them their own medicine by the spadeful.

I have known some good promising heavyweights in my time. I've sparred with some of the greatest fighters in the world, such as Nigel Benn, and I have never seen anyone match Lew for speed and power. He also had natural technique. Being in Lew's company while working in security or socialising in some dodgy area gave you a great feeling of safety. Not only would you feel you had this huge power by your side, but he gave you this immense confidence in yourself. Lew just knew he could handle anything, and that is how he made you feel. You would realise that this huge self-belief was a significant part of his power. You could see that when Mike Tyson was at his most fearsome. Fighters had lost the fight before they entered the ring, because they had no belief in themselves. Getting the right coaching and a few breaks could have taken Lew to the top. I now run a telecommunications company, and one of my best friends is Dave Hill, who owns a boxing brand called Ringside. Through him I have got to know Joe Calzaghe and other world champions. I have seen them fight up close. But I have no doubt whatsoever that Lew would have been a serious contender for a world-title belt if he'd had a few breaks in life. Where would Tyson have ended up without the legendary trainer Cus D'Amato?

I was with Lew when his wife left him with three kids. He had come to London to get his career on track. Just when he was getting well known and could have really made some serious impact on the fight scene, this bombshell was dropped on him. He went back to the north of England and brought the kids to London, where he raised them on his own. Lew had a dark side that, like a lot of people, came from drink. When he'd had a few too many, he could become unnecessarily aggressive. And with a force like Lew this was a very frightening experience, so you would need to keep your distance. Perhaps this was a result of his bad luck. I know it is a tragedy for Lew and British boxing that he never got just a little bit of luck. Whether he'd won or lost to one of the great heavyweights, he would have been exciting, thrilling and charismatic. As someone once said, 'He could have been a contender.'

Lew is not like any other tough guy I have ever known or heard of. He is sharp, witty, funny and has a huge personality. Then he can change in the blink of an eye into some dark monster with enormous power, like a runaway freight train. If he ever does lose it when you're near him, make sure you're not in his way, and make sure that when he has passed, you start running in the opposite direction as fast as your trembling legs will carry you and don't look back!

# JIMMY SHERIDAN
## East End entrepreneur

I first met Lew while he was working on the door of Lautrec's in Dagenham. We instantly took to each other, and for a number of years I mistakenly referred to him as Scouse, as I'd always thought he came from Liverpool. I have met some hard and very dangerous men on my travels around the globe, but this guy Lew, having seen him in several fights, is without doubt the best.

On one occasion I saw two black guys in Lautrec's fooling around. These guys would have made Mike Tyson in his prime look like a feeble midget; they were all muscle and brawn. Lew told them to behave, but they took no notice, so he walked back over to them and with two punches knocked both of them out. With the assistance of the other bouncers Lew dragged them both outside, and when I went to see if everything was OK, I saw that they had placed them still unconscious on top of each other in the sexual '69' position. I was standing outside with Lew when the police arrived and demanded to know what had happened to the men. 'I've no idea,' Lew replied. 'It looks as if they have been fighting, but it wasn't in here because they are banned.' The officers didn't reply. They just dragged the men into their van one at a time before driving off.

I have heard plenty of women say they feel safe going into clubs knowing big Lewie is on the door, and there are not many that can command that much respect in London. Lew is no gangster and no villain; he is just an all-round, decent, no-nonsense fella who, if he had been born a cockney, would undoubtedly have been promoted by the guys with the right connections to have taken him to the top. That, sadly, is what it's all about, particularly in the East End. It's who you know, not what you know or can do!

# PETER KOSTER
## Head of security for eighteen years at various nightclubs throughout London, boxing promoter and bodyguard to numerous celebrities

A massive broad-shouldered man walked out of the lift at the Room at the Top nightclub and into my life. It was 1976, and I was the head doorman at the venue. Lew told me that he was looking for work. I was regularly approached by hopefuls thinking they could work the door, but this lad was different. Lew was heavily built, sharp and looked you straight in the eye. His aura screamed violence! Lew proved to be the ultimate bouncer, fearless of names and reputations. He has had guns pulled on him, he has been stabbed, sprayed with ammonia and hit with every type of weapon you care to mention, but he's always remained the last man standing. A master of explosive controlled violence, Lew is unlike many doormen, who rely on drink or drugs for courage. What you see is what you get: a twentieth-century gladiator who came unknown from the north to become one of London's most respected hard men.

I'm qualified to say all of that because I have been around hard men and the club scene all of my life. Born and raised in the East End, I saw the Krays, the Readings and any other well-respected family you care to name at work. The thing about the Krays and their ilk is that they always did their business with the backup of a gang. When I lived in my father-in-law's pub, the Scots Arms in Wapping, the Kray gang used to take protection money from him. Most publicans in the area paid them a pension, as it was known, because it was the done thing back in those days. If the Krays protected your pub, they used to give you a small black-and-white photo of Charlie, Ron and Reg Kray shaking hands. This photo had to be put in a prominent position by the cash till so that anybody coming in the pub could see it. Customers would then know not to cause grief in the place, as it was a 'Kray-protected boozer'.

A fella known as Scotch Jack Dickson would usually collect the money from our pub, but when they were making the film *Battle of Britain* down in Wapping, Ron and Reg used to come in. There's a scene in the film which shows all of the old warehouses on fire. When they filmed that, there were loads of celebrities about, and Ron and Reg were in nearly every day hoping to bump into them. They would have all of their gang hanging about, and occasionally some fella they took exception to would get a clump. I have never liked the idea of gangs resolving issues against one man. That's something Lew never wanted or had to do. He always went into situations alone.

In any nightclub you'll get faces and their hangers-on taking liberties. They come into nightclubs without having to pay, because they know the owner, the manager or the door staff, but instead of acknowledging the hospitality they have been shown by offering the lads on the door a drink, they swan through without even saying good evening. If I told Lew that one of these disrespectful faces was in the club, it would be like showing a red rag to a bull. Lew would glare at them, bump into them and be rude all night in the hope they would say something to him. Few ever did, but occasionally we would end up having to carry one or two of the ones who did respond from the premises.

There is, of course, another side to Lew apart from his fighting ability. When my father, Jim Koster, sadly passed away, my mother, who was very ill, was brought from a hospital to attend the funeral in a wheelchair. I had not told Lew about the service because he was going through a terrible time of it himself, trying to raise three children after his wife had left him. There were only about 15 people at the church, and as one would expect, I was feeling really low. Midway through the proceedings I turned to look towards the back of the room for some reason, and there, standing alone, dressed in a black suit with tears streaming down his face, was big Lew. When the service had ended, Lew came back to the house, sat all of the mourners down, made them tea and sandwiches and went out of his way to make a very difficult day that little bit more bearable. His thoughtfulness that day meant so much to me, particularly as I knew he was enduring difficult times himself.

I was Lew's manager when he fought Roy Shaw in Ilford. I had been involved with boxing for some time, providing up-and-coming boxers for shows that my old friend Frank Warren was promoting. The fight between Lew and Roy was so crooked I couldn't believe it. When Roy was dishing out punishment, they let the round go on; when Lew was hammering Roy, they rang the bell. They just rang the bell whenever it suited their man. If that fight had lasted a week, they wouldn't have let Lew win. These days nearly all of Roy's fights are available on video, but despite there being two video cameras filming Lew's fight from a stage behind the ring that night, the footage has never appeared. I have asked Joe Pyle Jnr if he could get me a video of the fight to prove it was a fix, but Joe refused to comment either way.

Brian Gerard, Peter Lee, Ray Smithers and I put up the money for Lew's fight. Yet, when we arrived at the venue, Roy's people hadn't reserved our seats. They made it clear they didn't want us watching the fight because they knew, before a punch had even been thrown, that the outcome might be deemed controversial and that we may demand repayment. Eventually we were allowed in but had to stand at the back of the club against a wall.

Let's get this straight: I am not disrespecting Roy Shaw, Joe

Pyle or any of the lads who were in Roy's camp that night. All I can do is tell it as I saw it. I like Roy; he is a man with a lot of respect, especially when ladies are in his company. Boxing was how Roy was earning his money when he fought Lew, so I wouldn't expect him to do anything different to what he did that night.

Nobody who was at the fight believes Lew lost. Saying he had blood all over his face and an eye hanging out of his head is ridiculous. Lew had no blood on his face whatsoever and only slight swelling around the eye. We were all naturally gutted, but I suppose life is made interesting by the fact we win some and lose others. I'll never forget Brian Gerard phoning me the following morning and saying, 'How do you feel now the sting's gone out?' I still laugh when I think about it now. We had both lost a lot of money backing Lew. I guess Brian was saying what's done is done, wipe your mouth and move on. That's what I would like to see my friend Lew do now. In his time Lew has been stabbed, shot at, squirted with ammonia, beaten with fists and iron bars, but only one thing has ever really hurt him, and that's life. As his friend, I would like to hear him say one day that he had wiped his mouth, put the past behind him, life was now being good to him and his luck had changed.